RUTH ELLIS, MY MOTHER

Ruth Ellis, My Mother

A daughter's memoir of the last woman to be hanged

By
Georgie Ellis

WITH ROD TAYLOR

SMITH GRYPHON
PUBLISHERS

First published in paperback in Great Britain in 1996 by
SMITH GRYPHON LIMITED
Swallow House, 11–21 Northdown Street
London N1 9BN

First published in hardback by Smith Gryphon in 1995

A CIP catalogue for this book
is available from the British Library

ISBN 1 85685 105 2

Printed in Great Britain
by Cox & Wyman Ltd

For Peter and Phyllis Lawton

*'Perhaps after I die
the truth will be known.'*
Ruth Ellis, 12 July 1955

CONTENTS

CHAPTER ONE

Crime of Passion

The innermost secrets of the soul of Ruth Ellis went with her to the gallows on the morning of 13 July 1955. What final thoughts flashed through her confused and tortured mind in those few seconds between meeting her executioner and death will never be known. Yet there is scarcely a day goes by when I do not wonder about it and shudder at the inhumanity perpetrated against her in the name of society. Ruth Ellis was my mother.

In the forty years that have elapsed since that morning, her name and the case have refused to go away. She has been the subject of countless books by academics and investigative journalists alike, of at least two major television documentaries and, in 1985, of a full-length movie, *Dance With a Stranger*, in which she herself was portrayed by Miranda Richardson and her two lovers most relevant to her story by Rupert Everett and Ian Holm. In death she found a perverse starring role that brought her the fame and notoriety that had eluded her for all but the last dozen weeks of her catastrophic life.

The lure of the bright lights of post-war London had sucked Ruth Ellis into a sordid underworld, from which she sought to escape into respectability. The succession of people in whom she naively placed her trust to lead her towards her goal were mostly restless men who took solace in alcohol and sexual relief with prostitutes. My mother had tragedy engraved on her destiny from the start.

Those who have taken the time and effort to make detailed studies and assessments of her life-story all agree on one point: she was unlucky to hang and would certainly not have been executed even just a couple of years later. There is a consensus by and large that her death was directly responsible for the introduction of the previously unheard-of, in English law, defence to murder of diminished responsibility in the Homicide Act 1957. It is with the knowledge of how, in a more enlightened age and given a less callous Home Secretary, my mother would still be alive today that I have decided to rake over the coals and consider the effects her execution has had on me and the rest of our family.

If she had served the term of imprisonment that is more or less the norm for a murder conviction in parallel circumstances today, she would now be a woman of 68 and grandmother to my six children. Moreover, she would have already been a free woman for the best part of thirty years. The arguments have raged over whether or not she should have hanged for what was blatantly a crime of passion. It is true that she did little to help herself. It is also clear that her defence at the Old Bailey in London was conducted badly. It is known that key witnesses were either not called or told lies. These facts are beyond dispute. The judge was fair, and the jury had few choices, given the way the case was presented. The Home Secretary, Major Gwilym Lloyd-George, an inferior son of a great man, made the unilateral decision, vested in his office, not to recommend a reprieve.

Yet the various scholars who have tackled the case all insist that Ruth should not have hanged. All I know is that in each such case, be it Timothy Evans, Derek Bentley or Ruth Ellis, it is too late to show mercy in hindsight, once the neck has been broken. The repercussions of execution for those left behind, both to mourn the loss of a loved one and to serve their own sentence and live with the inevitable stigma that the unforgiving so readily attach, are as eternal as the ripples of the largest stone thrown into a pond. The aftermath of Ruth's violent death is recorded in two suicides, one death from a broken heart, a lawyer whose faith in justice was so shaken that he never practised again and my own stumblings through a life that, for some reason, consciously or otherwise, has weirdly mirrored my mother's.

The uncovering of coincidences in our respective stories has forced me seriously to consider what strange forces steered me into a life-pattern that Ruth would have instantly recognized: one of sex, poverty, rejection, humiliation, degradation and a fierce determination independently to conquer whatever fate and, admittedly, our own blind stupidity might throw at us. The more I have got to know her, the more I find to like in her. I freely admit, though, that her downside of manic, possessive jealousy, of social ambition at whatever cost to her self-respect, serve to keep a perspective on her character and curb any temptation I might have to gild her with values and qualities with which she was not, in truth, blessed.

I was only 3½ when she died and did not know she was my real mother until I was 8. Yet I came to feel some kind of bond with her, which, combined with a natural curiosity, has driven me to explore her brief life for my own personal satisfaction. When I was 28, the same age as Ruth when she died, I became racked by an awareness of how short her time on earth had been, albeit three years longer than the man she murdered. I began to perceive the need we all have for those simple ingredients of life that make tomorrow something to which we can look forward. None of us knows our allotted span, and it is this blissful ignorance that allows us to be optimistic and hopeful and thinly obscures the perils of existence. Time conscious though we may be, we go on in anticipation of a future.

Ruth knew the day, the hour, the minute and the second of her death as only the condemned can do. Only execution by the process of law offers this absolute certainty of the time of death. Not a second sooner, not a second later, with the grave already dug within the precincts of the prison. Ruth was aware that her twenty-eighth year would be cut short as required by those carrying out the law of the land and acting on behalf of society. Yes, even on my behalf. I do not intend to dwell over-long on a barbaric relic of not too distant history. However, it has served to heighten my appreciation of life, the gift of which, in my case, came from Ruth Ellis. It is the first, the last and the only thing she ever gave me, but I harbour no blame nor resentment. I am often reminded of something I once heard the late comedienne Joyce Grenfell say: 'Life is just this very minute and I, thank God, am in it.'

When Ruth was taken from the Old Bailey to the condemned cell at Holloway Prison, north London, the first thing that she asked for as prisoner 9656 was a copy of the Bible. She spent the last minutes of her life on her knees before a crucifix pinned to the wall of her cell. I will never be sure if, with the help of the prison chaplain and the compassion of the prison governor, Ruth found a faith with strength enough to support her right to the end, but the reports of the warders and the executioner suggest that she retained a composure that forced them to describe her as the bravest woman ever to go to the gallows.

Albert Pierrepoint, the semi-literate Manchester publican who was paid 15 guineas to pull the lever said years later: 'She was no trouble. She wobbled a bit, naturally. Any woman can do that. Nothing went wrong with her. She was as good as bloody gold, she was.' Pierrepoint hanged a total of 520 men and women, and Ruth was the last woman. He must have been strange. In 1987, at the age of 82 and living in retirement in the sleepy seaside resort of Southport, he said in an interview for Red Rose Radio: 'I enjoyed every bloody minute of it. I have been to so many places in the world, always staying in posh hotels.' The night before he broke my mother's neck, he spent the night in Holloway, presumably in the guest suite. I hope she did find requisite faith, but I find it impossible to conceive that, armed with the cut-and-dried, unambiguous certainty of death in a few seconds, the over-riding emotion could be anything other than sheer terror. To stand there hooded and manacled, face to face with a towering blank wall of hopelessness, waiting for the trap-doors to part to plunge her into convulsed and writhing darkness, is an image on which I prefer not to linger. Men have been known to ejaculate, vomit and defecate at the last. I doubt if my mother had an orgasm as her ultimate human experience, but it would be nice to believe she did. I would rather make-believe on the improbable than torture myself with the undeniable reality of her final human experience.

Much debate has gone on as to why the Ruth Ellis case captured the interest of the public to such an unprecedented extent. Why is she still remembered forty years on? She was the last of fifteen women to be hanged this century, a fact that most people whom I encounter appear to know whatever their age. However, I never come across anybody who can name any one of the other fourteen. Equally, her memory does not appear to invoke the venom and horror that greets the names of other murderers such as Myra Hindley, Peter Sutcliffe and Donald Neilson. Nor is she portrayed as a figure of fun like Lizzie Borden; nor one of mystery like Jack the Ripper; nor one of pity like Derek Bentley or Timothy Evans.

There is still a touch of glamour attached to the case, erroneously in my opinion. She was portrayed as the perpetrator of a crime of passion, which caught the imagination of the public and fed the voracious appetite of Fleet Street hacks who knew a good story when they heard one. A rejected lover who pumped bullets into the man who 'done her wrong' must have struck a chord with thousands of women at the time. How many identified with her and felt that old, 'There but for fortune go I' feeling? I understand how affairs of the heart, cruelty both mental and physical within a relationship and brutal rejection can destroy rationality. I have been driven to within a hair's breadth of wanting to kill a man myself. I have felt my own responsibility temporarily diminish with the pain and humiliation inflicted upon me by deranged, drunken and violent men. Of all the traits that I discover I have in common with Ruth, paramount is my talent repeatedly to select lousy men. Of all the bad apples in the crop, she and I harvested a barrowload between us.

It has been suggested that Ruth's case grabbed the head-lines almost to the exclusion of all else at the time because she was young, blonde and pretty and had, beyond dispute, been treated abominably by David Blakely, the lover she murdered. By contrast, her immediate female predecessor to be executed was 51-year-old Cypriot Mrs Styllou Christofi, who was not only not an attractive woman but indeed was described as ugly. Her crime was to strangle her daughter-in-law and then set fire to the body in a back garden in Hampstead. Her case rated few column inches and little protest other than from the abolitionist movements of the time. It must be true that Ruth derived publicity from her glamorous, if tarty, image, but it is equally true, as will be later seen, that her looks and appearance did her no favours with the judge and jury. I suppose if she had been unattractive the papers would have been reluctant to exploit her picture as much as they did and, from time to time, continue to do. The simple fact is that she still arrests media attention after forty years – and would she not be thrilled to know it?

There is a vast difference between reason and excuse, and it is beyond most of us to excuse murder. But a groundswell of public anger at Ruth's imminent execution grew nationally as the days for a reprieve ticked away. This indignation was in part nourished by press suggestions that Blakely deserved what came to him. He certainly was a weak and cowardly person who thought nothing of hitting a woman but shrank cowering at the prospect of fisticuffs with another man. Ruth was increasingly depicted as the victim, and to some extent she was. She was a battered woman and had the extent of her suffering been accurately described to the court, then almost certainly the jury would have recommended mercy. One could never submit that a battered woman has the right to go out and shoot her aggressor, but a relationship that knows repeated violence is bound to tell on those involved sooner or later.

As I have already intimated, my own experiences have brought about an understanding of the utter despair of extreme circumstances that can lead to a tragedy, and I cannot discount the outside chance of my or any other woman's reactions being triggered beyond rational contemplation. The law always speaks of the hypothetical 'reasonable' man or woman. Alas, judges of the High Court, Queen's Counsellors and Cabinet Ministers who shoulder the absolute responsibility for clemency rarely find themselves in unreasonable circumstances, so it was asking too much for the periwigged assembly at the Old Bailey to begin to comprehend how a woman had struggled from the nomadic poverty of her family, through intermittent prostitution to the promise of security and respectability, only to be callously and selfishly destroyed by the man who had made her false promises of marriage and flaunted his many infidelities in front of her.

Along the way she tasted money, moved in circles that were the realization of some of her earliest dreams, had an illegitimate child, my half-brother Andy, and married George Ellis, my father. On 2 October 1951 she gave birth to me. What follows is what happened to us and the other members of our family, but in order to make some sense out of the ensuing tragedies and, sometimes in my case, comedies of life, it is necessary to explore the backgrounds of both my mother and my father, my mother's lovers David Blakely and Desmond Cussen, who by bizarre connivance shared her simultaneously, and all the other extraneous and eccentric characters who surrounded us. The principal players mostly had two things in common: they were alcoholics and often inadequate in most of life's demanding departments.

CHAPTER TWO

Driving Ambition

My mother and I were each born into similar, far from ideal circumstances, but at opposite ends of the country. She was born in Rhyl, north Wales, and I took my first breath in the maternity ward of Dulwich Hospital, south London. By quirk of fate our respective formative years were spent in geographical reversal, she in the south and me in Warrington, Lancashire, not 50 miles from Rhyl. Though we were both born into poverty, she at least had the foresight not to stand in my way when my father found a wealthy, childless couple prepared to raise me as their own and provide me with the opportunities that were beyond her reach.

At least that is the way I like to think it was. It is more likely that she could not wait to get me out of the squalid little flat where she lived and entertained her clients, above the drinking club of which she was manageress. Even more probable is that David Blakely urged her to be rid of me, as my presence would have been an irritant to him and a cramp on his demands on my mother. Either way it seems she was not troubled by my departure, and there is not one report of her ever having mentioned me during her entire time in Holloway. She did, however, repeatedly enquire after the well-being of my half-brother, Andy, once she had been convicted. A psychiatrist who conducted an examination of her on 4 June 1955 in Holloway, reporting on her state of mind at the moment of the shooting of Blakely, said: 'An emotionally mature woman would have been prevented from this action by thoughts of her children. I asked her about this point, and she told me that she never once thought of them.' So much for us.

Ruth was born in Rhyl simply because her father Arthur Hornby was a professional cellist, and the resort was close enough to the port of Liverpool for him to find occasional work aboard the huge ocean liners that sailed the Atlantic. In between voyages he could find work in the hotels along the coast. For professional reasons, although I can find little wrong with Hornby, he adopted the name Neilson, and, ever after, that was the name used by the family. In an attempt to preserve her anonymity following the bull-dozing of the old Holloway prison, the remains of Ruth Ellis were removed to a church graveyard in Amersham, Buckinghamshire, where she rests in the shadow of a simple headstone bearing the name Ruth Hornby.

Arthur the cellist was to marry a part-French, part-Belgian refugee from the German invasions of the First World War, my grandmother Elisaberta, known as Lisa to some and Bertha to others. She had been orphaned when young and raised by nuns. Not surprisingly, she was a staunch member of the Church of Rome and bore Arthur six children, of whom with only one, my Aunt Muriel, am I still in contact. Muriel was the second child. Julian, the eldest, would later suffer ignominy when he turned up with flowers to Holloway, and Ruth refused to see him. Granville, the third in line, who was the brother closest to Ruth, was destined to spend the last night of her life fighting in vain for the missing evidence that just might prompt an eleventh-hour reprieve. It was in some part due to Granville's developing an illness as a child that the family moved from Manchester to the Welsh coast on the recommendation of a doctor that sea air would be of benefit to him.

Ruth was Arthur and Bertha's fourth child, born on 9 October 1926. Her birth came towards the end of a year in which Britain had moved ever closer to a General Strike, one that had become 'all out' on 3 May. By 12 May it was over, but the economy was ailing and would continue to do so for years, with unemployment steeply on the increase. Work as a musician became harder for my grandfather to find. Their fifth child, a boy, died in his second year, and the baby of the family, Elizabeth, was arguably destined to be the one most affected by Ruth's execution.

The first five years of Ruth's life were spent in Rhyl, then an agreeable enough town, a long way removed from the miles and rows of holiday caravans that today mar the once pleasant landscape. Muriel, who is five years older than mother would have been, recalls the early Ruth as short-sighted and indistinguishable from most kids her age, inclined towards puppy fat.

The slump hit the North in a big way, and many families joined the great migration to the promised lands of southern England. The Neilsons headed for Basingstoke in Hampshire, where Arthur got work in a cinema orchestra. Even before he had a chance to get started it was obvious that the end was in sight for such orchestras. Talkies, beginning with *The Jazz Singer* starring Al Jolson, were arriving from America, and the cinema musicians soon became obsolete. My grandfather found himself unemployed again, his pride sorely dented. He turned to drink and then to excessive drink. Where once had been a caring, loving husband and family man, there now raged a broken spirit who vented his wrath and frustration in violent verbal and physical abuse of his wife and children.

I am describing what I know of events of sixty years ago as they were related to me, but I detect no difference in the cause and effects that were to be so much a part of Ruth's life a generation later and my own life another generation down the line. The theorum seems to be as solid and unshakeable as Pythagoras: Poverty + wounded pride = alcohol + violence = misery.

There was no work as a musician, and Arthur had reluctantly to face this fact, as, too, did my grandmother who suffered as her husband failed to provide adequately for her and the children. Years later, after Ruth's death, Bertha told her recollections to broadcaster and author Godfrey Winn, who wrote them up in articles for the *Sunday Dispatch*. She told

Winn: 'Ruth hated us to be poor. She hated boys, too, at that time . . . she always liked clothes. . . . She wasn't like my other children. She was so very ambitious for herself. She used to say, "Mum, I'm going to make something of my life."'

I can well understand why she hated to be poor. I have never met anybody yet who enjoys having no money. Nothing is sharper in my own memory than finding myself in the early hours of a cold, wet morning, bruised and blood-stained courtesy of a man, with nowhere to go and less than £5.00 in my pocket to last me for the rest of my life. Not a pretty sight and not a happy circumstance. Like Ruth, I am determined never to let it happen again, but of course I cannot guarantee it.

To understand where Ruth Ellis's attitude and driving ambition came from requires some grasp of the desperation of poverty and all its knock-on effects. For Ruth, her attendance at Fairfields Girls School was a relief from the constant tension and rows of home, where food was in short supply, and spare cash for having fun was out of the question.

Arthur finally found a job, not playing the cello, at which he was acknowledged to be particularly adept, but as a telephonist and hall porter in a nearby mental hospital. The dent in his dignity at such a demotion would have been tempered by the relief that a house came with the job. Muriel has total recall of this time and remembers finding herself with an increased burden of responsibility as her mother slowly but deliberately abnegated much of her own responsibility. Her spirit weakened by the continued hardship, she had withdrawn into isolated activities such as knitting and devotion to prayer.

Ruth's nature was rebellious, and she had become a handful. Her looks were starting to blossom, and she habitually went missing, for which Muriel was made to shoulder much of the blame. There is no record of when Ruth began an active sex life, but it was certainly early. She was quick to see the value of sex as a means to her ends. Later, when she frequented the West End of London, it would not take her long to realize that what she had previously given away was, in fact, a saleable commodity. Years on, when I reached the nadir of my own despair, I came to the same conclusion, about which I have no regrets.

11

What was seen at the time as precociousness is now clear to me as the first stirrings of a perception that life had more to offer than her parents' experience suggested. Arthur lost his job at the mental hospital and hit the bottom of the social pile by becoming a caretaker in Reading, Berkshire. This necessitated further domestic upheaval, and Ruth began to despise her home, wherever it was. The war had started, and, just 14, she left school. To judge by her letters, what schooling she had does not appear to have penetrated far into her brain. She was an atrocious speller, and her grammar and syntax would shame an 8 year old, though towards the end of her life she did show some inclination modestly to further her education, even if the motivation were merely to impress David Blakely and his inner circle, all of whom were light years of learning ahead of her.

A woman who figures large in Ruth's story once David Blakely arrived on the scene was Carole Findlater, destined to bear the brunt of Ruth's venom from shortly before the shooting all the way to the scaffold. Carole was well read, a successful journalist and Woman's Editor of the *Daily Mail*, as well as a former lover of Blakely's. Their relationship was not harmonious, and, while Carole mocked her ignorance, Ruth could give as good as she got. With her barbed retorts, Ruth could cut the pomp out of any pretence of ceremony. She just employed a different language; one in which the word fuck was the most useful verb and noun, and its accompanying participle, fucking, served her well as both adverb and adjective.

Having left school, Ruth took a job in Reading as a waitress, where the basic pay was humble, but where she rapidly learnt that she could easily make use of her pert looks and flirtatious charms substantially to increase her earnings with tips. What she earned she spent, and, according to Muriel, she showed no responsibility at all where money was concerned, opting to squander it on clothes and entertainment to keep her away from the depression of home as much as possible. In all the books and reports that I have read, Muriel is portrayed as a martyr who was purer than the driven snow and who sacrificed her own adolescent and youthful years to act *in loco parentis* to the other siblings.

Muriel did meet and fall in love with a man and wait five years before she changed her name to his to become Muriel Jakubait. She has always said that her suffering after Ruth's execution was made worse by an endless stream of vicious jibes at her, calculated to make her feel guilty in her own right. These appear to have been particularly numerous at the time of the murder of any child, when she claims to have been taunted that, had it not been for Ruth Ellis, we would still have the death penalty and that child would, in the opinion of the taunter, still be alive. I'm sure there is truth in what she says, and I am sure she has at times been deeply wounded by such unfair treatment.

During Albert Pierrepoint's retirement he recounted a macabre tale, in which he and Muriel, in the company of a couple of others, went to visit Ruth's grave. He said: 'I went out with her one afternoon. I had a meal with her . . . in this place in London.' Afterwards they all went to the grave. He went on: 'Then they said we are going home now, so we'll run you home . . . and, on my God's honour, this is the truth. You couldn't believe it, but we were all singing as though we were going on a trip.'

Of his time actually spent by Ruth's grave he said: 'All of a sudden I heard some groaning. I thought she were comin' up from t' grave. It was a fella as drunk as a clot hiding at t' back . . . He was boozin' just behind her grave.' I trust Mr Pierrepoint's honour has been severely tested by his maker.

Arthur Neilson was not to spend an eternity in the caretaker's job, and by a stroke of good fortune he found himself for once in the right place at a right time when he took a job as chauffeur that required him to base himself in the Southwark district of London. Bertha opted to stay put in Reading, even though a two-bedroomed flat went with Arthur's position. Notwithstanding the Blitz and all the inherent dangers of wartime London, the lure of the capital was irresistible to Ruth, and she took the other room in her father's flat. She patently derived a deal of excitement from the bombs that the Luftwaffe dropped almost every night.

By all accounts Ruth made a girlfriend of her own age,

and all was fine until Bertha paid a surprise visit and found Arthur in bed with this friend. My normally passive and docile grandmother revealed a latent pugilistic streak and physically attacked my grandfather, something that she had doubtless longed to do on previous occasions. Whether she went home and prayed for it we will never know, but very shortly afterwards the Luftwaffe dropped a bomb close by the flat, and Arthur, quite severely injured, was buried beneath a pile of rubble. Ruth, with her own bare hands, was the one to dig him free.

With this, Bertha changed into forgive-and-forget mode as the entire family moved to Camberwell, and Ruth embarked on a black period in her life, being forced to find work in the OXO factory, something not remotely to her liking. Her boredom threshold was to remain low all her life, and the pursuit of her pleasures, dancing and men, were all that made life tolerable for her. She was very forward with men by this time, and Muriel would often hover in embarrassment while Ruth practised her charms and conducted her sexual experiments. She was determined to get through the war with a 'here today – gone tomorrow' attitude and not waste her youth because of it.

Granville was a prisoner of war in Germany, and Julian had been gravely injured, with wounds that would always plague him and ultimately kill him. Ruth's licentious days were temporarily drawing to a close, although she did not immediately realize it. What began as aches and pains and creeping lethargy, she at first put down to too many late nights. As her symptoms intensified, she was diagnosed as suffering from rheumatic fever and admitted to hospital in March 1942, where she languished with impatience for a couple of months. She must have been delighted when her doctor advised her to take up dancing to help her convalescence.

Ruth needed no further encouragement and told OXO to stuff its machinery up its corporate backside as she determined to dance for England. She managed to find a string of men, soldiers and GIs, all willing to whisk her round the popular dance joints of the time, all responsive to her manipulative flirting. Some say she even sang for a while with a band, while others have remarked that she was atonal all her life, though that would not have stopped her taking centre stage. Indeed, were Ruth a young woman of today her role model would be Madonna. How she would have relished playing the public slut, flaunting her ribald sexuality for vast sums of money to an audience ever ready to excuse excesses of outrageous behaviour.

The closest she came to this was on the dance floor, where she displayed a total lack of inhibition and outdid all her rivals. There is no doubt that through dance she attained the recognition and popularity that were so desperately important to her. In her mind the worst fate that could befall a girl was to be insignificant, and, though small of stature, dainty even, she was energetic in her resolve to stand out from the crowd.

About this time her naturally fair hair had darkened, and she discovered peroxide, one of the important crutches for her fragile ego. To the very end of her life she bleached her hair, which some experts say played no small part in her downfall in Number One Court at the Old Bailey. When my turn came to make the most of my own attributes in my mid-teens, I, too, believed that blondes have more fun, and I have remained unnaturally blonde ever since. In Holloway Ruth's hair assumed an importance out of all proportion to her situation, but I can understand why. Had she wanted to defend herself, it would have been to her advantage to appear in the dock looking mousey, pathetic and grey, a broken victim of human suffering. Instead, having decided to die, she chose to do so looking her best and graced the dock as a high-class, high-heeled tart, a sort of slimline Barbara Windsor. The broken mouse was not a role within her repertoire.

Over the weeks in prison Ruth's hair had lost its colour and texture, and it was only thanks to the prison governor, Dr Charity Taylor, acting with well-intentioned humanity and contrary to Home Office regulations, that Ruth's regular hairdressers, Shack's of Shaftesbury Avenue, were permitted to send in the raw materials to restore her platinum coiffure. Thus was her self-esteem renewed as she protested almost to the last that she was quite content to die, a belief justified for her by the biblical dictate of an eye for an eye.

But beneath her commitment to that doctrine lay a more covert, feminine fear. What, I believe, bothered her most was the prospect, if reprieved, of spending ten or a dozen years locked away and returning to the outside world an old, spent woman. On release she would be 38 or 40, which to her spelt finished. If only I could tell her my own experience.

My life, as will be revealed, has been just as fraught and traumatic as Ruth's, and it is only in my early forties that I found true independence and the ability to live joyfully without fear of being hurt or rejected by others. Before I had never known what normality was and over the years I have regrettably placed all my six children in abnormal surroundings and circumstances. Ruth was a fool, and she inadvertently made us all pay for her selfish vanity in those bleak days during which all her thoughts and passions were focussed on one worthless man, David Blakely. In parallel, I have had my own obsessions of the heart, and I have allowed myself to be driven to the end of my tether. But I am learning from my experiences, and I have vowed that never again will I allow myself to be pushed outside the parameters of my own control.

So the newly peroxided queen of the south London dance floors, five feet two inches tall and teeming with the enthusiasm of youth, went out to take the Streatham Locarno dance hall by storm. She found work as the personal assistant to the in-house photographer at the Locarno, a job that temporarily gave her the touch of the glamour she craved and access to the more important clients of the venue. It was there that she would soon meet the first big love of her life, and there, too, in that self-same Streatham Locarno, that one of those eery coincidences that have plagued me throughout my life had its beginnings.

Having spent all my childhood, bar the first couple of years, in Warrington, when I was in my mid-teens I became a model and discovered the bright lights of the big city, in my case Manchester. It was the early 1960s, and after the Beatles had placed Liverpool firmly on the map, Manchester was basking in the secondary glories earned by the Hollies, Freddie and the Dreamers, Herman's Hermits, and Wayne Fontana and the Mindbenders. The city's clubs thrived, a glittering cornucopia of discos and nightspots. My favourite hang-out was Tiffany's on Oxford Street, where the resident group – they were pop groups in those days, not bands – was the Nocturnes. Within the confines of Manchester, the Nocturnes were as famous and highly regarded as their aforementioned contemporaries, and enjoyed widespread and loyal support to the extent that queues of eager young Mancunians formed round the block on most nights of the week. Being a model on the books of the top agency in the north, Lucie Clayton's, I was spared the need ever to join the queue and had privileged access as and when I wished, which was nearly every night.

The Nocturnes were three guys and two girls. The girls, Lyn Paul and Eve Graham, later enjoyed international fame with the New Seekers, whose recording of a jingle for a Coca-Cola advertisement, 'I'd Like to Teach the World to Sing (In Perfect Harmony)', reached the number-one spot in the pop-music charts in the first week of 1972. The drummer with the Nocturnes was Ross Mitchell, the lead guitarist Kenny Taylor, but I only had eyes for the singer and bass player, Nicky Walker. Neither Nicky nor I were to know it at the start, but he was destined to become my first husband and the father of my first child, Scott.

Following his long stint as a Nocturne, Nicky joined the resident musicians who worked at the Streatham Locarno, and I, trailing in his wake, moved with him. I doubt we were ever in love, but we certainly thought we were. We were certainly in lust, and I was resolute in my determination to marry him. My adoptive parents in conservative Warrington tried every guile to dissuade me, but the teenage rebel was not for turning and spurned their advice, plunging headlong into a first, disastrous marriage. More than twenty years further down life's rocky road, we remain on the best of terms, though we are both quick to admit that domestic bliss could never have existed between us.

In Streatham, Nicky had formed a best friendship with a charming young chap, Andy Simmons, and we all hung around together, inseparably. Andy always seemed to have plenty of cash on him, and he drove round in a gorgeous soft-topped Morgan sports car, a present from his doting father. When the day of our wedding came, there were just the three of us – hardly the dream day of days for the 17-year-old bride, marrying with the reluctant permission of her adoptive parents, who had added a codicil to the permit making it clear that henceforth she was on her own.

Andy was best man, and he drove Nicky and me, squashed into the two-seater Morgan, to Brixton Register Office. Nicky was no better at orthodox planning than I, and it came as a total surprise to us when the registrar stated the need for an independent witness to the ceremony, aside from himself, ourselves and Andy. Ever the most resourceful of our triumvirate, Andy trawled the Brixton streets and returned with an unsuspecting passer-by who satisfied the registrar's statutory demands. Though I was a married woman, child bride even, I cannot recall any feeling of emotional metamorphosis as a result of our signing a piece of paper and being legally pronounced man and wife.

One weekend Andy told us that his parents were going away and asked us if we would like to spend the weekend at their home. It was a golden opportunity for Nicky and me to break with the routine of non-stop work, and although we had a very pleasant flat in Streatham, it was hardly green belt. The Simmons home turned out to be a large house in Northwood, tastefully furnished and clearly cherished. Andy's Morgan sat proudly in the driveway, inviting any *Country Life* photographer to immortalize archetypal 1960s upper-middle-class England. I recall a relaxed weekend with laughter, good food and a few drinks, of course. When I casually asked him what his father did for a living, he said, without embarrassment: 'He used to be a lawyer, but, a few years ago now, he was involved in a case which so disturbed him and destroyed his faith in the British judicial system that he has never practised law again.'

'Oh,' I said with no more interest than anyone might show, 'and what case was that?'

'The Ruth Ellis case,' he replied.

I must have concealed my inner reaction for Andy did not pursue the conversation, and the subject was quietly dropped. If Nicky overheard our conversation, he certainly betrayed nothing to arouse Andy's suspicions. My mind was working nineteen to the dozen. Here I was, sitting in the home of a lawyer who had been involved in the infamy of my mother's case, and, from what I had just heard, it had destroyed his professional life.

I determined never to make Andy privy to my origins; I just thought it would be unfair, and make him uncomfortable in my presence, destroying the camaraderie that we shared. However, I found the revelation disturbing, and Nicky must have found me in strange mood when we went to bed that night.

The end of the weekend brought an even greater shock, which again I felt compelled to keep to myself. I admit that at this stage in my life I had given little thought to my mother, and I had never had any desire to flaunt her. In particular, I had never been conscious that there was any strong physical similarity between us. I was slim, as she had been. In those days I never weighed more than eight stone, and with my long blonde hair I would be a liar if I claimed not to know that men found me attractive. I was not overendowed in the breast department and to be so in later years would cost me £1000 in surgeon's fees. But, in retrospect, I can see that I have inherited some physical attributes from Ruth: small bones, a strong neck, and legs that can be exposed on any beach without shame.

I would not instantly have added my mouth and my eyes to the list of inherited similarities, but, in 1975, when the *News of the World* newspaper tracked me down, photographer Terry O'Neill deliberately had me made up in the style of Ruth, and the end result took my breath away. There I was in my mother's image. It curdled my blood when I compared our photographs. Although I am a rational person and have never had any truck with contact with the hereafter, I cannot help but wonder whether I have lived out vicariously Ruth Ellis's remaining years.

On the Sunday afternoon Andy's parents returned home. There had been no rave-up, no party, so there was no last-minute panic to restore order to the house. When his parents walked in, Andy's father turned ashen when he saw me. What he saw, or imagined he saw, I will never know. In a quivering voice he asked: 'And where do you come from?'

'Warrington,' I replied, and with that all the remaining blood drained from his face, and he looked as though he were about to faint. Instead, he drew a deep breath, pulled himself up to his full considerable height, recovered his dignity and, with a half bow, left the room. I never saw him again. He was Leon Simmons, the lawyer who had represented Ruth in her divorce from my father, and the man to whom she turned just a few hours before her execution. He was the only member of the legal profession whom she trusted implicitly and with whom she ever achieved a close working relationship and understanding. It was to him that she wrote, just two hours before her death:

DEAR MR SIMMONS
THE TIME IS 7 O'CLOCK A.M. – EVERYONE IS SIMPLY WONDERFUL IN HOLLOWAY. THIS IS JUST FOR YOU TO CONSOLE MY FAMILY WITH THE THOUGHT THAT I DID NOT CHANGE MY WAY OF THINKING AT THE LAST MOMENT. OR BREAK MY PROMISE TO DAVID'S MOTHER [to atone for his death with her own]. WELL, MR SIMMONS, I HAVE TOLD YOU THE TRUTH AND THAT'S ALL I CAN DO. THANKS ONCE AGAIN.
GOODBYE.
RUTH ELLIS

Yes, she had told him the truth, but too late for him to effect any change. With only 24 hours remaining before her scheduled death, she dramatically changed her story and, for the first time, sought to implicate Desmond Cussen, the man who had been described in court as her 'alternative lover'. Not surprisingly Cussen, who I fervently believe should have stood in the dock alongside Ruth, had disappeared and proved untraceable, in spite of the frantic efforts made by Mr Simmons and Victor Mishcon, now Lord Mishcon, his senior partner in the law firm. Ruth's brother Granville joined the all-night search, but unable to produce Cussen for questioning in person, all last-minute pleas were ignored by both Scotland Yard and the Home Office.

Where the Home Secretary, Major Lloyd-George, was during these final critical hours is not generally known, but my own researches indicate that he and his staff were far from being on the case. At perhaps the most crucial moment in this eleventh-hour panic, the Permanent Under-Secretary to the Home Office, Sir Frank Newsam, was in the Royal Enclosure at Ascot racecourse. Leon Simmons was distraught and thereafter relegated himself to the legal sidelines. Taking his pension several years ahead of retirement, he quietly left the profession that he had served with pride and commitment. He could hardly have blamed himself, for no one could have been more diligent in defence of his client. If Ruth had told the truth from the start, instead of suppressing most of the facts that could have served in mitigation, it is not beyond the bounds of credibility that she would be alive today, her case forgotten, possibly a couple of suicides averted, and everyone involved might have lived reasonably happily ever after. There again, perhaps not.

There is something that still strikes me as totally illogical and that concerns parliamentary procedure. Notable members from both Houses were revolted by the Ruth Ellis case and campaigned vigorously for a reprieve. A leading voice was the member for London, North Kensington, George Rogers, with vociferous support particularly from Sidney Silverman, Anthony Greenwood and Emanuel Shinwell. Their eloquent protestations appeared daily in the columns of the national newspapers. However, under parliamentary rules, the case could not be raised in either House until the sentence had been carried out according to the law. Well, I am sorry, but that is a bit bloody late.

So through the Streatham Locarno I came face to face with Leon Simmons and, by coincidence, walked in my mother's footsteps. During the war years that she worked there, the Locarno was a favourite haunt of servicemen on leave. They were mostly Americans and Canadians, all a long way from home and with a lot of money to spend in comparison with their British counterparts. Ruth, curvaceous in all the right places and turned out like a Hollywood siren in the Jean Harlow–Carole Lombard mode, caught the eye of many a prowling soldier, sailor or airman. She was as free with her charms as she had always been generous with everything she had. Muriel recalls with annoyance how Ruth would regularly give away her toys or best clothes to school friends who admired them, all items that had been scrimped and saved for from the Neilson family's shoestring budget.

There was one man on whom she set her sights, Clare, a French-Canadian soldier. His surname is not known, but it was he who won the affection and eventually the love of 17-year-old Ruth. Clare was not the classic tall, dark and handsome Clark Gable clone that one might expect to have swept her off her feet; those who remember him do so as a short, rather dumpy man. His appeal for Ruth lay in his sophistication. He sent her flowers, wined and dined her in the restaurants of Soho, afforded her the luxury of travelling by taxi and generally introduced her to the delights that money could buy. He presented her with clothes and jewellery and flattered her with protestations of undying love. In return she willingly gave him her body and discovered the joys of a regular sex life with the partner of her choice. Totally ignorant of contraception, a word never used in the house of my staunch Roman Catholic grandmother, the inevitable happened, as it did with so many other girls in wartime. Ruth became pregnant.

Ruth's initial reaction to her pregnancy was one of shock and fear. Clare was ten years older than her, and she dreaded his response to the news as much as she anticipated the wrath of her mother. Her apprehension appeared to be unfounded when Clare reacted with joy and immediately proposed marriage. The family had taken an unreserved liking to the personable Canadian, and Bertha's fears of public shame and disgrace at the prospect of becoming grandmother to a bastard child were soon tempered by the announcement of the forthcoming marriage. Enthusiastically she gave her full support for the union.

Clare said that he would need to approve the arrangements with his commanding officer, though he foresaw no obstacles. Within a week he confirmed that his CO had raised no objections, and Ruth and her mother began making plans for the wedding. Each time they tried to pin Clare down to a date, he came up with conflicting orders from his unit that made it impossible to name a day. His procrastinations continued, and his excuses wore thinner and thinner. Bertha sensed that all was not well, and to allay her suspicions she wrote to Clare's commanding officer to establish exactly what was forcing the delay in the wedding arrangements. It was just as well she did, since Clare had omitted to tell them that he already had a wife and two children back home in Canada.

It is interesting that all the books up until now that write in any detail about my mother have been by men, and none has come close to understanding the extent to which she was traumatized by this revelation. All her trust and emotional security were swept away in this one act of treachery. She was carrying the child of the man to whom she had entrusted her life and spirit, and he had rewarded her with a pack of lies. Only a woman who has been on the receiving end of such heartless treatment can come close to understanding the long-term damage of such a cruel blow. I know, I have been there. I have been assured that a lover had left his wife once and for all, when I was carrying his child. I miscarried, and while I was going through agonies, the wife whom I had wanted to believe he had left more than a year previously gave birth to another of his children.

'What's this,' I asked, 'the second immaculate conception?' He never answered, but only I know the pain I felt at his deception. Fortunately, I was old and experienced enough to handle the betrayal, but for Ruth, a strip of a girl at the age of 17, it must have destroyed whatever limited emotional reserves she had.

Clare opted to brazen it out by repeating his declarations of love and attempting to convince those who would listen that he had never loved his wife and wanted to divorce her and marry Ruth. Whether Ruth believed him or not was soon irrelevant. To her home in Brixton one morning a florist delivered a bunch of red carnations addressed to Ruth. The flowers were a reminder of the first bunch Clare had ever bought for her, and red carnations were to have an on-going significance for her throughout her life. Attached to the flowers

23

was a goodbye note. Both had been sent from the troop ship that was returning Clare to Canada.

He sent her money at sporadic intervals for the best part of a year but was then never heard from again. To spare the family blushes Ruth was sent 250 miles north for her confinement. There she told anyone curious enough to ask that her husband was an American pilot who had been killed shortly after they were married. On 15 September 1944 she gave birth to a son in a nursing home in the Cumberland village of Gilsland, just north-east of Carlisle. She named him Clare Andrea Neilson, ever after known as Andy. He was my half-brother, and he, in turn, would come to a terrible end, another victim of the gross aftermath of mother's hanging.

CHAPTER THREE

Life in the Fast Lane

With Clare gone, Ruth returned alone to Brixton with her infant child. Arthur, now an invalid whose once nimble musician's fingers were gnarled and crippled by arthritis, averted his gaze from his daughter and grandchild in a gesture of disapproval. Bertha, ever vulnerable to the prejudices of society, burst into tears at the shame that Ruth had inflicted upon them. The sniggers of bigoted neighbours were of far greater importance to her than the welfare and needs of her daughter and new grandchild. The only genuine care from within the family came from Muriel.

Muriel had married and produced two sons. Her heart reached out to baby Andy, which was just as well since most of the responsibility for his early upbringing was to devolve upon her. Ruth had no malicious intent to neglect her son, nor did she deliberately exploit the goodwill and stability of her older sister. What was uppermost in her mind was the need to earn a living. I can empathize with the emotional tug-of-war that was her plight. When my own first born, Scott, arrived I had to face a similar predicament. I was little older than Ruth had been at the time of Andy's birth and already estranged from my husband Nicky. Once my figure was restored to normal I needed to return to modelling, and so I willingly shared responsibility for Scott with Peter and Phyllis Lawton, my adoptive parents in Warrington. I felt no sense of relief in doing so, merely an acknowledgement that I had no other choice and an appreciation of how lucky I was to have a mother figure like Phyllis, who had spent the major part of her adult life taking care of those in need. She rallied to my cry for help when she was most needed. For six months I travelled home from London every weekend.

When Ruth's figure returned to normal she found her breasts were bigger and more shapely than they had been before her pregnancy. She was even more the object of men's instant attention, and she was quick to detect that her sexual attraction had increased. She was the sort to enjoy the wolf whistles that followed her down streets, and, privately, she vowed to fulfil the maximum potential of her assets and turn them into cash. With this in mind as a means of generating an income to support herself and her son, she answered an advertisement that was to launch her on the path towards the vice dens of London's Soho, Mayfair and Kensington.

The advert appeared in a local newspaper and was for a model to work evenings only in 'artistic nude poses' for members of the Camera Club. To shed her clothes in front of men was no problem for her as she did not suffer from prudery, was stoically proud of her attributes and rather wallowed in men ogling her with sexual hunger. Apart from anything else, the pay was £1.00 an hour; money for old rope and more than she had ever earned during her brief working life. Of course, nine years later, when news of the Blakely murder was first splashed across the news-stands and front pages of the papers, several of the men who had leered at her in the Camera Club through their Box Brownies crawled out of the woodwork to try and sell their vulgar and, by the standards of the time, pornographic pictures. Their expectations of wealth were thwarted by Fleet Street editors who had standards of decency and, without exception, rejected the pictures on principle. Today it would be a different story, as principled editors of the British popular press are as rare as dodos.

To be fair, the Camera Club was not exclusively peopled by perverts, and Ruth is recorded as saying that most members treated her with respect. Sometimes, after a session, she would go out with one or two of them for a drink in a club, usually in Mayfair. There she could manage to forget the pain that she had suffered and dream that she was living the Mayfair existence that was then the social zenith of the debutante and others of the more privileged classes. She saw Mayfair as it would later be romantically portrayed in Anna Neagle's films, *Spring in Park Lane* (1948) and *Maytime in Mayfair* (1949). Unfortunately for her there was to be no Michael Wilding as her leading man, but a succession of conmen, prefaced by one of London's worst, Morris Conley. After Ruth's death, a reporter on *The People* newspaper, the late Duncan Webb, wrote in his column: 'Right in the centre of corruption in the West End of London stands the figure of Morris Conley . . . I hereby name him as Britain's biggest vice boss and the chief source of the tainted money that nourishes the evils of London night life.' In 1961, on 10 September to be precise, *The News of the World* carried a story of a trial, in which Conley was convicted of keeping a brothel.

Conley, Maurie to his pals, owned several drinking clubs. It was in one of these, in Duke Street, just off Grosvenor Square, following a photographic session, that my mother made his acquaintance. With him a club owner, and her a young, ambitious model, Ruth was flattered by his attentions. Conley, rich by any stretch of the imagination, had become wealthy from an imaginative variety of criminal activities dating back to at least 1934. He was fat and unattractive, but Ruth was overwhelmed by his obvious power and association with a string of famous names. He, in turn, saw her naive vulnerability and potential for work in one of his drinking clubs as a hostess, then as now, a euphemism for prostitute. She was hooked into his kingdom, oblivious of his criminal record and his total lack of ethics. In an earlier court case he had been found guilty and imprisoned for operating one-armed bandits that 'were so rigged that the jackpot could never be won if the machines were played on for a hundred years'.

In short, Conley was a convicted criminal, a pimp, a ponce and a fraudster. But he did have a soft side and turned up at Ruth's trial to offer his services as a defence witness, an offer that was not surprisingly turned down. It must be remarked that in those early days he in no way exerted any undue pressure on her to become a part of his flesh empire, but he enabled her to see clearly how she might best profiteer from her youth and sex appeal and escape the fetters and deprivations of poverty once and for all. Though she was ripe for exploitation, she entered the depraved world of Maurie Conley with her eyes wide open.

Conley was active in the worst kind of post-war property development, whereby he bought up blocks of derelict flats, hardly improved on their dereliction and leased them to the desperate homeless. They then lived in fear of his dangerous heavy squad who settled for breaking arms and legs in lieu of unpaid rents. Many of his flats he kept back for the use of his girls, his hostesses, who were allowed them for a reasonable rent, provided their youthful bodies were available on demand for his personal use.

Ruth revelled in the novelty of this brash, self-satisfied man, who flaunted his prosperity at a time of general austerity. With the twin advantages of time and distance, it is easy now to look back and see what a shady world she had entered, one where Mickey Mouse promises of earth's great joys and physical gratification were part of the everyday currency traded between hostess and client, and where sex and money were inextricably mingled.

Ruth never did anything by halves, and the cruel blow she had received from Clare had given a hard edge to her character. She knew full well what was involved in taking a job with Conley, but the prospect of having £20 a week in her pocket was all that seemed to matter. This would be made up by a low basic wage, commission on drinks ordered by clients as payment for her company within the clubs, tips and 'presents' from those whom she chose to entertain on a personal level in her flat. Conley provided free evening dresses but otherwise took a slice of all other earnings. Not only did he expect his girls to accommodate his lusts whenever his whim demanded but also those of any business associates he considered worth sweetening for his own gains. For these services there would, of course, be no 'presents'.

The licensing laws of Britain were restrictive and avidly enforced by the police. Having a club that only admitted members was a way of circumventing the liquor laws, and Conley owned at least four of them. Ruth began at his Court Club in Duke Street, where alcohol was served from three o'clock in the afternoon until eleven at night. When that closed he liked his more popular hostesses to cross to Welbeck Street, where his Hollywood Club opened its doors at eleven and served until three in the morning.

The clientele in these clubs was a mixed bag that embraced most social strata; a black marketeer might have rubbed shoulders with an out-of-town businessman, or a group of wealthy young playboys, who enjoyed the devilment of drinking out of hours, might have exchanged chit chat with a couple of demobbed servicemen with money to burn. Most came from the respectable middle classes for which Ruth so hankered, and, by and large, she enjoyed associating with what she considered to be a good class of people. The men in the drinking clubs would treat the girls with polite respect, and any client who transgressed would be unceremoniously removed.

Nothing has changed today. I find that the men who pay for the services of escorts that I supply through my agency are perfectly mannered, well respected in their own circles and from time to time enjoy being seen with a glamorous ornament on their arm. If the girls find the man attractive, then what private arrangements they may make beyond the basic escort service that I provide is entirely up to them, but if they choose to augment their income I can only say good luck to them. I can also say with hand on heart that I have met and enjoyed far more considerate and appreciative men who have paid for my company than those who have taken me for granted and beaten me up for my troubles.

And so it would appear to have been with Ruth. There is no record of her ever having problems with a professional client, yet the men she took as husband or full-time lovers knocked her from here to eternity. If there is no emotion on either side but simply a desire for distraction, there seems to be almost no risk, but when the heart becomes empassioned, that is the danger signal. Then and only then does the great green monster, jealousy, rear its ugly head and, if plied with sufficient alcohol, wreak its havoc.

Conversations recorded by subsequent researchers with some of my mother's contemporaries suggest that she gave a good service, and no man complained of not getting his money's worth. She took care with her whole appearance and was pleased if she excited comment. She keenly enjoyed any reaction. She had no affinity with the labouring classes and delighted in their absence from the clubs. She laughed and joked freely with the middle and upper classes, many of whom felt as trapped within their own sphere as she did in hers and equally fettered by convention. Once inside the anonymity of London's watering holes everyone was free to behave as they wished. A favourite bar became the axis on which a transient world in miniature revolved. My mother proved to be very popular in Maurie's clubs, though she retained a prudence that quickly enabled her to spot the bar-room bullshitters and potential troublemakers. Her later choice of lovers would suggest that this is not true, or that she somehow shed her discretion along the way.

There were half-a-dozen hostesses who worked the Court Club, and among them Ruth found something that had eluded her all her life, a best friend. Vicki Martin was the same age as Ruth and came from a similar background to her own. They shared ambition for money and worked as a team. While Ruth had always made a point of trying to spend Sunday with Andy, Vicki's arrival on her scene meant they could accept lucrative invitations from wealthy business men to weekend in the country, usually south of the river in rural Kent or Surrey. Once having tasted the champagne and brandy way of life, they were a united pair of working girls with no qualms about soaking rich men for as much as they could possibly get out of them, be it in the clubs or the privacy of a country house.

It was these visits to a world previously outlawed to her that stimulated Ruth's softer, more feminine side, which would occasionally manifest itself in her dreams of a home, a settled family and security within what she perceived as the upper echelons of society. What she didn't know was that her expectations could be only met with disappointment and disaster. The respectability that she craved was impossible for her to attain because her club activities had already tainted her with disrepute; she was on course for the final rejection that would turn her into a murderess. In all her time with David Blakely she asked for little save acceptance on an equal footing from those who formed his inner circle; people such as journalist Carole Findlater, Ruth's *bête noire*, who didn't get on with her. Had Mrs Findlater not been so hostile to Ruth and her husband Anthony so weakly compliant, both Blakely and my mother would still be alive today. The role the Findlaters played in the tragedy was never revealed at the time of the trial, but deep digging by Laurence Marks and Tony van den Bergh for their 1977 book, *Ruth Ellis*, exposed the extent to which the couple contributed to the double tragedy.

Vicki and Ruth loved to party and found no shortage of volunteers to ply them with the expensive food and drink to which they had rapidly become accustomed and escort them around the better clubs of London to dance till dawn. Vicki dreamt of movie stardom but never progressed beyond the casting couch. Together they laughed and played unreservedly and whored energetically. My mother, however, in spite of her worldly experiences, or maybe because of her Catholic upbringing, had either not discovered or failed to master elementary contraception. One of the club's wealthiest members from the business community made her pregnant. When she confronted him with the news he vanished without trace, and she took herself off to a private clinic, where she underwent the first of several abortions. Meanwhile the other girls and Vicki in particular covered for her, and few were any the wiser.

Ruth had mastered her trade and was one of Maurie's best. The talents she most needed were the ability to persuade the clients to eat and drink as much and as quickly as possible. When a man offered her a drink, she would order champagne, but more often than not a glass of cider would be surreptitiously substituted to swell the profits. Likewise, a small tot of ordinary tap water with a bottle of tonic looked just like the gin and tonic that she had ordered. If it became obvious that the client wanted to bed her, and she was not averse to the idea, she would endeavour to prolong their retirement until he was either incapable of further consumption or his libido was diminishing. Ruth was a skilled flirt and knew the value of the tease. The longer she could play him like a fish on a hook, the more bottles of champagne he was likely to buy to impress her. The old hostess trick of waiting till the man turns his head away, however briefly, and emptying one's glass into a potted plant was in her repertoire.

The hostesses had a strong mutual bond, as they still do in the latest proliferation of similar clubs in London. They did not see themselves as tarts. Tarts hung around on street corners or in shop doorways. I doubt they even thought of themselves as prostitutes, for they were selective in their choice of bedfellows, and it was by no means compulsory, unless presented with one of Maurie's specials, to sleep with anyone. However, the rent had to be paid, and Ruth, as much as any of the others, enjoyed the buzz that she got from carrying a handbag stashed with cash. She was a free spender herself, and the contents of the bag needed to be regularly replenished. Aside from that, she was a sexual enthusiast and not averse to deviating from straight, up-and-down missionary intercourse – if the price were right. Given a good education she might have made an astute business woman, and in modern parlance she would assuredly be described as having 'street cred'.

A cursory glance through today's London papers reveals a plethora of advertisements for club hostesses. In the fifty years since the war, the West End has gone full circle. The drinking clubs died off when licensing laws were relaxed to allow all day alcohol consumption. If you wanted a drink, the pubs and those 1960s inventions, the wine bars, were there to supply the demand. If it was sex that was wanted, the massage parlours advertised without restraint. Now, it seems the clubs, which offer both with a veil of respectability, are back in fashion.

The sophistication that Ruth believed she had found estranged her more and more from her family. Andy was pushed from pillar to post between Bertha and Muriel, and visits home offered little to Ruth other than boredom. Her vivacity needed constant outlet, and what she had once called home she now saw as a lifeless and depressing place. The values that she came to hold so dear were, of course, phoney, and she would have to wait until she was locked in the condemned cell to discover who her real friends were.

Life in the fast lane is highly addictive, as I was to discover for myself in protracted affairs with footballer George Best and film star Richard Harris. Any hours not spent sleeping or tarting oneself up are spent in search of new satisfaction, whether derived from spending, jetting, eating and drinking or screwing. Mine were the days of sex, drugs and rock 'n' roll and, though Ruth died three months before the phrase rock 'n' roll entered our vocabulary, she clearly would have loved the liberations that came with the swinging sixties.

Her play period was conducted during the years of sweet rationing, clothing and petrol coupons and even basic food rationing. There were never any shortages in Maurie's clubs. Steak, all but unknown in the average household, was freely if expensively available, as were whisky, gin and extra coupons for whatever you might fancy. On the other hand, no government managed to ration sex, which is in demand equally in war time and peace time. If what I hear is correct, there were housewives doing it in Bradford for an extra bag of coal; Lincolnshire farmers offering half-a-dozen eggs for a roll in the hay, and what the butcher could not get for a pound of bacon was probably not worth having. 'Twas ever thus and ever more shall be, which is why I am a strong advocate for the legalization of prostitution, of which more on later pages.

The all night parties and the endless topping up of high spirits with alcohol and other stimulants inevitably take their toll. Ruth was drinking more and more. The tots of water were now really gin, and in the champagne stakes she liked the real thing. The hours of partying are inevitably followed by the body's refusal to take any more. The resultant lethargy demands greater effort to be shaken off, and the eyes, the greatest giveaway of all, lose their lustre. Ruth's drinking had dramatically increased though it still had a long way to go. She and Vicki Martin talked for hours about what the future might hold and how they might best scheme to realize their ambitions. Vicki was a tough, much tougher than Ruth, sensation seeker. In wild bids to publicize herself she took to smoking cigars whenever asked to pose for pictures and, as fashion and the laws of the club jungle decreed, bleached her hair platinum blonde. Her eyes were alert to every opportunity, but any avenue with promise inevitably ended between some set of sheets or other. She never gave up.

Vicki had been born Valerie Mewes, and the fact that she deemed it necessary to change her name is indicative of her endless quest to be what she was not. She finally found her brief moment of fame in the early 1950s, when she featured regularly in the gossip columns as the girlfriend of the fabulously rich Maharajah of Cooch Behar. The Maharajahs of the old Raj were the ultimate symbol of wealth in those days, for the Sheikhs had not then struck oil in the Gulf. In, as it turned out later, yet another parallel between my own life and Ruth's, Vicki was to die in a car crash only three months before the murder. Mother had lost one of her best friends.

I, too, had a best friend. Her name was Kathy Anders, and she was, beyond a shadow of a doubt, one of the most beautiful girls I ever saw. She came from Rochdale, famous for its bus station, the Co-op and Gracie Fields. Kathy had the wonderful rich accent that abounds in that Lancashire town, liberally spiced with solecism, and, nowadays, whenever I hear an interview with the Rochdale pop singer Lisa Stansfield, I close my eyes and see Kathy.

In 1974 she was crowned Miss England and shortly afterwards married David Moores, son of Cecil Moores and one of the heirs of the Littlewoods empire created by his uncle John and his father. From that point on Kathy had few friends. She moved to live in Halsall, near Formby, a well-to-do resort between Liverpool and Southport that was home to numerous Moores. David was extremely possessive and watched her like a hawk. He rarely let her out of his sight. She was only permitted friendships if he approved, and I was one of the chosen few.

Once a Moores, Kathy had an open cheque book, and while I was shopping for my clothes at Oxfam and other second-hand outlets such as Manchester's Elite Dress Agency, Kathy swanned round all the most expensive shops of the city, as well as Southport, signing her name without hesitation. The trouble was she had no clue about co-ordination and would buy top and bottom garments that no more belonged together than fish and custard. Consequently I was her frequent companion on these sprees, and we would shriek with laughter as she attempted to mismatch everything in sight. One time she desperately wanted a gold beret, and though we searched high and low it was without success; so I went home and crocheted one for her. From her reaction I might have just presented her with the Crown Jewels, so overwhelmed with gratitude was she. To me it was very little. I have a facility with all types of sewing, skills inherited from Bertha whose old Singer sewing-machine I still have at home. I can never look at that great heavy machine without marvelling that, as a refugee, she carried it halfway across Belgium with her. It was her trade; her tool whereby she could always earn a crust. Her talents were extraordinary, especially when she worked the daintiest and most delicate of lace.

My son Scott used to love me to pick him up and take him to Kathy and David's house with its vast tended gardens and modern swimming pool. Kathy kept the fridge stocked with ice cream in readiness for Scott, though she never ate it herself. I remember sitting with her one deliciously hot summer's day while Scott splashed around happily.

'Come on,' I said, 'let's jump in the pool.'

'Oh no,' she replied, 'I would never go in there.' She had a total fear of water.

At this time I was married to my second husband, Peter Bunting, who became singularly disenchanted with my almost daily visits to Formby. I continued to go because, quite simply, I enjoyed her company, and Peter was always busy with his new job. I have never had a better friend than Kathy before or since. She had a premonition that she was going to die. One day we were driving into Southport, she at the wheel, no shoes on her feet – she always drove without shoes – and out of the blue she suddenly said to me, 'You will make sure David is all right if anything happens to me, won't you?'

'What are you talking about?' I asked.

'You know, if anything happens to me, you will look after David for me?'

I promised her I would and quickly steered the conversation off the subject, but echoes of her nagging concerns were to come back to haunt me shortly afterwards.

Kathy rang me at home one day to say that she and David were eating out that evening in one of their regular restaurants in Formby and asked me if I would like to join them. For a variety of reasons I was not able to go. I was in a hurry and tried to get her off the line as quickly as possible, reminding her that we were scheduled to model together the following Monday, and I would see her then. That night she never made it home. Less than a mile from their house, the car left the road and ended up, passenger side down, in one of the small irrigation ditches that are a feature of the agricultural land in those reclaimed areas. Kathy drowned in just a few inches of water.

Thus began some of the worst days of my life. True to my word I went straight over to the hospital to find David. The front entrance was surrounded by press and news cameras, so I discovered a back entrance. The doctor there told me that David would not talk, but as I walked into his room, he said, 'I knew you'd come.'

I sat in a chair in that room for two and a half days, day and night, with David asking me not to leave. Eventually I asked, 'Can I go now?'

'Yes,' he answered. 'I'm all right now.'

Kathy was the latest in a long line of Moores' family tragedies. Just a few months earlier, David's older brother Nigel had been killed in a motoring accident in France. All the money in the world cannot buy life.

So I know the devastation Ruth must have felt when she learnt of the death of Vicki Martin with whom she had been through so much. All those times at the Camera Club and the Court Club, and with Maurie Conley and all the others, must have flooded back.

Vicki Martin had been another forced to lie down and close her eyes whenever the repugnant Maurie fancied his afternoon delights. Though sex with Conley must have been something of an ordeal, Ruth was able to laugh off whatever disgust and revulsion she might have felt. For her, perfunctory sex was never a problem, and this is another of her characteristics that has rubbed off on me. Faced with the option of a park bench and starvation or a roof over my head and a full belly leaves no gap for prudery and principle. Such sex rarely lasts more than a couple of minutes, no matter what they like to think of their prowess. There are times when it is expedient to lie back, but to hell with England, think of oneself, and tomorrow is another day.

Though the hours were long, and one day in the drinking clubs could be very like another, it was still the best life Ruth had known and presented her with the best opportunities to prosper. Many of those hours would be spent perched on a bar stool, wearing a mechanical smile, while some lost soul drank the broth of oblivion. Among those who frequented Maurie Conley's Court Club was a man whom the hostesses referred to as 'the mad dentist'. His name was George Ellis. He was to be the only man who ever married Ruth and who sired her only legitimate child, me. George Ellis, too, was destined for a grisly end.

CHAPTER FOUR

Marriage and Separation

Geoorge Johnston Ellis was born on the second day of
October 1909 in the Manchester suburb of Chorlton
upon Medlock. He met my mother in the Court Club
in 1950 when he was 41. Ruth was 24 at the time and had
recently had another abortion. Her feelings towards men in
general were fairly hostile, and her prime reaction to George
was that he was a pathetic species in the extreme, regaling
with crazy stories whoever would grant him attention and
splashing champagne around like water. It was certainly not a
case of love at first sight, at least not from her side.

My father was born with a fine brain and into comfortable
circumstances. His father, of Irish descent, had a thriving
business, which embraced both the wholesaling of fish from
Manchester's Smithfield Market and a retail outlet on the city's
Oxford Road, where George and his younger brother Ted
helped out after school and at weekends. My paternal grandmother was the dominant partner, however, and she it was
who pushed and encouraged the boys to make the most of
their considerable potential. Though both became dentists,
George in particular remained in slight fear and awe of his
mother for most of his life and never believed in himself
enough to feel up to her great expectations. His weaknesses

grew finally to outweigh his strengths, as he slowly but surely self-destructed.

He did well at school, though, and was rewarded with a place at the University of Manchester, where he attended the highly respected dental school. This did not offer the chance to escape the strictures of maternal influence as the dental department was but a short walk from the Ellis home and the shop where he continued to work, gutting fish before going off to learn about teeth. He became a highly skilled technician, but the talent that sticks uppermost in my memory was his skill at the piano. He had the deftest of touches and could play anything quite beautifully by ear. I play, but nothing like he could. Whenever he was at our home in Warrington, once he got out of bed, he would make his way to the piano and play 'As Time Goes By'. On top of the piano would be a tumbler of neat gin with two raw eggs – his heart starter, as he called it, followed by Andrew's Liver Salts.

By all accounts he was a very good dentist and made a deal of money from his practice, particularly during the war years. I have no idea when he became an alcoholic and can only guess that his drinking was a progressive affair, but it assuredly was a tragedy in that it destroyed both his marriages, his career and his body. Not only that but he was also one of those people who respond to excessive imbibing with physical and verbal violence, yet no violence that he inflicted on others would come close to that with which he secured his own death.

When George met Ruth he was living alone at 52 Sanderstead Hill, Sanderstead, following a divorce from his first wife, Vera. They had lived together in her home town, Warrington, where they moved in the upper circles of professional society. Vera was from an upper-middle-class background and very keen on amateur dramatics. She bore him two sons, Richard and John, who were never part of my own childhood. I cannot even recall my father speaking of them, but, in 1989, one of them saw me being interviewed about something or other at the BBC's Pebble Mill studios in Birmingham. They determined to make contact, and, through the efforts of a journalist friend of theirs, they traced me, and we met up in London's Westbury Hotel. We found, not surprisingly, we had much to talk about, and we have kept in touch ever since. Both have secured their own niches, Richard in property, and John as a lawyer.

Vera took the batterings and the abuse until her tolerance was exhausted. She fought to keep the family together, but one day she snapped. When my father came home from work that evening he entered an empty house. She had cleared out the lot – furniture, fixtures and fittings, pots and pans and the boys. She divorced him on the grounds of cruelty, both physical and mental, and she was awarded custody of the children.

George found solace in the bottle and in the clubs where he tried to buy friendship and favours. He, like so many of the other members, was desperately lonely and in the first stages of hopelessness. He was frequently morose and fast losing the little social standing that remained. His behaviour, so it is reported, was tinged with madness, even pretending to neighbours that Vera and he were still happily married though she had long left.

George Ellis became besotted with Ruth Neilson. She played hard to get – not by way of a game but because she really was not attracted to him. He was a pesterer and refused to take no for an answer. He spent lavishly on champagne for her and invited her out for dinner or to other clubs, all of which invitations she declined, while accepting his champagne and pocketing the commission. Eventually, he must have thought his persistence had paid off when Ruth told him to go to the Hollywood Club where she would later meet him. In fact she had no intention of meeting him at all but merely said so in order to be rid of him. She had intended to stand him up all along, as she and some of the other girls were going to a party. (Robert Hancock, in his 1963 book, *Ruth Ellis*, claims Ruth actually slept that night with a dress manufacturer in exchange for a couple of frocks. I have no reason to dispute his account.) Anyhow George, who was not a popular man among his own sex, was left high and dry by Ruth, and some other clubbers began to taunt him. Some sort of scuffle ensued, and George was slashed with a razor, necessitating eight stitches to close the wound on his face.

In a perverse way this was the best thing that could have happened to him, for Ruth was so overcome with remorse and guilt for the trick she had played on him that she began to go out with him frequently. She blamed herself, wrongly of course, for the injuries that he had suffered that night and was filled with compassion for his suffering. She later learnt that the trouble had arisen when George danced with some villain's girl in one of the other clubs. He told her the whole story at his golf club in Purley, and, of course, during the telling they both got drunk. He had a driver, and they went back to the West End clubland, where they got progressively drunker. The next thing Ruth was able to recall was waking up in George's house in Sanderstead, but it must be highly improbable that either had been capable of any coitus.

They began to date on a regular basis, wining and dining after her working hours at the club were over and then, more often than not, dancing the early morning away. Slowly but surely she began to see George from a different perspective. She developed a new purpose, to save him from the ravages of his drinking habits, and they planned a holiday away together. Perhaps she was already thinking that George Ellis, dental practitioner, might just be the one to satisfy her lust for respectability and security. Andy was almost 6 years old and living with the Neilsons in Brixton, a situation that she cannot have viewed with much satisfaction. Whatever her thoughts, Ruth kept George a secret from the family and, in fact, would not present him to them until after their marriage.

Their holiday was planned for Cornwall. Ruth was not used to luxury hotels and the seaside, but she settled easily enough for their romance to grow. Having her to himself made George less dependent on the booze, and he made one of his many pledges of abstinence, which he was never able to keep for very long. In his sober moments I am sure she found him stimulating company. He had been fond of sailing and even had a pilot's licence in days when private flying was a rare pastime. All his promises came to nought as he turned repeatedly to liquor.

After the holiday he briefly found work as a locum for a Hampstead dentist, but that employment was short-lived. Ruth returned to the clubs and spent most of her time working another Conley venue, the Little Club in Knightsbridge. George was possessive and whisked her away for a few days alone to a Surrey hotel. Dropping by at Sanderstead, there is a report that George was staggered to find his mother in the house and blurted out that he and Ruth had married. Ruth was forced to go along with the lie. The prospects of actual marriage were becoming distinctly real, and Aunt Muriel remembers Ruth telling of being in love for the first time with a man with whom she felt she could be settled.

Separating the fact from the fiction is not easy at this juncture, and there are conflicting versions as to who proposed marriage to whom and who made threats of whatever nature to the other. Their relationship was already volatile, and rows of high decibels were not uncommon. They lived together at Sanderstead in trial marriage, and George made new resolutions to give up the demon drink. Like a fool she believed him, especially when he agreed to dry out as an in-patient at nearby Warlingham Park Hospital. Before long he pronounced himself cured and, having been admitted on a voluntary basis, checked himself out against the professional advice.

Ruth became Mrs George Ellis mark 2 at Tonbridge Register Office on 8 November 1950. In a scene that I was to re-enact in my wedding to Nicky Walker, the witnesses were unsuspecting passers-by hauled in off the street; hardly the most romantic of beginnings and made even more depressing by the fact that, the day after the wedding, George returned to the mental hospital at Warlingham Park in lieu of a honeymoon. I do not know what the motivation was, but it strikes me as odd to go through with a wedding and then return to hospital for psychiatric treatment.

Money was in short supply, and Sanderstead had to go. On 28 December 1950 George re-registered his National Identity Card and gave as his new address 7 Herne Hill Road, London SE24, which was the home of my grandparents Arthur and Bertha. So, for a while, it would appear that the newlyweds lived with Ruth's parents, although Muriel remembers much family hostility towards the union, particularly from brother Granville. Whatever the circumstances, George could not have stayed there long as he was soon back in Warlingham Park for yet another attempt at a cure. While there he wrote to a dentist in Southampton who ran a group of practices in that area, and, hard to imagine how, he was offered employment together with a house at Oak Bank, Warsash Road, Warsash on Southampton Water. His new boss was Ronald Morgan who believed his story that a nervous breakdown had been responsible for his recent unemployment, and that he was fully restored to health and raring to go, supported by his lovely young wife. When called upon to do so and in sobriety, my father could always turn on the charm, and it is no wonder Mr Morgan professed himself pleased with the new appointment.

The status quo of peace and harmony could never have hoped for long life with two such extreme characters as Ruth and George. He discovered a network of local pubs and clubs and new sets of drinkers with whom to socialize. He became unreliable about the times by which he told Ruth he would return home and, little by little, unreliable in his work. The first tell-tale signs of the extent to which Ruth was vulnerable to jealousy and possessive behaviour, and which would eventually lead to the murder of David Blakely, began to appear through the veneer of domesticity and contentment. When they went out together, she would be as she had always been: exuberant, oozing vitality and a great natural flirt. The trouble arose if George so much as spoke to another woman. She would blow up any such encounter out of all proportion and bombard the poor man with wild and wilful accusations, figments of her imagination of which he was totally innocent. His alcohol dependence was by then total, and in drink he responded to his wife's suspicions and charges by punching and hitting her.

Once under way their troubles gathered momentum, and Ruth was forever packing her bags, with or without Andy in tow, and returning to Brixton for a few days. It is said that there is certain type of woman who incites men to violence, and I have sufficient evidence to admit that there may be much in that submission. In all probability I am one such woman myself, yet I totally abhor violence. I have been on the receiving end of so much, and yet never have I witnessed any man raise his fist to me unless his brain is addled with alcohol.

By this stage I was on the way, conceived in Warsash, and I must have spent much of my gestation being shipped from pillar to post, lodged in my mother's womb as blows showered down upon her tiny frame. Vera had experienced such treatment at the hands of George during her marriage to him. Ruth had seen her own father hit her mother and her sister Muriel on frequent occasions. I have vivid memories of my father's appalling displays in the Warrington home where I later grew up; and I have had children by men who have blackened me all over. So if there is something within me, that indefinable aspect of my personality, that provokes men to beat me up and throw me around by my hair, then I must have got it from mother, and she must have got it from Bertha, and Lord knows how far back it goes. Woe betide the man who tries it on my little ones. I am bigger built than Ruth, but no match for the strength of a man. Few women are. Ruth, on the other hand, was tiny. At the time she was hanged, her weight was recorded as 7 stone 5 lb.

The marriage was all but over long before I was born. The beginning of the end came when my father lost his job with Ronald Morgan. Reports that George had been bingeing and neglecting his work had filtered through to the Morgans and were common gossip in the village. The straw that broke the camel's back came when he irrationally opted to take a day trip to Cowes on the Isle of Wight, leaving a surgery full of patients who had all made appointments. By the time he condescended to telephone the receptionist to say where he was and that he would not be back that day, he was well and truly plastered, and, as they say, it's a funny way to give in your notice. He was fired.

Surprisingly, though, he was a long way from finished and landed on his feet almost immediately with a post with a practice in Newquay, Cornwall. Simultaneously Ruth had her pregnancy confirmed and opted to return to the family in Brixton. He moved into a private hotel in the Cornish resort. This separation did not stem the tidal flow of accusations of adultery that Ruth continued to level at her husband. She schemed plots to catch him unawares and moved to the resort briefly where she worked on elaborate plans to trap him, whereas all he was interested in doing was making enough money to feed his expensive addiction. That they even made a further attempt to patch up their marriage is probably due to the fact that I was on the way. In their book Marks and van den Bergh suggest that I would have been aborted had my grandparents not promoted their enthusiasm for Ruth to have a legitimate child. I will never know, but if that is true I offer them due thanks for the great gift of life.

Meanwhile my father was again falling down on the job, and he returned to the place that had become his bolt-hole whenever he felt pressured to absolve himself from responsibilities, the mental hospital at Warlingham Park. There Ruth's propensity to launch into a tantrum and tirade of vindictive mumbo jumbo reached a startling crescendo. Convinced that George was spending his hospital days engaged in sexual relations with both female patients and members of the staff, she visited one day with her temper inflamed and barged her way all over the hospital ranting and raving, screaming abuse in the language of the gutter, of which she was total mistress. So out of control is she said to have been that she had to be forcibly held down and sedated.

The doctors who had always tended George, in particular one Dr Rees, a psychiatrist, prescribed drugs for her from that point on until her arrest for the murder of David Blakely. One of the more surprising omissions by her defence lawyers at the trial was the failure to call Dr Rees to give any evidence that she had ever been treated for any psychiatric disturbance or that she was, at the time of the murder, taking legally prescribed sedatives. Combined with the alcohol she had consumed, the pills would have made her incapable of rationale at the time she pulled the trigger.

So my nine months inside my mother's womb were mostly spent with my father in detoxification and my mother showing serious signs of mental disturbance. The war of attrition intensified with both parties intent on wearing down the other's reserves. If there was any love left between them, no one has ever been able to recall it. Ruth went to Muriel's and would never again return to George Ellis. On the second of October, my father's birthday, coincidentally, and my mother was a Libran too, in 1951 I was born in the maternity unit of the hospital in Dulwich, south-east London. I have been told the delivery was difficult and prolonged, an experience that I shared when my first born, Scott, made his debut at 10 lb 12 oz, when I was a mere stripling at 7 lb.

Ruth took quite some time to recover, and at one point I understand there was some concern for her life – not a concern shared by George who, so I am told, chose to ignore my arrival, though he was notified at Warlingham Hospital. I think it was really the fact that he did not want to be saddled with the inevitable expense of a new baby that made him suggest that I be offered for adoption. Ruth would not agree, and she, Andy and baby me moved into Aunt Muriel's already overcrowded dwelling. Any correspondence between George and Ruth was now conducted through solicitors.

Without bothering to tell Ruth, George Ellis went back up North and to Warrington, the town where he had met his first wife. He had several acquaintances there from his earliest years in the dental profession. His name was still good, and word of his indiscretions down South had not preceded him to Warrington. He found employment as a schools' dental officer with the Warrington Health Authority, but his chronic drinking meant that he was always ducking and diving and spraying his breath to avoid detection. He still had a very significant role to play in my life, however.

Once Ruth recovered, and her figure was restored, she wasted no time in seeking out Maurie Conley who, in turn, was pleased to have one of his more popular hostesses back in action. Whatever doubts might have assailed her decision were smothered by necessity. Her brief bid for middle-class respectability had ended in failure and with another mouth to feed. The Court Club had changed its name to Carroll's and had a full late-night supper licence. The Little Club, too, was thriving, and London's West End clubs were going through a boom period. Financial constraints were freeing up as the post-war years gathered momentum, and shortages of luxuries slowly, but not instantly, became history.

Those who had a nose for easy money were edging into position. Rachman and his gang of thugs were moving in on the potential of cruel, unscrupulous property speculation, and the Krays were securing the boundaries of their own territorial conquests. Young men and old appeared to have more money to burn than ever before, and the everyday features of the capital had lightened.

At the other end of the scale the Neilson parents had been forced into another move, this time further into South London from Brixton to Tooting Bec, neither the one nor the other much different from the other grim addresses Ruth had known. They were not the districts of her dreams, so it was back to Mayfair and Knightsbridge with a vengeance and a single-minded determination, more fierce than ever, to better her lot. Carroll's had moved up-market, and its clientele numbered several international members of highly monied fraternities. She was back in the job she knew best, and with Aunt Muriel doing her best for me Conley provided Ruth with a small flat in Oxford Street, central London, where once more she was installed and available whenever Conley snapped his podgy fingers.

The only apparent legacy from my father was his name. Ruth had taken it and stayed with it and, indeed, had appropriated it for Andy. He was known henceforth as Andrea Ellis, and, of course, so was I known by my father's family name, though over the years I was destined to change it almost more times than my underwear.

In November 1951, with the marriage one year old and me in my first month of existence, George entered an application to file for divorce on grounds of cruelty. In those days the Probate, Divorce and Admiralty Division of the High Court did not dish out premature divorce petitions in the way that today's morally devalued society has come to expect. Marriage was a legally binding contract and was respected as such. His application was refused.

Ruth took a cursory look at her status quo and concluded that she was neither financially, nor in the eyes of the social classes for which she hungered, any better provided for than she had been at the outset of her working life as a waitress in

47

Reading. The greener grass in which she perceived the world of George Ellis to be located turned out to be just as arid as the pavements of Brixton. Her dreams were in tatters. There is no doubt she felt she had offered her all to him; her time and her body had been his exclusively. She would have no future need to furnish other men with sexual satisfaction, and she, George and Andy would live happily ever after.

Everything had disintegrated, and Ruth was right back to square one. It would have been reasonable to assume that George, with his education and professional experience, could have faced the responsibilities of his second marriage with greater maturity than his young wife, but that was not the case. Ruth had been left to worry about money, which he rashly spent on drink, much as he had done in his bachelor days between marriages. They were not long wed when he took to going to London's Astor Club, where he manifested generosity by offering drinks to all and sundry though he could ill afford it. The source of all their quarrels was the drinking, and the toll it took both emotionally and financially on the family purse and the running of the home.

It is easy to paint Ruth as hard done by, but I can well believe that she was difficult in the extreme. Her irrational accusations of infidelity are almost impossible to explain. There must have been blame on both sides, and the vast chasm between their respective ages, education and interests would have launched them on a matrimonial path that was inevitably a cul-de-sac. I myself have trodden the same path three times and been perilously close on a fourth occasion. I will never venture down it again.

CHAPTER FIVE

Me, Georgie: Life with Ruth

The first two years of my life I was cared for by my grandmother and Aunt Muriel. Since Muriel had a large family of her own, I probably spent most of my time with Bertha, and, from her correspondence in later years, she had forged a strong attachment with me. Furthermore, from the letters I have, it appears she bore no bitterness towards my father even after Ruth's death and wrote to him too, never missing our shared birthday.

The acrimony between my mother and father must have mellowed at some point because, on his visits to London from Warrington, he would visit, showing a growing interest in me after that initial rejection at my birth. He also frequented the clubs where my mother worked and, so I have read, occasionally slept on the sofa at her flat. Not surprisingly I have no memory of those days, but Ruth can have seen very little of Andy or me as she was in full-time work as a hostess, a job that left few daylight hours for anything other than sleep.

During those months, when she plied her trade against gynaecological advice, she began to feel out of sorts, a feeling that progressed to nausea and considerable abdominal pain. It was round about Christmas 1952 that she was finally admitted to the Middlesex Hospital, London, where doctors diagnosed an ectopic pregnancy: one in which the embryo grows in the Fallopian tubes rather than the womb. My own dictionary, *Chambers Twentieth Century*, defines ectopia as: 'morbid displacement of parts'. I think that just about sums it up. She was hospitalized for a couple of weeks and unable to return to work for about three months.

Even then she was patently not fit for the rigours of hostessing, and in an uncharacteristic act of compassion, or maybe just because it suited him, Maurie Conley offered her the managership of the Little Club, but not until after David Blakely had made his mortiferous encounter with her at Carroll's. Above the Little Club was a one-roomed flat that Maurie allowed her to use as part of her terms for the job. She took Andy and me to live there with her, and from all accounts it was a squalid little hole.

When Andy and I met up again in 1972, although he was highly confused about many things, he clearly remembered that room. My own recall is dim. I had long lived with a fear of puppets and had a vague recollection of Andy or someone else often frightening me with some hideous wooden doll. Andy was able to verify this and admitted he had delighted in terrifying me with one of his Christmas presents, a model of the radio dummy Archie Andrews. Though millions of listeners loved Peter Brough's famous talking doll, I still cannot look at a picture of the ghastly creation without recoiling in trepidation. My other immovable memory is the perfume my mother used. When as a teenager I strolled round the cosmetics counters of Manchester's department store, Kendal Milne, I picked up the scent of Miss Dior and knew instantly that this was the smell she had favoured – a memory again confirmed by Andy. Other than those two specific images and flavours, I have retained only a sketchy recall that my mother was blonde.

From August 1953 David Blakely spent most nights of the week in that tiny flat. The inflamed passions of both he and Ruth were in their infancy and insatiable. Andy was at school, and, as far as Blakely was concerned, I was a nuisance and in the way. His presence and interference were to shape my entire life, for my father took one look at Ruth's domestic set-up and concluded that something must be done and done quickly. My grandmother would have taken me back, but he had other ideas, and Ruth, obsessed by both her managerial post and her new lover, was hardly in a position to impose demands, especially when his proposed solution was so patently in my best interests.

The ménage of Blakely and myself vying for my mother's attention lasted beyond my second birthday. I know that because I have a letter from my grandmother in which she painfully reminisces about making my birthday cake:

HOW I WISH I WAS MAKING YOUR CAKE THIS YEAR, FIRST ONE CANDLE THEN TWO WHAT FUN WE USED TO HAVE.
HOW I MISS YOU. BUT I KNOW YOU ARE HAPPY AND THAT'S ALL THAT MATTERS.
FONDEST LOVE TO YOU
MY DARLING YOUR NANNY

I have no idea on what precise day or month my father acted and 'stole' me away, but I suspect it was either at the end of 1953 or early in 1954. My mother connived at the arrangements he had made, and, anyway, in March 1954, she had an abortion of a pregnancy conceived with Blakely. Where I was exactly I do not know, and it is not particularly important to me, but I do remember the day, whichever day it was, from beginning to end.

My father carried a case in one hand and held on to me with the other. First we took a bus and after that a train. It was exciting, and he told me we were going on holiday. They had, of course, conspired to tell me that so, hard though it may have been for Ruth, the goodbyes to her and to Andy were of no special significance and carried no suggestion that the parting was terminal. We went off cheerily.

The train, which was long and smelly with that mixture of bodies and soot that steam-train enthusiasts drool over, set off slowly. Almost immediately my father began to drink. The journey seemed interminable though I suppose it was no more than five or six hours. He got progressively inebriated, and his conversation went into decline. What began by pointing out some of the sights as we puffed away from London became incoherent mumblings before he at last fell asleep.

We arrived in Warrington. We climbed down from the train, crossed a bridge, I think, went through the ticket barrier and out of the station approach. George had slept off some of his excesses. Waiting outside was a big black car, as big a car as I had ever seen and, to my child's eyes, the size of a modern limousine. In the back of the car was Phyllis Lawton. My father said to me: 'This is your new mother. Go and sit on her knee.'

I did not understand and was frightened. The car with Peter Lawton at the wheel and my father alongside him in the front drove until we reached the driveway of a large house in a green area dotted with similar large houses. I was shown a bedroom and cried, lost in the vastness of the alien space that surrounded me. Though I did not know it, this was to be the home where I would live until I married, and it is the place to which I still refer as home today. I call the Lawtons my parents, but I still think it was a rather callous introduction on the part of my father.

It was all very mysterious, and my mother was never mentioned. What it transpired had happened was that my father had returned from one of his London trips and confided his fears for my security in his colleague, Phyllis, herself a dentist with the Warrington Health Authority, working to and with George who had the grand title of chief dental officer. Phyllis was married to a veterinary surgeon, Peter Lawton, and between them they generated a handsome income. They afforded the trappings of 1950s luxury and lived in the finest part of town. Their one regret was that they had no children, though both badly wanted to raise a family.

Phyllis was and is one of the world's saintliest of people, who has always done her utmost to promote the welfare of others. She listened attentively to all George's anxieties, and no doubt he painted a sordid picture of Ruth, the life she lived and the undesirable company she kept. Ever hiding his own humiliations and deceiving himself over his chapter of disgraces, he always explained away the weal across his face left by the razor-slashing as having been inflicted as he fought valiantly to protect Ruth from a gang of thugs. Just as he never told prospective employers that he had been regularly treated in a mental hospital, so he was economical with the truth whenever it fitted his purpose. He was a man of stubborn resistance, and his facility with words when sober and his natural charms spun webs that held firm against the falsehoods of his tales being exposed. Whatever story or stories he embroidered for the benefit of the Lawtons' ears, Phyllis fell for them, and she it was who proposed that he bring me to live with them for a while.

I was cute. I had curly hair, a winning smile and a bouncy manner. Inevitably I became their surrogate child. What they had not bargained for were the constant comings and goings of my father, at his will not theirs, and the disruptions he would bring in his wake. The sole cause remained his drunkenness. We shared a room, my father and I, me in a cot lying terrified and feigning sleep while he stumbled and reeled around the room, incapable and falling over, before, on a good night, collapsing into a stupor. There can be few more frightening spectacles for a small, or even a large, child to behold than a parent smashed out of their brains.

George would disappear for periods of time, leaving me with the Lawtons, and return after whatever binge he had ended.

What else I do recall from those early months or maybe even early years is that my real mother, Ruth, was never spoken of in my presence. I suppose her memory faded, along with the residue of my former life. I did think about her, and I was always aware that the Lawtons were not my real parents. I called them my step-parents and, at some stage began to call Phyllis 'mummy', which I still do to this day. Though I wondered to myself where my mother was, there was an atmosphere, which I cannot put my finger on, that made me aware it was expedient to keep my thoughts to myself. There cannot be many children who have not bombarded the adults in their life with whys, whens, hows and wheres, but I never did, at least not on that subject.

When my father died in 1958 I was told by Phyllis that I should now call Peter 'daddy', but I never did, until I was about 12 years old. Instead, I invented my own pet name for him, 'Boom', which replaced the previous 'Uncle Peter' and has stuck to this day.

Life with the Lawtons was a joy, I have to say. Kinder people have never existed. For holidays we used to go to a house in Rhosneigr, on the beautiful west coast of Anglesey, where all was wonderful unless father, as was his wont, suddenly inflicted himself upon us, got drunk and dominated the piano in that house as well. Though I can never condone his outrageous behaviour, his regular presence must have in some way eased the transition from my mother and grandmother to total strangers. For that I am in some way grateful, but, sad to admit, I never think back to George Ellis and feel any love.

Quite early on the Lawtons wanted to adopt me, but Ruth, maybe promoted by Blakely, refused to give her permission. My grandmother wrote to me on a fairly regular basis and sent numerous letters to George imploring him to let her see 'Georgina, my baby'. He did not accede to her request.

At some point during this formative period of my childhood the murder, the trial, the accompanying publicity and the execution occurred, all skilfully and successfully kept from me. I was 3½ by then but unaware of any appreciable change. It was only when I was 8 years old and stumbled upon the truth that certain events in my past assumed a different interpretation.

One particular incident struck me as strange at the time but not to such an extent that I made a particular song and dance about it. Phyllis was getting me ready for a visit from the child-welfare people. She washed me, this was in the afternoon, and put me into one of the many pretty dresses that I had (they always spoiled me). When she was turned away I clambered up on to the window sill and looked out on what seemed to be a sea of people, mostly men, all clutching cameras or some such.

Before I had chance to take in the scene, she had grabbed hold of me and hauled me down, and begun to scold me in a way that was not normal for her. This must obviously have been at the very height of the trial publicity, and the press were encamped, possibly on the day before or the day of the hanging itself, to try to obtain a newsworthy picture of Ruth's small daughter.

It was more than five years before all that dawned on me, and I am deeply appreciative of the effort they must have made to protect me. It cannot have been easy for them, and they certainly had no notion that they would be parenting the daughter of a murderess when they took me into their home originally. Lesser folk would have returned me more or less whence I came.

My grandmother continued to write to me without disclosing any hints about my mother's fate. She also wrote to George following Ruth's death. I have one letter that she sent to him, which adequately conveys her feelings. It was on the occasion of one of our joint birthdays:

DEAR GEORGE

HERE'S WISHING YOU ALL THE BEST FOR YOUR BIRTHDAY SEEING IT'S A TWIN BIRTHDAY PARTY IT OUGHT TO BE ALL THE MERRYER. I AM SENDING SOME SNAPS OF GEORGINA MY BABY. I HOPE YOU WILL LIKE THEM, ALSO A FEW CIGARETTES

ANDY IS AT SCHOOL AND SETTLING DOWN VERY NICELY. I HAVE LEFT BROMPTON RD AND I AM NOW IN SERVICE. I CANNOT GET OVER THE LOSS OF MY BABY. I MISS HER SO VERY MUCH. ANYWAY WISHING YOU BOTH ALL THE BEST ON THIS DAY. EXCUSE WRITING FOR MY EYES ARE FULL OF TEARS.

YOURS B NEILSON

I DIDN'T SEND GEORGINA A DOLL BECAUSE I KNOW YOU MUST HAVE BOUGHT HER ONE BY NOW.
GIVE HER A NICE BIG KISS FROM HER NANNY.

My father then decided it would be better all round if my grandmother ceased to write, and if all contact with the Neilsons were broken off. My grandfather journeyed to Warrington to confront him on this issue but found him intractable. He was forced to return home with news that could only add to Bertha's already great distress.

George Ellis was an irrational man, and in another volte-face he caused heartache to the Lawtons. With Ruth dead, there should have been no obstacle in their way in their plan to adopt me. He refused to allow it. He and Ruth had finally been legally divorced in January 1955 with the decree made absolute on 25 February, just a month and a half before Blakely was shot. The Court awarded legal custody of me to him. The Lawtons had no reason to contest the Court's ruling at that stage, for they had no anticipation that he would stand in their way on the matter of adoption. The only thing that might ever have gone against them was the fact that they were both middle aged, but George Ellis himself was no spring chicken and certainly not a fit man to whom a young child should be entrusted.

This drove a greater rift between the three of them, and the entire stability of the home was under threat. Peter demanded of Phyllis that George be thrown out, banned from the house and left to his own inadequate devices. Compassionate Phyllis could not bring herself to expel him, and their whole marriage, built on the most solid foundations of mutual trust and love, came to a head in a ferocious fight, which I can see as clearly as if it had taken place yesterday. My father was drunk, and Peter accused him of deliberate provocation of all members of the household. It was lucky that nobody got killed, and it all ended with George being led away by the police.

He had lost his job with the Health Authority for two reasons. First and foremost was his drunkenness, but the excuse that the Authority used was that he suffered badly from psoriasis. I never understood the full horror of this affliction until I saw Dennis Potter's drama *The Singing Detective* on BBC television in 1986, in which actor Michael Gambon portrayed a writer of trashy fiction with a similar, if more extreme, condition. The skin becomes uncomfortably flaky and scaly, and it would be problematic for a dental practitioner to work in such a state.

He stayed away from us for longer periods of time, and the mountain of gin bottles atop the wardrobe in the bedroom grew at a slower pace. The atmosphere at home improved, and

I wanted for nothing. Intermittently throughout my childhood I had been rather sickly and had spent some time in hospital. Such ordeals were always lightened by presents and beaming faces at visiting time.

My first school was Stockton Priory, a small private school in Stockton Heath, a town on the banks of the Manchester Ship Canal not far from Warrington. It was quite expensive and attended only by children of the wealthier parents in the area. I was happy there, and I felt I had nothing to hide. Home and school life were gentle and ordered, and I was a good learner. I cannot single out any particular friend, just that I had lots of them, and I played and worked as hard as anybody. I made progress and could read and write with the best of them. I am still an avid reader whenever I can find the time.

George visited at irregular intervals, as it had become impossible for him and Peter to live under the same roof. In order to get out of the house, he would insist on taking me for a walk, whether I wanted to or not. Once we got out of sight of the house, we would go from pub to pub, with him urging me not to tell, embellished by ghoulish stories of what happened to tell-tales.

Aside from these visits my life was ordinary with no unusual dramas; those began shortly before I was 8, on 2 August 1958 to be precise, the day on which my father died. My parents, that is the Lawtons, sat me down quietly and told me that he had died instantly in a motoring accident without any suffering.

I did not feel sad at all. My first thought was one of relief, knowing that I would face no more of his drunken nights, during which I lay rigid in my bed, dreading his sobbing or his frustrated kicking at objects at random or whatever other undignified behaviour accompanied him as he fell finally into his bed.

I will never forget the day of the funeral. Everyone wore black, and there was a great deal of muttering, which I was not privy to, and many pitying glances cast in my direction. There were not that many people there, as he was a man with few friends. The curious must have swelled the congregation.

When they returned, mummy Phyllis told me that Uncle Peter was going to be my new daddy.

I was shocked. I had already been given a new mummy, even though I secretly believed my old mummy would one day come and find me. The thought of a new daddy was just too much. However, with both my natural parents dead, the Lawtons now moved without further obstacle to adopt me. I was no longer to be Georgina Ellis but Georgina Lawton.

After the adoption papers were signed, sealed and delivered, I went to secondary school, a boarder at St Hilary's in the beautiful Cheshire village of Alderley Edge. This was a Woodard School, one of a group of public schools with a strong Christian tradition. I think it was selected because Peter had been a pupil at another Woodard school Ellesmere College in Shropshire. St Hilary's was all right in its way, but I shall never forgive one of the teachers, a Mrs Molyneux, for making me stand in front of the whole school to announce that I had changed my name and that henceforth I was to be called Georgina Lawton. It may not sound like such a big deal, but for me it was a devastating moment.

Some years later, after I had left school for good, I learnt the true circumstances of my father's death. He had not been killed in a motoring accident. What had in fact taken place was all part and parcel of his chronic alcoholism. With his money all but run out, he had gone to Jersey at the height of that summer of 1958. I suppose he selected Jersey because alcohol there was free of tax. He checked himself in to Le Chalet Hotel at Corbière, the most south-western point of the island, and embarked on a binge. When his depression hit rock bottom, he found himself penniless. He did not even have the money to pay his hotel bill, and on Saturday, 2 August, he took his own life. The extract from the Register of Deaths of the Parish of St Brelade, Jersey, reads under Cause of Death: 'He took his life by strangling himself with the cord of his dressing gown whilst the balance of his mind was disturbed.'

He chose to hang himself, surely no coincidence. How he managed it would do credit to a gymnast. Somehow he had looped the cord around his neck, attached the ends to each side of the bedhead and pushed with his feet. The second drama for me of that year took place after George's death, after the funeral and after my eighth birthday.

CHAPTER SIX

Fatal Attraction

At the time of my eighth birthday I had never heard of David Blakely, and I retained only a half-hearted fantasy of my mother. My home in Warrington and my school in Stockton Heath were the foci of my world. The only clouds on the horizon were the repetitive sicknesses from which I suffered, and which denied me the normal rough and tumble that a child of eight usually enjoys. My great joy in life was riding, either my horses, which we entered in shows, or my beautiful bicycle, on which I used to accompany Peter on his fishing trips. He had a special fibreglass rod made for me, but all these activities were curtailed as my health declined. As though it were not bad enough being brought up as an only child, what was worse was the fact that my illnesses confined me indoors, either in hospital or at home. Though I lacked for nothing materially and could not have been given more tender loving care, my parents were hardly great fun for me as an 8-year-old, spirited child. I longed to shriek and run around and simply be a child, and I envied all those other children who came from larger families and went home each evening to someone to play with. Though I had an imaginative mind and had learnt to keep my own company and my own counsel, the chief result was hours of boredom. Even children's television in 1958 was only broadcast for about an hour a day, and, anyway, I have never been a telly addict. I suppose I was often lonely and had to create my own amusement. What happened was what usually occurs when a child gets bored: I became mischievous, looking for something to do.

It was a weekend, a damp, dreary and depressing Sunday afternoon, one of those dismal days when autumn mists hide all the beautiful colours behind a pallor of grey as a portent of the drab winter to come. Phyllis and Peter were sitting arguing over the relative merits of ICI or Brooke Bond tea on the stock market. There was an overall atmosphere of aimlessness, as though the clock had stopped, and the household were frozen in sympathy. I sauntered unnoticed out of the room and ambled without purpose up the stairs. At the top I noticed that the door of my parents' bedroom was ajar. Now this was unexplored territory for me; I had rarely been allowed inside. It was private, and equally I knew that I should not go in, yet something, possibly the devilment that is a fundamental part of my make-up, compelled me to do so. I tiptoed in as quietly as a mouse.

Not content with merely glancing around and taking things in or just peering out through the windows, my curiosity took over as I opened the top drawer of an old-fashioned, heavy oak chest. Before me on the top I saw all those garments that were known in the 1950s as unmentionables and are now called lingerie. Ever incautious, I started to rummage. The truth of who I was lay underneath, just below Phyllis's underwear.

My little fingers moved bras and pants from one side to another as I found some paper, no, papers. I lifted out the whole bundle. They were mostly newspapers and cuttings, and they had yellowed with age. The one on top stared out at me with its four-word headline that would stick with me for the rest of my days: RUTH ELLIS TO HANG. Below the headline was a photograph of the blonde beauty whose image I had dimly retained from infancy. I had not a second's hesitation. I knew she was my mother. With the photograph and the word Ellis emblazoned in the top line of the paper, there was simply no room for doubt.

I began to spread out the pages over the carpet. It was clear she had done something terrible, but what? Under the first cutting I found her death certificate. The words in it made no sense to me. What they actually said, under Cause of Death, was: 'Injuries to the central nervous system consequent upon judicial hanging'. I went back to the yellowed paper and found something I could understand: 'She shall be hanged by the neck until she be dead.'

CERTIFIED COPY OF AN ENTRY OF DEATH

Given at the GENERAL REGISTER OFFICE, SOMERSET HOUSE, LONDON.

Application Number Exhib 150029/58.

No.	When and where died	Name and surname	Sex.	Age.	Occupation.	Cause of death.	Signature, description, and residence of informant.	When registered.	Signature of registrar.
25	Thirteenth July 1955 H.M. Prison Holloway N.7	Ruth Ellis	Female	28 years	a Club Manageress of —— Egerton Gardens Kensington London	Injuries to the central nervous system consequent upon judicial hanging P.M.	Certificate received from J.Milner Helme Coroner for the City of London Inquest held 13th July 1955	Fourteenth July 1955	Doris L. Stanley Registrar

DEATH in the Sub-district of Tufnell in the Metropolitan borough of Islington

REGISTRATION DISTRICT ISLINGTON 1955

CERTIFIED to be a true copy of an entry in the certified copy of a Register of Deaths in the District above mentioned.

Given at the GENERAL REGISTER OFFICE, SOMERSET HOUSE, LONDON, under the Seal of the said Office, the 10th day of November 1968.

DA 294744

I went cold. It was beyond my understanding that someone could die like that. I read on. I learnt that she had shot her lover dead, a man named David Blakely, and that her dreadful deed had meant that she too had been killed. Now, at last, I understood why she had never come back for me, why no one ever spoke of her, and why I had been taken away. My longed-for real mother whose hazy image of perfection I had cherished secretly was dead, and I would never see her again. I did not cry, but I felt an overwhelming sadness for her. I wondered what this man had done to make her kill him.

Suddenly I remembered the time I had stood briefly in the window wearing my party dress, when Phyllis had pulled me ferociously away. All those cameras had been there to try to take my picture. I didn't spend much longer poring over the papers. There was little else to know. I had taken in the basic facts that my mother, Ruth, had shot a man called David, and she had been hanged by her neck until she was dead. I was more anxious to put everything back where I had found it and leave no trace of being a snoop. I must have covered my tracks well as my parents never suspected anything. It would be seven years before I told them of that Sunday afternoon, of how I came to learn the stark facts of my pedigree, and how I had kept the knowledge as my own secret for all those years.

Who was David Blakely? I often wondered, and it is so easy for me now to sit and pass judgement on him as a spineless, inadequate, ne'er-do-well who destroyed himself and my mother with his vainglorious conduct and disregard for others. Easy indeed it would be, but entirely subjective. I wanted to discover more about him, and the more I read, and the more I battled with men through the passage of my own life, the more I came to recognize in him the sort of man for whom I might likely have fallen and who might well have driven me beyond the point of tolerance. The facts of his life have been told before but always from a man's standpoint and from the viewpoint of those investigating the crime rather than the personalities. In my own case, they are all personalities who have had an effect on my own life.

Blakely was a Yorkshireman, born in Sheffield on 17 June 1929, thus making him almost three years younger than Ruth. His father, John, was a well-respected doctor, a Glaswegian, whose general practice was in Crookes, a suburb of the city. David was the youngest of three boys and one girl born to Dr John and his wife Annie, but although there was money in plenty and the local society was theirs for the asking they were not a happy couple. Dr John – surprise, surprise – was a womanizer. He was a tall, good-looking man, popular at the golf club, at the bedside and, patently, between the sheets. Evidently he was kind, and in the days before the National Health Service it is said that he never refused treatment on the grounds that a patient was not able to pay. On the downside he was not much of a husband or father, nor was Annie any great shakes on the maternal duties. The children were raised mostly by a nanny, and David, the youngest, was nanny's favourite. He needed nanny all his life, and she was still responsible for the upkeep of his flat when he died.

However, whether he were a good or a bad family man, there is no doubt that Dr John Blakely was a hugely popular member of the community, whose popularity was put to the test when David was $3\frac{1}{2}$ – the age, incidentally, that I was when mother was executed.

One Saturday night in February 1934, a 25-year-old unemployed waitress, Phyllis Staton, who had been missing from her parents' house for two or three weeks, returned home, where she collapsed. She later died in hospital. Dr John Blakely was arrested and charged with her murder. He was also charged with the unlawful supply of a pituitrin-based drug for the purpose of procuring an abortion. He appeared before Sheffield magistrates on 21 and 22 February.

The prosecution sought to establish that Dr John and Phyllis had enjoyed each other's company for almost two years, and when she told him of her pregnancy he administered the drug to terminate it. When he realized she was dying, they submitted, he drove her home and dropped her at the rear door of the family house, attempting to make a getaway unrecognized. But someone saw him, and, furthermore, before losing consciousness, Phyllis was able to tell a member of her family that it was the doctor who had brought her back. The defence admitted the affair between the two but blackened the character of Phyllis by saying she had had many lovers and, when she found herself with child, picked on Dr Blakely as the wealthiest among them. No other lovers were called to give evidence.

On the drugs charge, Blakely admitted supplying Phyllis Staton with an abortifacient substance but pleaded not guilty on the grounds that it could not be proven she had actually taken it. The prosecution case was theoretical and offered a supposition that Blakely had deliberately chosen a pituitary extract in the full professional knowledge that it would be untraceable in a post-mortem. There was medical corroboration from a City General Hospital superintendent that the prosecution contention was feasible.

In their wisdom the magistrates threw out the charges on the grounds that the evidence against Dr Blakely was so weak, there was no prima facie case to answer. To my untutored ears, that is a nonsense, but the upshot was that Dr Blakely walked away with an unblemished character, and, if the reports are to be believed, his practice unaffected by the local publicity and his admission of adultery.

Half a dozen years later – had she been asleep or what? – Annie divorced him for adultery. Shortly after that she married a former racing driver, Humphrey Cook, who was very much richer than the doctor and who was highly influential in David Blakely's development. The Cook money had been passed down through a family drapery business, and there had been enough of it for Humphrey to become a star of the pre-war race track and for David to avail himself of sufficient funds, at least to begin with, to support his own racing ambitions.

David was 10 when his parents divorced. It was wartime, and the family was further fragmented when his brothers went away to fight. Annie had been awarded custody, and her life with London-based Humphrey Cook moved them away from Yorkshire to Mayfair. Annie was as taken by the material quality and social status of Mayfair as Ruth would be a few years later. The difference was that Cook had the money for her to shop in Bond Street, while Ruth would be called upon to use her hard-earned cash to support David.

It was also Cook money that dispatched David to public school at Shrewsbury, a Shropshire market town and one of the lovelier and more privileged settings in which any boy could spend his school days. While there he displayed no academic flair, neither did he shine on the sports field; nor was he sufficiently personable to be popular just for his own sake. He was a loner whose only interest lay in motor racing: the cars, the circuits and the drivers. When home from school and staying with his mother and step-father, he immersed himself in all the racing magazines to which Humphrey subscribed. David rarely saw or communicated with his own father and forged a much more meaningful link with Humphrey through their mutual interest, which for David Blakely became first a fixation and then grew into an obsession.

To be a star of the race track was his only ambition, but when the time came for him to leave Shrewsbury he was faced, as were all young men, with National Service. Possibly the only benefit he ever derived from his public-school education was that it softened his time in the Forces, where he was conscripted into the Highland Light Infantry with a commission. In the army, as at Shrewsbury, he was industrious only when it came to the assembly or dismantling of objects mechanical, especially engines.

After serving his time he was demobbed and had to work out how best to make a living. With neither the inclination nor the aptitude for anything other than cars, the decision was taken out of his hands by Humphrey Cook who, while sympathetic and in many ways encouraging, had the experience to know that jobs and opportunities in motor sport at the end of the war years were few and far between. Humphrey decided that David should be trained in hotel management and used his contacts to secure an opening at London's Hyde Park Hotel. If David were grateful, it seems he did not show it and complained loud and long that the pittance of a wage that the hotel paid him was not an adequate living; so his mother, foolishly, topped up his weekly wage packet from her own generous allowance.

Marks and van den Bergh, in their researches, conclude that David was uncomfortable with female company of his own age during this period and moved with much greater ease through the bedchambers of some of the more middle-aged ladies who were staying at the hotel as single guests. The fact is that his only real early female bonding was with his nanny, and this, combined with his cloistered years at public school and in the army, away from mixed company, made him uneasy initially with women. The only other close relationship he had previously had with the opposite sex was with his sister Maureen, so it is likely that those encounters with sex-hungry women at the hotel were his baptism in carnal relationships.

In their company he found a taste for alcohol, which released his inhibitions, so that drinking and sex became congruent activities to relieve the tedium of hotel discipline. He learnt to turn on the charm, dazzle with his smile and relax, as long as conversation never ventured beyond trivia or cars. His step-father took him to race meetings, and he wasted no opportunity to mingle with the sporting fraternity. The sullen, sulky young man of school days and management training became an animated charmer with a smooth line in chat. He became friendly with some of the drivers and mechanics in the various racing classes and basked in their reflected glories, determining to become one of them.

Humphrey Cook overindulged his stepson in many ways. Whether this were to please his wife or out of genuine affection for David is open to conjecture. One of his errors of judgement was to buy a second-hand sports car for David and give him free access to his own petrol account. That car, though nothing special, was good enough for David to enter some lowly races and get a primary feel for the sport. From that point on the car occupied almost all his time, and it was only the intervention of Humphrey that stopped the hotel kicking him out sooner than they eventually did. If Humphrey, in rare moments of wisdom, tightened the purse strings, David would drive north, demonstrate his affection and loyalty to his doctor father and come away with extra money in his pocket. He was devious in the extreme to meet his financial needs.

David's stability, if indeed he ever had a chance of being so, was not helped by the fact that just across the road from the Hyde Park Hotel was an eating and drinking establishment called the Steering Wheel Club. It was a favourite meeting place for those involved in motor sport, and David thrilled to be on the fringe of circles that included Stirling Moss, winner of the London Trophy at Crystal Palace, up-and-coming drivers Peter Collins and Roy Salvadori, and occasional visiting stars like Italian ace Alberto Ascari, who beat Juan Fangio into second place to win the 1953 British Grand Prix at Silverstone. But the king of the court at the club was undoubtedly young British driver Mike Hawthorne, a tall 23-year-old Adonis who drove for the famous Ferrari and who was later, shortly after Ruth shot David, to die tragically in a car crash in his Jaguar on the Guildford by-pass.

David, like so many hangers-on, spent whatever cash he had on buying their companionship. From all accounts the club members were similar to the popular image of those of any rugby club, and their idea of fun was to squirt soda syphons at random or stick ice cubes down each other's trousers. Momentary acclaim would be awarded to upside-down champion beer swillers who, like performing seals, had expectations that something may be thrown them as a reward for their demonstrations of loyalty and willingness to entertain.

Blakely, of course, went over the top with his protean talents for having a good time, and one such story ends with him cowering in fear behind a bar. If one were to indulge in the soda squirting japes, it was as well to pick the right victim. On this occasion Blakely made the worst possible choice and emptied a bucket of ice cubes down the neck of golden boy Hawthorne. To compound the offence, he then squirted the star with soda water. Hawthorne reacted violently, and if others had not intervened would probably have killed him, thereby saving Ruth the trouble later on!

David Blakely had another stroke of fortune, which did him no favours. His father died suddenly and left him £7000. This gave him the freedom to wine, dine and bed a string of girls and to drink in the club to his heart's, if not his liver's, content. Like father like son, David acquired a reputation as a womanizer and revelled in it. Close by the hotel was the Little Club, and David found a side entrance to the hotel, through which he could surreptitiously slip without the hotel bosses being aware of his absence. With his inheritance tucked under his belt, his laissez-faire attitude at the hotel turned to indifference both to guests and his superiors. He was fired.

One of the hotel's regular clients had been a Yorkshire girl, Linda Dawson, daughter of a successful Huddersfield businessman. Attracted to each other, he visited her parents' estate, and entertained her in London. He whizzed her around in his HRG car and took her to bed at every opportunity. Bedding women was no problem since Humphrey had provided him with his own flat, and, even after the Cooks moved to Penn in Buckinghamshire, he was given a flat in the large house there with its own separate entrance. He and Linda enjoyed good times spending freely from his inheritance, which had proved just the cushion David wanted to avoid all forms of work. She fell in love with the man she perceived as being worldly and glamorous, and he in turn must have liked what he saw in her because they became engaged.

The engagement, which lasted almost to the end of David's life, did nothing to curtail his promiscuity. He enjoyed a cinema usherette on a regular basis and casually laid anything else in a skirt. He juggled his social and sexual encounters as a full-time occupation and embarked on an affair with a married woman in Penn, which would later cause much angst to Ruth. David saw himself as a playboy and while he still had the money, played the role to the hilt.

He met the Findlaters through his passion for racing. Anthony Findlater, known to all as Ant, was the son of pre-war racing driver Seaton Findlater; Carole Findlater, Ant's wife, the daughter of refugees from Tsarist Russia. They were both destined to play a major part in the events that built up to the tragedy of David and Ruth.

Accounts of precisely when David Blakely met the Findlaters vary, but apparently David answered an advertisement placed by Ant that offered for sale an ancient Alfa Romeo. The two men clicked immediately and Ant, a skilled mechanic and a lowly paid engineer, eventually joined David in his new project to design and build a racing car, named 'the Emperor'. It is probable that they embarked on this some time after they had first met, but in between David had a passionate affair with Carole, which, it is said, reached the point of her planning to leave Ant for him. Whether it was her staunch Jewish upbringing by her proud parents who had escaped the pogroms or not, Carole backed out at the last moment to stay with her husband. It is, therefore, surprising that Ant, Carole and David became almost inseparable and the very best of friends, with Ant pulling out all the stops and using his considerable skills as a mechanical engineer to assist David in his ambition to become a racing star.

The two men had much in common apart from motor racing. Both were public schoolboys – Ant had attended Hurstpierpoint – and both came from wealthy backgrounds but, apart from David's dwindling £7000, both shared impecunious foregrounds. To begin with, before the Emperor became a reality, they shared racing expenses and co-drove David's HRG at various meetings. The ins-and-outs of the Emperor project and the complexities of their business relationship together with Carole's burgeoning career have been extensively documented by other writers and have no real interest to me here, nor do they play any significant part in my own story. It was not until later, when David met Ruth and was consequently presented to the Findlaters that they become relevant to the fate that befell my family.

When David's capital started to look a little thin, and day-to-day cash to support his boorish delights was in short supply, he was forced to seek employment. Once more it was Humphrey who helped him to find something suitable, and David was given an undemanding job with Silicon Pistons, a light engineering company in Penn. This was conveniently close to the Crown, the pub where he evidently spent as much if not more time as he did at work.

He continued to flit between Penn and London, where he still had his flat, drinking in increasingly heavy bouts and behaving loutishly as alcohol turned him more and more obstreperous, to the point at which a large percentage of Steering Wheel Club regulars shunned him and did their best to avoid him. It was around this time that my mother, Ruth Ellis met David Blakely, the man she grew to love and hate and finally came to murder.

CHAPTER SEVEN

The Alternative Lover

Most of the principal characters in the Ruth Ellis story are now in place. Many of those in my own life have yet to make their first appearance, and before they do I shall introduce the last of Ruth's significant lovers – one of the great rogues of the piece, Desmond Cussen.

Cussen was not a villain in the same way as Maurie Conley – in fact, far from it. A gentleman of breeding and education, Cussen's only act of wickedness was in the last few hours of the life of his bitter rival and enemy, David Moffat Drummond Blakely. Little is known of Cussen's formative years other than his failure to impress either academically or socially, dismissed by one of his former colleagues as 'a bit of a drip'. This certainly tallies with my own impression of him. His later years are more certain, as he was traced, by television reporter Peter Williams, for a Thames Television documentary, to the fabulous city of Perth in Western Australia, where he was living and running a flower business.

My mother was no angel, and David Blakely was a fool. Desmond Cussen, on the other hand, was older and should have been wiser, but instead he ministered to Ruth like a well-trained pet poodle. Of wisdom had he none. At the Old

Bailey, he was to be described by learned counsel as 'the alternative lover'. How he ever managed to have sex at all is a mystery to me as he quite clearly had no balls. But enough of this vitriol.

Desmond Cussen was born with the proverbial silver spoon in his mouth. His childhood knew no deprivation, and his smooth passage into the family firm, Cussen & Co., a wholesale and retail tobacconists with outlets in London and south Wales, was assured. The war intervened, of course, and this is where Cussen must be given his due. He was only 17 when he joined the RAF and underwent training, mainly in South Africa, to be a bomber pilot. He flew Lancasters throughout the war and was not demobilized until 1946. Whether or not he saw much active service, I do not know, but one would have thought that his experiences would have hardened him to the world rather than moulded such a weak character.

His training in accountancy prepared him for the position earmarked for him by the family in executive finance. The business headquarters were at 93 Peckham High Street, in south London, where Desmond had an office, but his first responsibility was for two or three shops in Aberystwyth. Within a short period of time he was appointed to the board of directors and received a salary commensurate with his elevated position. As a wealthy bachelor he lived in the splendour and comfort of a self-contained flat at 20 Goodwood Court, Devonshire Street, W1. This address, just off Harley Street in fashionable Marylebone, would later be the scene of some of the high points of the dramas that ensued.

Desmond was a car enthusiast. He was never a racing driver, but all reports suggest that he drove a black Ford Zodiac about town as though he were qualifying for pole position at the Euston Road traffic lights on a Monday morning. He, like Blakely, was a fringe member of the clique that frequented the Steering Wheel Club and other social circuits within reach of London. Though in himself he was a nobody, his sycophancy bought him a marginal affiliation to the society to which he aspired. He was, among other things, another worshipper at the temple of Mike Hawthorne.

Desmond Cussen's acquaintances from those days have described him as a solitary man, which is, I think, a description that would apply to many of the men who were regular punters at the drinking clubs. Writer Robert Hancock describes him as having 'a faintly oriental look', but, in photographs, it's rather as if he were trying to look like Cary Grant or perhaps Robert Taylor or Erroll Flynn; with the over-obvious application of Brylcreem in inimitable Denis Compton fashion, he ends up looking not only like a Scotland Yard detective but also old before his time. He had a small moustache and always dressed conservatively in a suit and tie. No matter what I read about him there appears to be no evidence of lightheartedness, no suggestion that he enjoyed a joke, and no indication that his pomp was ever reduced by his circumstance. One thing he had in common with all the other men in the life of Ruth Ellis was an addiction to alcohol. The one thing he did not share with them was that, as far as I know, he never hit her.

There is no trace of anything vital in Cussen's personality, except when he sat behind the wheel of his car, living out his fantasies of Brooklands or Silverstone. He was an old-fashioned man, always polite and never a user of foul language. He did not belong in the circles in which he moved, and it would have been much better for everyone, including himself, had he kept away. Alas, he was soon to fall in love with Ruth.

One of the several reasons why I am so antagonistic in my appraisal of Desmond Cussen is because of his treatment of Andy, my half brother. But, more crucially, it is my belief that Desmond Cussen supplied my mother with the Smith and Wesson .38 revolver with which she shot David Blakely. Moreover, Cussen not only taught her how to use it but also drove her to the scene of the crime, having plied her earlier with quantities of Pernod. With the prescribed drugs that Ruth was taking, this cocktail diminished her responsibility for what came next. This is, of course, something that I will explore and justify in greater detail later.

Prior to the murder, Ruth had come to an agreement with Cussen. If he gave her the gun, she would never admit it to anyone nor incriminate him in any way, on one condition:

no matter what happened, he would take care of Andy. I realize that such an arrangement makes the premeditation of the murder appear even more damning, and I cannot argue with that. Desmond wanted Blakely dead as much, if not more than Ruth did, and that was the deal. She was to kill Blakely, Desmond would be exonerated from all prior knowledge of the crime, and he would assume all subsequent responsibility for Andy's welfare.

When my mother was executed, Andy was staying with MP George Rogers and his wife. They had become involved in my mother's cause and with our family. There is no question but that the Rogers acted only with absolute correctness and according to the wishes of Ruth and all the family when no one told Andy what was going on. How they hoped to keep such a secret from a boy approaching his eleventh birthday is beyond me, but that is the way it was played. At what stage Andy learnt the appalling truth, I have no idea. By the time he re-entered my life his mind was incalculably scarred, and he was manifestly schizophrenic.

Andy, or Clare Andrea as he was registered at birth, was never an easy child. This was perhaps to be expected. His father had left before his birth, and he was raised one week by Muriel, by Bertha the next and then whisked off in between on some expedition by Ruth. He was shifted about and carted around without a thought of what was best for him. Bertha, I know, was horrified at his treatment and tried various ploys to keep him with her, but an aggressive husband and an irrational daughter made it impossible for her to do anything about it. Of all the victims in the whole scenario, my heart reaches out most to Andy. He was treated like a piece of human baggage on a conveyor belt, often unclaimed.

Andy lived in the flat above the Little Club and was privy to most of what went on there. He also stayed for a while with Ruth at Desmond's smart flat. The boy, not yet into adolescence, saw his mother share her bed with two different men on different nights of the week, witnessed the ravages and loss of control brought about by daily alcohol abuse and watched his mother thumped until she was black and blue and bleeding at the hands of David Blakely.

Andy would be put to bed each evening at seven or eight o'clock and left on his own throughout the night. What and whom he would discover on reawakening was always unpredictable. Yet Ruth loved him. She desperately wanted to settle him and provide him with an orthodox life. His welfare is possibly the only reason she ever married George Ellis. It is perhaps the only advantage she saw in staying in with boring old Desmond Cussen, and it is just credible that, in the absence of David Blakely, she and Desmond might have made something of their relationship; he asked her to marry him on several occasions and was emotionally available and in a financial position to set up the family home that Ruth always said she wanted.

But this was not to be. Cussen was stupidly prepared to tolerate a status quo in which he set up Ruth and Andy in a small service flat of their own, knowing full well that Blakely was living there from Monday to Friday as Mr Ellis, the only name by which the landlady knew him.

In that oddest of arrangements Blakely would stagger out of Ruth's bed and drive himself to work at Penn. Mid-morning Desmond would arrive and spend the rest of the day with her and, if he were around, Andy. Unlike Blakely, who never even gave the boy the time of day and made him feel totally unwanted, Desmond did at least buy him presents and take both him and Ruth to the cinema or the zoo or out for a day in the country. But, mostly, Andy did not know whether he was coming or going, and if his mother had had a particularly heavy night, he would be left to fend for himself as best he could. He spent so much of his young life being ignored that he withdrew into his own cocoon, which was often mistaken for sulking. Any child who finds no one to listen will stop talking, and Andy ceased to communicate. He was considered a problem child.

On the night of the murder Andy saw Desmond Cussen place a gun in mother's handbag. He was not capable of inventing such a story and was able to describe to me precisely where he was in the flat when Cussen deliberately armed Ruth. It was not the first time Andy had seen guns in Cussen's possession, and he would tell anyone prepared to hear where, in which drawer, his armoury was located. Nobody listened. With modern forensic science, Cussen's fingerprints would have been found on the murder weapon. As it was, the off-duty police officer to whom she handed the empty gun took no care to preserve any prints, and by the time it was examined it was smudged and printed by many hands.

After the murder and prior to the trial, Desmond continued to curry Ruth's favour by sending flowers, food parcels and make-up to her in Holloway. Neither the members of the press nor the authorities considered him an important character; his role was seen as a bit-part player among the *dramatis personae* of the story. He was only one of a string of well-wishers, yet his generosities were his way of assuring Ruth that he would be true to his side of their agreement. He was called at the trial as a prosecution witness merely to establish that he had been Ruth's 'alternative lover', and that he had witnessed fights between her and Blakely and the resultant bruising. Neither in examination nor in cross-examination by Melford Stevenson QC was Cussen ever asked a question about the gun or to account for his own whereabouts on the night of the killing.

Once Ruth Ellis had been found guilty and sentenced to death, Desmond Cussen disappeared. He opted to lie low just in case she changed her story, which, of course, she did but too late. He had cleverly protected his hideaway, and when Granville, the lawyers and the police were desperately seeking him as the final hours before the execution ticked away, he was impossible to locate.

Andy, staying with the Rogers for the days leading up to and just after the execution, found their house rather peculiar. He could not understand why a Member of Parliament should have no radio or television and should take delivery of no newspapers. He had been told that his mother was abroad on a modelling assignment. On what precise day he found out the truth, he had no distinct memory, but when he did it all clicked into place for him, and the significance of seeing his 'Uncle' Desmond give his mother the gun became clear to him.

Desmond kept his word to Ruth about Andy but only financially. He took no interest in the boy's development and made no attempt to communicate with him from that point on. He paid the fees for his education at a Roman Catholic boarding school, St Michael's, in Surrey. My grandmother saw him in his uniform and told me how proud he had felt, particularly of his cap with its badge and neb. It was all too late, though, and his early difficulties were amplified by the loss of his mother. Though he was an intelligent child, his personality was already split, and his mind damaged irrevocably. The school was unable to turn the tide, and his psyche was confused by the debris of his childhood.

When Andy left St Michael's he went to live with Bertha who was then in service in Hemel Hempstead. Bertha, on the verge of a mental breakdown herself, was in no fit state to handle a disturbed youth. For much of the time Andy sat at home silently and turned himself into a zombie. With my grandfather seriously ill, my grandmother was unable to cope, Muriel couldn't really help out as she had her own family to deal with, though, as always, she did try to find time for her nephew. Elizabeth was starving herself to death, her heart broken by Ruth's fate, and Granville had his own problems to work through. Of Desmond Cussen, whose solemn promise to take care of Andy had saved his skin, there was no sight.

When Andy found me about fifteen years ago, he was a destroyed man, unable to fulfil a useful role in society. He was dishevelled and unkempt but not dirty, his appearance born more of careless indifference than desperation and degradation. He was living in a poky flat in the run-down area of London that encircles Euston Station. I saw him four or five times from then on, but I still wish I could have done more or supported him better by living in closer proximity. He had absolutely nobody. My grandparents were both dead by then, and, in a pattern that was repeated throughout his life, he had been left to fend for himself without adequate means, skills or powers of reasoning to do so.

During our first meeting he sat writing while I tidied his living area. I asked him to show me what he had written, and he presented it to me with enthusiasm. The page was full of gobbledygook; there was not one word that made any sense at all, and although I didn't say so it frightened me. Even more alarming was the realization that Andy actually thought, for much of that time, that I was his mother and addressed me as such. He wanted to know where I had been, but the question was always phrased in the short term, as though Ruth had just popped out to the shops a little while earlier. Equally suddenly he would revert to relating to me as his sister. I never felt menaced by him, though, in any way. He had a gentleness about him that reassured me.

Andy's behaviour could be eccentric and disturbed. In the course of a trip with him to Land's End Muriel felt so threatened at times that she was convinced he was about to push her over the cliffs. Once on a visit to Bertha, he turned on the gas as she slept. They would both have died had someone else not come in and discovered them. On another occasion I sent him a sweater that he adored so much that he never took it off. Another time he rang me at my home in the north and asked what lipstick I used. I told him Estee Lauder's Ashes of Roses and thought no more about it. The next week a delivery van arrived with a parcel that contained a whole box of the lipsticks, scores of them, from Harrods. It would have taken me twenty years to use them up.

Andy lived very much in a world of his own. He spent hours travelling on trains to no particular destination, just riding round for the sake of it. He had tickets to all sorts of places, which he had no reason to visit; he just liked to go there by train, to travel and never arrive. Yet though he was strange, confused and schizoid, introverted to the exclusion of most of the rest of the world, he could be acutely perceptive. He had got into the habit of telephoning me frequently, and I never knew what to expect from one call to the next; it could be a buoyant, jovial Andy or a simpering and pathetic, drowning rat. On one particular occasion he was unusually lucid with all his faculties in place, not confusing characters or chronology, and he began to talk about Ruth. It was one of the last things he ever said to me: 'You know, Georgie, you inherited all her strengths, and I all her weaknesses.' I have thought a lot about this over the years, and I have to agree with him. When I analyse my own character and compare myself to him, I understand precisely what he meant.

Andy killed himself with a concoction of drugs and alcohol in his Euston flat during a very hot August. When his body was discovered, he had already been dead for three weeks. He was only found when another tenant noticed flies crawling out from under the door. Once inside the stench of putrefaction overwhelmed the building. I went with Muriel to the funeral, and the smell of my brother's rotting flesh lingered with us among the congregation.

Ruth had needed to shield Desmond Cussen on the understanding that he would take care of Andy. What she had told her lawyers, her parents and her brother Granville the day before her execution was sworn to secrecy. She made them promise not to reveal the name of the man who had supplied the gun and driven her to Hampstead where she killed David Blakely on that fateful day. It was almost twenty years on, with my grandmother in hospital and my grandfather approaching the end of his life, before they revealed the name of Desmond Edward Cussen in a letter that my grandfather wrote to anti-hanging campaigner Sydney Silverman MP. Written but never sent, it was only when my grandfather died that my grandmother handed the letter, which he had tucked away inside a Bible, to Muriel. Ruth's personal sacrifice of her life had been in vain.

CHAPTER EIGHT

Ménage à Trois

The dawn of the second Elizabethan age was the signal for political and social relaxation. The horrors of war began slowly to recede, though Londoners and other city dwellers had daily reminders of them as they walked past the devastation that was the legacy of Hitler's bombing raids. London was eager for change, desperate to replace the drab blacks and greys with elements of colour and create new heroes who were not soldiers. This climate spawned a clutch of new film stars, while television breathed life into everyone's living-room, and sport, especially dangerous sport, provided the catharsis for youth's pent-up energy, frustrated by the restrictions of war. Hillary and Tensing conquered Everest, Roger Bannister ran the four-minute mile, test pilot Neville Duke broke the world air-speed record, and the stars of motor sport risked and often lost their lives on international circuits.

It is hardly surprising that David Blakely, young and feckless, and Desmond Cussen, wealthy and bored, should both be drawn towards the excitement that was the essence of motor racing and its après track activities, particularly drinking. Blakely and Cussen were acquainted before either had met Ruth, and while they had no particular liking for or special affinity with each other, they did spend time in each other's company. At the Steering Wheel Club, where neither featured high in the popularity stakes, Cussen is remembered for drinking alone in a corner for hours on end and Blakely for his schoolboyish pranks and ability to irritate. They were associated principally because Blakely was a sponger and a ponce, who would feed his drinking habit at another's expense, and Cussen was a willing purchaser of company. Thus were two complete opposites thrown together by destiny, the one good-looking, supercilious and spoiled, the other unprepossessing, unattractive and manipulative.

It was Cussen who met Ruth first in one of the clubs. He was also part of the social scene at Carroll's when Ruth first encountered Blakely. She was impressed by neither man and is quoted as saying of her introduction to Blakely: 'In strolled David wearing an old coat and flannel trousers. I did not like his manner from the start. I thought he was too hoity-toity by far.' This quote is taken from Robert Hancock's book, which goes on to say that Blakely then made some derogatory remarks about the club's hostesses. Not being blessed with tact, one can only assume that he couched his lascivious observations in offensive language.

The ridicule Blakely attempted was to bounce back on him. For once, as it happened, Ruth was not in the club to work but as a guest of some of the members. As such she felt indignant and free to speak her mind: 'My hackles began to rise, and I turned to the other boys, and, in a plainly audible voice so that he could hear, I said: "Who is that pompous little ass?"' Hardly the most auspicious start for a love affair that would in the future be so all-consuming. Their second encounter as reported by Marks and van den Bergh, was equally antagonistic and bore no clue that, within a couple of weeks, they would be inextricably entwined. It took place at the Little Club, a venue to which Blakely had originally been taken by Cussen or vice versa. Her reaction on that occasion was patently conditioned by his boorish comportment, alcohol induced, which prompted her to remark to a fellow employee: 'I hope never to see that little shit again.'

These early exchanges took place some time towards the end of 1953, Coronation year. None of the other writers, whose integrity I do not quesion, is agreed on the precise timing, but the facts suggest to me that the most likely date is around

Ruth's birthday, her twenty-seventh, on 9 October 1953. I am not suggesting that was the date of their first meeting, but for this birthday she was given a party at Carroll's.

It was on or shortly after her birthday that Ruth was made manager of the Little Club by Maurie Conley and given the use of the flat above it. The date is significant because Ruth herself was to say that the first customer she ever served in her new capacity was David Blakely and that he began to live with her two weeks later. She claimed in her evidence that it was August, but she was not living at the flat in August, so the timing was impossible.

If it was not love at first sight, nor even at second sight, an infatuation, mutual and requited, was born out of, or in spite of, their hostilities. If Cussen were already besotted with Ruth, he had not made his feelings known, and she had paid him scant attention. Indeed she may not have noticed him at all among the racing crowd and its satellite groups.

Ruth took her new job very seriously and was well rewarded with a basic weekly salary of £15, plus commission on all bar sales, an entertainment allowance of £10 a week and a flat that went with the job.

To put this into perspective, you could buy a solid gold wristwatch then for £14 and a Lloyd Lounger chair for £4. Britain was still in the grip of food rationing, and my favourite ad from the time goes: 'Let's make it a banquet; we've got a tin of Nestlé's Cream,' but Ruth had none of these hardships and was flying high. Any need for her to entertain punters on the side took a back seat, though she remained happy to give away her charms free. Neither David nor Desmond ever had to pay her, though perhaps Desmond did so indirectly; there are many testimonies that she was generous with her sexual favours if the fancy took her.

Ruth was a woman ahead of her time, who came to terms with her sexuality and its value and understood her own sexual needs without embarrassment. Ingrained into so many women then, and even now, was the idea that sex was something to be tolerated in marriage, and not for a woman to pursue for profit or pleasure alone without social censure. The hypocrisy of then has hardly been attenuated today. I am from good Roman Catholic stock yet I seethe with indignation and incredulity at its stance on contraception. Ruth would never have had to endure so many illicit, back-street abortions had contraception been an acceptable part of life in the fifties.

After making such a disastrous first and second impression on Ruth, David must have turned on the charm to get her into bed within the fortnight. He spoke with the refinement derived from his years at Shrewsbury, and he still had money to match his playboy style. When sober he had good manners, and innumerable women yielded to the spell cast by his dark-brown eyes. He cut a rakish figure and was slimly built and generally appealing. Of course, he was already engaged to the Dawson girl, but he had no moral qualms about bed-hopping with Carole Findlater and one or two other women of his acquaintance. He saw himself as a womanizer and promoted his reputation both at the Crown in Penn, where he started a long affair with the married woman, unnamed at the trial, and in all the clubs that he frequented. Though he had yet to win a motor race, he moulded himself in the image of those at the top of the racing tree and boasted of his exploits on the tracks.

One person who was close to him was Cliff Davis, a fellow driver, older than Blakely, who had enjoyed considerable success driving a Cooper in the 1500cc class. After the murder he was one of the few people who knew my mother and Blakely, and who spoke out freely about them. He is alleged to have said that David's first opinion of Ruth was that she was merely 'one of the best fucks in London'. He went on to tell Marks and van den Bergh that he, too, had enjoyed mother's ministrations on one memorable occasion and confirmed her renown for giving full satisfaction, calling her an artist with special reference to the deployment of her tongue. Davis was also one of the few people to speak up for Ruth Ellis as a person, aside from her sexual activities. He held her in high regard as a woman of principle. In contrast he found Blakely a man of few principles. As a pair he felt it was a tragedy they had ever met and described their relationship as being as unstable as a stick of dynamite.

Ruth was generous by nature, and Davis has testified that she was never slow to stand her corner. If she were socializing with the boys rather than working, she always bought her round, and this side of her character is corroborated by Muriel's family recollections. Blakely was not backward in taking advantage of her generosity once he embarked on his project to build the Emperor with Ant Findlater and his own money started to run short.

The early days of the affair were coherently described by Ruth at her trial when her Counsel, Mr Melford Stevenson QC, asked her: 'How did he show his feelings for you?'

Ruth replied that 'In the December of that year [1953] I had an abortion by him [she meant pregnancy because the abortion happened in March 1954], and he was very concerned about my welfare. Although he was engaged to another girl, he offered to marry me, and he said it was quite unnecessary for me to get rid of the child, but I did not want to take advantage of him.'

Melford Stevenson asked how she reacted to the marriage proposal, and she said: 'I was not really in love with him at the time, and it was quite unnecessary to marry me. I thought I could get out of the mess quite easily.'

In the beginning David was not at all possessive of Ruth. Just when the tide turned, and the lust turned to something more is not clear, for although Blakely continued to spend four or five nights a week in Ruth's bed, he attended all formal social events, such as dinner dances, with Linda Dawson on his arm. Apart from the pregnancy, by then a mere trifle to Ruth, there is no suggestion that either of them took the relationship seriously: David's offer of marriage is ridiculous considering that he was engaged, and Ruth was technically still married to my father.

Once Maurie Conley heard that David was living in the flat above his club he was furious. He demanded that Ruth pay rent and told her in no uncertain terms that the association was bad for club business. The rent was a drain on her own weekly income, so she began to entertain gentlemen again but only in the afternoons. David did not like this but does not appear to have raised any objection or made any contribution to the rent or other costs. He did not even help with financing the abortion, although Ruth admitted that she had not asked him for money.

Ruth must have seen through him. He never took her anywhere, nor did she meet any of his friends other than those who frequented the Little Club. Theirs was a two storey existence, drinking on the first floor and fornicating in the flat above. To be fair to them both, each was preoccupied at the time with a front-line interest: Ruth with her job as manageress of the club and David with his car. The car was sapping his resources at an alarming rate, and she stupidly allowed him to drink and run up a tab behind the bar. The club takings fell as the affair intensified, and she allowed him more and more latitude. Eventually it would cost her her job.

Throughout those months Desmond Cussen became infatuated with Ruth Ellis, and his dislike of Blakely turned to hatred. Cussen had usually paid for sexual favours, and no one recalled an earlier serious affair or relationship. What is on record is an observation that he never again looked at another woman once his infatuation had taken hold. The only other woman to whom he had previously demonstrated such devotion was his mother.

Quite when he began to make his protestations of undying love to Ruth I do not know, but she must have strung him along to a certain extent. It was he, not Blakely, who took her to an occasional weekend race meeting, and it was probably such outings that fuelled her discontent with the way Blakely was taking her for granted.

Ruth's affair with Blakely was off and on, sometimes from one hour to the next. Though they made sporadic visits to the cinema and theatre together, this was not enough for her. She began to nag him to include her in his social set. She wanted to go to race meetings with him rather than with Cussen, and she pestered him constantly to include her in his world beyond the drinking clubs. He capitulated and took her to a party that had been organized to celebrate Ant Findlater's birthday. That was April 1954.

If it had not been love at first sight with David, it was certainly mutual hate at first sight when Ruth Ellis and Carole

Findlater met. They obviously both knew about each other, and all but ignored one another's existence. Ruth thought Carole behaved like Mother Superior, while Carole disdainfully dismissed Ruth as a brassy little tart in a skimpy dress who chatted flirtatiously with almost every man present. Following this unfortunate initial encounter, both Ant and David were subjected to bitchy remarks from both women about the other. Needless to say Ant sided with Carole, and David was caught between the devil and the deep blue sea. The Findlaters were his best friends, and Ruth was his lover. Moreover, Ruth grew jealous of the time Blakely spent with Ant on the Emperor project. A second meeting between the two women was no less cordial, with Carole walking out of a party as soon as Ruth arrived.

David had started to take Ruth to the race circuits, where, according to Findlater, she stuck out like a sore thumb, and none of the crowd wanted anything to do with her. Cliff Davis disagreed with Findlater on this issue and after her death spoke of what great fun Ruth had been, and of how all the crowd had enjoyed the champagne and other goodies that made up her picnic boxes. Either way, the antagonism between the two women grew so intense that if the Findlaters knew that Ruth was accompanying David to a race meeting, they would stay away themselves.

Findlater worked for Aston Martin, but as work on the Emperor increased, Blakely persuaded him to work full time on the new car and offered to pay him £10 per week to do so. This further drain on Blakely's remaining capital made him more and more dependent on Ruth, and she found she was all but keeping him. Money was tight all round, and the Findlaters were plunged into deeper financial turmoil when Carole announced she was pregnant and would have to give up her own job.

Ruth began to question the relationship with Blakely to herself. She was more deeply hurt than anyone imagined by the rejections of David's friends. Carole was not alone in treating her as a social inferior. Several of the other wives and girlfriends of men she knew in the clubs shied away from her, and to add insult to injury Blakely himself rarely behaved

Ruth Ellis, my mother,
executed 13 July 1955 when
I was 3½. In relaxed and
informal pose, *left*, and
photographed modelling a
striped sweater *above*.
(Above: Syndication International)

Above: George Ellis, my
father and Ruth's ex-husband,
an alcoholic who hanged
himself three years after
Ruth's execution. (Popperfoto)

Right: My grandparents,
Arthur Neilson, the frustrated
musician, and his refugee
wife, seamstress Elisaberta.
They had a hard life and
taught us that poverty and
wounded pride lead to alcohol
and violence and equal total
misery.

Above: Muriel, Ruth's older sister by five years, who bore much of the family responsibility. She watched with anger as Ruth squandered her earnings on clothes and having fun and was embarrassed as a young woman by Ruth's flirtatious ways with men.

Above: a dark-haired Ruth on holiday in Cornwall, before she had discovered peroxide and that gentlemen prefer blondes.

Right: Me, aged 2½, just before I was taken from my mother and sent to live with my new parents, Phyllis and Peter Lawton, in Warrington.

Above: Ruth, third from the right, out on the town with friends. She relished the high life but secretly yearned for respectability. Desmond Cussen is on her right. (Syndication International)

Left: Desmond Cussen, described at Ruth's trial as her alternative lover. A wealthy company director, he was obsessively in love with my mother and wanted to marry her. (Syndication International)

Above: left to right: Carole and Anthony Findlater with Ruth Ellis and David Blakely. The Findlaters were Blakely's good friends with whom Ruth enjoyed a less than harmonious relationship.
(Syndication International)

Left: Ruth's lover David Blakely, the wannabe racing driver and the man whom she shot in a drunken moment of extreme and misdirected passion. He gave Ruth this photograph of himself shortly before she killed him.
(Syndication International)

To Ruth with all my love
David

Above: Actor Richard Harris swept me off my feet and introduced me to many of life's finer pleasures. With him I lived an international jet set life in the lap of luxury.
(Popperfoto)

Above: The greatest footballer ever and my first lover George Best, who remains a good and stalwart friend. In the sixties, being a part of the Best Set was like a dream come true for me.
(Popperfoto)

Right: Me, Georgie: my model-agency portfolio. Like Ruth, I had an appetite for glamour, and like her I came to realize the bonus of being a blonde.

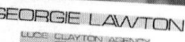

GEORGIE LAWTON
LUCIE CLAYTON AGENCY

Top and above: Happy times with David Beard. And our children.

Right: Scott, my eldest son and Ruth Ellis's first grandchild.

Me, Georgie: relaxing on the
beach *above*; feeling
mischievous in Paris, my
favourite city *right*.
(Both photos by David Beard)

towards her with gentleness, and often shouted and become jealous if she paid too much attention to other customers in the Little Club. Ruth was bitter about the fact that she was not considered worthy enough or sufficiently sophisticated to take her place alongside the man with whom she had fallen in love. Notwithstanding David's engagement to Linda Dawson, the passion between Ruth and David was volcanic and liable to erupt in fits of temper or wild sexual desire. She adored him but was not totally blind to the reality that their long-term future looked bleak. She seriously considered ending the whole affair, although we will never know how close she ever came.

The birth of a daughter, Francesca, to the Findlaters in 1954 came as a great strain to them. Ant was working all day and most of the night with David on the Emperor at the garage that David had rented in Islington, after which the two men would retire to the drinking clubs. Carole not unnaturally resented all the hours her husband spent with David, and, though he was her former lover, she grew almost as hostile to him as she remained towards Ruth. Carole was equally disgusted that David had continued his association with Ruth after she had so clearly lectured him on the crass stupidity of prolonging an affair with a woman so unsuitable. For a while David felt the welcome far from warm at the Findlater flat in Tanza Road, Hampstead, which is probably just as well since Ruth issued him with an ultimatum either to stay away from the Findlaters or to stay away from her.

Desmond Cussen's infatuation had in no way dissipated, and his was often the ear into which Ruth spoke of her concerns. A taciturn man, Cussen was a good listener, and Ruth told him much of her life story. He urged her to terminate the affair with Blakely and asked her to marry him. He could offer her all she desired in terms of creature comforts and security for both her and Andy. Unfortunately Ruth did not love him and saw him as more of a father figure than the man to whom she could devote the rest of her life.

I found myself in a similar position after divorce from my second husband. I became engrossed in an affair with a wealthy and eligible businessman. For a while I thought it was wonderful to drive a smart car and be granted material things at will. I remember standing with him in Manchester's St Ann's Square, an expensive shopping area, as he invited me to select anything I wanted from any one of the shops. However, I had already met the man destined to become my third husband, and I had a split-second realization that I was simply not in love with the other man. I rejected the offer and put an end to the relationship as kindly as I could. Money can buy companionship, sex and attention, but no amount of it can make you fall in love if the spark is not there.

David Blakely's life was becoming even more complicated than was normal even for him. The schedule of work on the Emperor was falling behind, and the costs were spiralling upwards. His step-father, though to that point encouraging and supportive financially, had heard rumours that David was spending prolifically on drink. Having confirmed the stories himself, Humphrey determined that next time his stepson came for a loan he would have to refuse. Blakely's relationship with Ant, his best friend and mechanic, was also fraught because of the open warfare between Carole and Ruth. While he continued to live with her, and she was his woman, he wanted her to be accepted by his friends. He was also still engaged, and involved in the affair with the married woman in Penn. His resources, both economic and physical, were stretched beyond the limit.

It was out of this quagmire of drowning no-hopers that my father George plucked me to take me to Warrington. I wrote earlier that I was unsure precisely when I was removed from the flat above the Little Club, but it would have been no later than May 1954. In the early part of June, David Blakely drove in the Le Mans 24-hour race in France. He sent Ruth a postcard dated 11 June, which read:

ARRIVED OK. HAVEN'T HAD A DRINK FOR 3 DAYS!!! WISH YOU WERE HERE. WILL SEE YOU TUESDAY. LOVE, DAVID.

The Tuesday came and went, and Thursday, 17 June, was Blakely's birthday. Ruth had planned a surprise party for him, but he had still failed to return. Whether out of spite, fury or mere mischief she gave Desmond Cussen the shock of his life when she invited him to join her in the bed upstairs in the flat above the club. At her trial, during examination by Melford Stevenson, she described this occurrence: 'David then went away to the Le Mans motor race, and he stayed away longer than he should have done. That was when my affair with Mr Cussen began.'

She slept with Cussen on a regular basis for about two weeks, during which period Blakely had moved on to Reims for more racing. From Reims he sent another postcard to Ruth, this time with an ironic postscript attached:

DARLING, HAVE ARRIVED SAFELY AND AM HAVING QUITE A GOOD TIME. THE CARS ARE GOING VERY WELL. LOOKING FORWARD TO SEEING YOU. DAVID. PS LOVE TO DESMOND!!!

It is highly improbable that anyone had informed him that something was going on between Ruth and Desmond, so I suspect the postscript was merely a sarcastic aside, Blakely's feeble attempt at a joke. He was aware that Cussen was aflame with desire for Ruth. At her trial, Melford Stevenson asked Ruth what she thought might happen as far as she and Blakely were concerned as a result of the affair with Cussen. She responded: 'I thought it might finish it. I thought that Desmond would tell David we had been intimate, and I thought that would finish it.'

As it transpired neither she nor Cussen told Blakely of their sexual activity. Desmond maintained his devotion, gave her money and offered again to marry her. As soon as Blakely returned from France, he went directly to the club and picked up where they had left off, as if he had never been away. Belatedly she threw a birthday party for him, at which an incident took place that forced Ruth to apologize to Carole Findlater. Taking a leaf out of David's book, in high spirits she had squirted Carole with a soda syphon, to which Carole took umbrage and stormed out. The apology was later accepted, apparently with little grace.

David turned up at the party very late and in a bad mood. In spite of the incident with Carole the revels were in full swing and continued through the small hours of the morning. For some reason that will never be clear, David did not give her any explanation for his late arrival, nor did she demand one. It was days or even a couple of weeks later that he told her he had been at the Hyde Park Hotel with his fiancée, Linda Dawson, and that their engagement was off. No news could have further strengthened the attachment Ruth felt for Blakely, and for his part he talked of marriage to her, as she explained at her trial: 'He told me that he would never have any happiness if we didn't get married.'

Unfortunately it was not the start of eternal happiness but rather the beginning of the end. Along with the pronouncement that the engagement was off, Blakely delivered the news that he was broke. His step-father had remained firm in his resolve and refused David any more money. He could no longer pay Ant Findlater, who was forced to take a day job and work on the Emperor only in his spare time. Ruth spent some of the money that she extracted from Cussen, mainly by insisting that she wished to finish with Blakely, on paying for David's rounds of drinks, and when there was no more left she allowed him to sign for them or, possibly, even drink free at Maurie Conley's expense.

The barmaid at the Little Club, a French woman married to an Englishman, Jacqueline Dyer silently watched Ruth neglect her managerial duties to indulge her selfish lover. The Emperor project had to be moved from Islington, where David could no longer pay the rent on the garage-cum-workshop. It was moved to the garage of his step-father's flat in Mayfair. Because she was the only one with access to any money at all, Ruth assumed the role of dominatrix in their relationship. She again forced him to cut off any social intercourse with the Findlaters on pain of exclusion from the Little Club. He was more or less at her mercy since without her he did not have the wherewithal to feed his alcohol habit, which was already a chemical dependence.

His jealousy, however, was fired as he suspected Ruth of continuing her afternoon activities, which, indeed, she did. He could not rant and rave too much, because he needed her money so badly. Desmond also continued to get into Ruth's bed whenever opportunity presented itself, in exchange for which he picked up the tab for the rent of the flat. The lethal web of complicity was being woven. In spite of his declared intentions towards Ruth, David continued his extra-curricular activities with the married woman in Penn. Ruth was just as possessively jealous as he was. At what precise time in this chronicle the violence started I do not know, but the storms were already brewing. Ruth made great issue of one episode during her trial when she said of David:

One night he got into bed and was stretching over to switch out the light when I noticed love bites all over his shoulders, back and neck. I went quite cold with shock, and I told him to get out and leave the flat. He said he could explain everything and started to tell me that someone had bitten him in the neck while he was playing darts at Penn. I said, 'Please get out of my bed and out of my flat and don't come near me again.'

The next night, according to Ruth, he was back at the club, and although she had instructed Jacqueline Dyer to say she was out, he found her in the flat and went down on his knees pleading forgiveness and swearing his love and allegiance. What a miserable hypocrite! What a limp excuse he had proffered. Ruth might not have been educated, but in her own special field there was none more expert; she knew a love bite when she saw one. Men, as I know, trot out the lamest of excuses when caught with their trousers down, but, mugs that women can be, we take them back; Ruth was no exception. He was back between her sheets and legs that same evening, having once more asked her to marry him. When Ruth suggested that his mother and family, whom she had never met, would always be an obstacle to any marital plans they forged, he brushed her fear aside, saying they could always marry in secret.

Whether he was ever serious in any of his proposals can never be known, but my mother withdrew her defence to my father's divorce petition and allowed it to go forward uncontested, without any claim for maintenance and renouncing all claim on me. She must have felt she was in with a chance at last, though Robert Hancock in his book *Ruth Ellis* states that the decision at least to be free of me was made a few months prior to her dropping her defence absolutely.

In August 1954 David asked Ruth to accompany him to Holland for a race in which he was to drive an MG belonging to a friend. In a moment of considered responsibility she turned down the invitation on the grounds that the club was going through a difficult time, and she ought not to leave it. There may have been an ulterior motive. My half-brother Andy was fast approaching his tenth birthday, and she needed to work out what to do with him for the best. The flat was crowded; Andy was quite difficult, and, possibly as a result of an accident when he was 6, in which he banged his head quite severely, he was clumsier than the average child and prone to breaking and bumping into things. On top of that Ruth was genuinely concerned about the way he amused himself. Even then he would ride the London Underground for hours on end, just as he would later take steam trains with no specific destination in mind. She thought his best interests would be served if he went away as a boarder at a preparatory school.

Allowing the mouse to play while the cat was away in Holland, Ruth broached the subject with Desmond Cussen, her limitless crock of gold. Cussen drove them to visit a school of his recommendation, and they met the headmaster who arranged for Andy to register in time for the start of the first term of the new school year. Desmond paid for the uniform and all tuition fees.

David returned to London after an unsuccessful race. His drinking was now an all day long business. He sponged off Ruth and the club itself, and when he went off to his day job at Silicon Pistons in Penn he would regularly be in the Crown as soon as the doors were open. Ruth's own drinking habits were also on the rise. On top of her daily intake of gin and champagne, she had discovered Pernod, known by many as 'lunatic soup' for its powers of intoxication. Presumably Pernod, which was not a fashionable drink in the 1950s, had been introduced to the club by Jacqueline Dyer. It was more expensive than other tipples that Ruth consumed, yet another increase in outlay if she were ever to pay for her own drinks. It was abuse of Pernod that contributed to her zombie-like condition on the night of the murder. Desmond Cussen, whose fondness for alcohol had never abated, was also drinking prolific quantities.

With Andy away at his prep school, all restraints on Ruth's time were removed, and she was increasingly able to play her men with her not inconsiderable skills. But David in particular had a very low boredom threshold. Hour after hour in the Little Club grew tedious for him, and he loved to pub and club crawl. Ruth's possessiveness was already reaching alarming proportions, and she hated him to go off drinking on his own. All too often she went with him, where, of course, there was no free booze and no 'tab' to pick up the bill, and Ruth's money was disposed of with abandon. To satisfy David's wanderlust Ruth spent time away from the Little Club for hours on end, and several regular clients for whom she was perhaps the main attraction began to drift off elsewhere. Takings plummeted.

The storm clouds gathered and darkened through the autumn. No member of the Ellis-Blakely-Cussen triumvirate was happy. Alcohol could only temporarily wash aside the resentments, jealousies and suspicions that festered in all three. There was no logical assessment of the status quo as they all dug themselves in deeper than ever. Ruth financed Blakely, and Cussen provided for Ruth. Whether or not Cussen knew his money was paying for Blakely's smoking and drinking, he turned the blind eye that only those who have ever been besotted with another person could comprehend. He made himself believe that the tempestuous relationship between Ruth and coarse, loud-mouthed, foul-tongued Blakely was doomed to peter out quickly. Then Ruth would marry him. He flattered her and treated her with total respect, no word of profanity ever leaving his lips. By October the violence had begun. Ruth underplayed it at her trial:

It was always because of jealousy in the bar. At the end of the evening when we got upstairs, it was always about the things he had been seeing me do, and so on and so forth. . . . He only used to hit me with his fists and his hands, but I bruise very easily, and I was full of bruises on many occasions.

There were many witnesses to the beatings, thumpings and consequent bruises that Blakely inflicted on Ruth yet, incomprehensibly, not one was called as a trial witness. The only time the subject was raised was very briefly during Cussen's evidence, and in any case he was a prosecution witness.

Maurie Conley grew alarmed by the plunge in turnover at the Little Club, and his ill-tempered response increased the stress with which Ruth was coping less ably. She struggled to improve sales by flirting with clients to encourage them to spend more money, but such behaviour only drove Blakely into renewed frenzies of violence. The situation became intolerable, and Ruth was faced with the choice of keeping either David or her job as manageress of the Little Club.

If she ever believed that David would marry her, she was an idiot. She did not fit. He had never taken her to Penn to meet either his Buckinghamshire set or his mother and stepfather; she was his support rather than the other way round, and in gratitude for her undoubted generosity he knocked her frail body about in drunken displays of arrogant and arbitrary fits of jealous temper. Yet, for some reason or compound of reasons, Ruth made the wrong choice and quit the club in December. Did she jump or was she pushed? Some reports claim that Conley relieved her of her duties; others that she resigned her post. Either way she was out of work and, because the flat went with the job, out of a home.

Andy was due to return from school for the Christmas holidays. She had to live somewhere. Step forward once more Desmond Cussen. It was his golden opportunity, and he seized it with both hands. Faced with no alternative, Ruth accepted his offer to move in with him at Goodwood Court. Andy was also made welcome when the school term finished. If ever there was a ménage with a 'light-the-blue-paper-and-retire' label attached to it, this was the one. Blakely was livid, but he could not provide a roof for them, so he just had to tolerate the situation. The curtain had come down on the second act, and the stage was set for the dénouement.

CHAPTER NINE

Me, Georgie: Sexual Awakening

When I was about 12 my health improved considerably. Having been hospitalized so often, many of my childhood memories are of intense physical pain. The condition from which I suffered, cystitis or inflammation of the bladder, is an unusual complaint for a child but, then again, to be different is par for my course. It had made me seriously ill, and the pain, which I endured for long periods at a time, drove me to screaming point.

My parents, that is to say Phyllis and Peter Lawton, could not have been kinder or more understanding and showered me with love and an endless stream of presents to compensate for my ill-health. I often wondered why the Lawtons' union had been childless, but it was not a subject that was ever broached. They were older than parents of children my own age, and I never tried to talk about anything that might make them uncomfortable. It simply was not worth it. Although they could not have shown me more affection, I was rarely totally at ease and never felt quite secure that the house was mine in the way that other children have explained to me their feelings for home. Perhaps the drunken violence that my father had introduced to an otherwise peaceful place had lowered my confidence and absolute faith in my safety there. The fears and confusion I felt when he was around may well have contributed to my constant sickness.

Much later in my life I discovered why the Lawton marriage had been barren. Phyllis, much to the surprise and delight of her parents, followed her father's calling into dentistry. They already had a boy who had entered the profession, but never thought that their only daughter would do likewise. Certainly it was most unusual in those days for women to undertake dental training. The family were thrilled with Phyllis's decision and drummed into her the value of the lifetime security that her qualifications would give her. In particular they stressed that she must never throw it all away for a man – oh, what a great lesson that is, and Phyllis learnt it well.

One might say she learnt it too well, for when she met Peter, who was training to be a vet, though they fell deeply in love, she refused to marry him until he could demonstrate to her satisfaction that he could provide a home and guarantee his income. The result was an engagement that lasted for an incredible sixteen years, and by the time they were married, they were both well entrenched in their respective careers and gave no immediate thought to procreation. Time ran out and so, when I came along with my pretty little curls and cherubic face, I was just what they needed.

The cherub embarked on the process known as growing up, and with the advent of better health my mind was free to explore new thoughts and ideas. I still carried the private secret that I had uncovered in the chest of drawers, but it did not prey on my mind. I had accepted with precocious calm and resignation that my mother was a convicted and executed murderess. I presumed, quite incorrectly as it transpired, that nobody else, be it friend, neighbour or the milkman, knew anything of my ancestry. Obviously, on reflection, with George Ellis having staggered from pub to pub all across the locality, there could have been no way that who I was and where I had come from could have been anything other than common knowledge. No doubt he milked her notoriety and spun all kinds of tales to his fellow drunks, at the same time painting a saintly picture of himself as the wronged husband who did all he could to save a loose woman from the amoral lowlife in which he discovered her. Still, I never saw anyone sniggering or pointing at me from behind trees, so I can only think that neighbours either kept the truth away from their children or, most likely, kept their children away from me.

Phyllis and Peter had set their hearts on my schooling taking me to university, where I would study medicine and become a doctor. I listened to all they had to say and said little in reply. I was only 12, and it all seemed like light years away. The prospect of studying into my twenties was like asking me to abandon my whole life and move directly on to old age. Like Ruth, who at 28 could not face the prospect of growing old in prison for eight or ten years, I saw everyone over 30 as hopelessly over the hill. It was 1963 and of far greater import to me than any thoughts of medicine or schooling were the Beatles, Jean Shrimpton, fab gear and boys on TV in outrageous trousers and high-heeled boots. *Top of the Pops* on my actual birthday broadcast the Beatles latest single, 'She Loves You', to which I could only say 'Yeah, Yeah, Yeah'. Like so many kids of my age I was ready to be swept along with the changes of the sixties, just as Ruth had been ready to lead from the front in the quest for post-war fun and adventure.

I became rebellious and difficult. I feel bad about it now, but it was inevitable. The home in which I lived felt elderly, and Warrington, midway between Liverpool and Manchester, was undergoing a vibrant change. Lancashire cities were leading the world, and I could not wait to become a part of it. I knew my future had to be glamorous, as either a model or a film star, but definitely not a doctor. Why is wisdom the exclusive province of the elderly? Now it goes without saying that I acknowledge the wisdom of my adoptive parents, and I wish I had become a doctor. They afforded me every opportunity, and I turned my back from the start. When God handed out obstinacy, I got it in spades!

So I approached boarding school with great excitement, an approach not unique to me. For some children it is a harrowing experience, others take it in their stride. I soon realized that much of the regimented routine at St Hilary's, Alderley Edge, was tiresome in the extreme, and my anarchic impulses, never absolutely dormant, were put on red alert. There was nothing wrong with the place itself. It had reasonable facilities, and Alderley Edge is one of the most beautiful locations in Cheshire, a high ridge that offers breathtaking views west over the Cheshire Plain and equally stunning vistas east over the Pennines and the Peak District. The problem for me lay in the uninspiring teachers and the drudgery of the curriculum. We were young teenage girls living in the midst of the swinging sixties, where, outside the school gates, tradition was being swept away, and new ideas were finding global outlets. Yet there we were at school, corseted in dowdy school uniform with our only leisure a game of netball or singing meaningless olde English ballads in the school choir. For a modern girl with modern ideas, it was hard to raise enthusiasm for the incomprehensible Chaucer, even the sexy bits, when Bob Dylan was our poet, the one we could all understand, as the times they were a'changing.

Sexual awakening was self-evident in all the songs, films and fashions that were part of the new explosion. We talked about boys but never saw one except through the school gates or while out on some embarrassing school walk in our unfashionable uniforms. Make-up was not allowed, even for the older girls, and some of us got a feeling that time was passing us by, and, just as Ruth must have felt, by the time we were released from the beastly place, it would be all over. I would not say I became wilful, but I would admit to being mischievous. It was a way of livening up the place and injecting a little innocent spice into the turgid pomp of compulsory behaviour, which seemed archaic and pointless to me.

I found it was good fun and daring to try to undermine authority and ridicule the folly of the whole set-up. Sometimes I was punished for my impertinence, but most of my misdeeds were just a simple breach of school rules, such as listening to Radio Caroline after lights out or running a poker school in the dorm. I never ran amok or caused any real damage but simply deployed my energies to break the boredom. Needless to say, word of my behaviour reached home in Warrington, and, not surprisingly, Phyllis and Peter adopted a critical attitude. It was during one of the holiday breaks that a violent row erupted. I was told in no uncertain terms that I was a disgrace and that if I did not improve and take my studies seriously, I would stand no chance of getting to university and becoming a doctor. I screamed at them:

'I don't want to be a bloody doctor. I'm going to be a model and an actress.'

'Oh, no, you're not, young lady!'

'Try and stop me,' I sneered.

'We will do everything we can to stop you because we love you,' they chorused in unison. And then it came out, by accident and in a fit of petulance:

'I bet my real mother would have let me!'

Silence. Shock waves reverberated round the room in the wake of my brutal outburst. They knew I had discovered the truth about Ruth. I slowly and deliberately repeated: 'I am going to be a model' and walked out of the room. I can now understand why they were so horrified. Not only was I defying their wishes and advice and displaying no gratitude in their ambition for me but I was also showing the first signs of turning into a clone of Ruth Ellis. The rebelliousness, the resentment of school, the yearning for clothes and glamour, the determination to become a model and the frivolous approach to all serious matters were, in their eyes, the realization of their worst fears.

Once they were aware that I knew the truth about my real mother, they dreaded that I might try deliberately to recreate her in my own way. In fact nothing was further from my mind, because, although I knew who she was, what she had done, and what her final fate had been, I knew nothing of her background. I could hardly have emulated her at that stage.

The incident in itself was no bad thing, because from that point on from time to time Phyllis would mention Ruth's name, though what she said was uncomplimentary as she would have no truck with a woman who had been on the game and shown no interest in her daughter. They had never once met her, so their opinions must have come from my father and what they had read in the newspapers. Still, it must have been a great relief for them to have everything out in the open.

They did not ask how I had found out about Ruth, and I did not volunteer to tell them.

Back at school the out-and-out tyranny of adolescence continued, and my impish high jinks won me modest popularity with certain girls. For perhaps the first time in my life I made a best friend. Her name was Melissa, and we were extremely close, sharing our spare time and food parcels as best friends do. I trusted her more than anyone I had ever met. One day in a quiet part of the school grounds, we sat chatting and giggling about boys and clothes. On impulse I asked her if she could keep a secret. She nodded and crossed her heart and hoped to die in the customary way, and for the first time ever I revealed my most carefully guarded, classified information about my mother and her crime. I spoke in whispers and can still see Melissa's jaw gaping wider and wider. She urged me to tell her more, but I had told her all I knew, and I felt better for having offloaded so many years of bottled-up anxiety and comfortable that my best friend was privy to my fiercely protected secret.

Unfortunately Melissa's idea of keeping a secret was to beat the jungle drums, and within a day it was all round the school. In Chinese whispers it went from Georgina's mother's a murderess, to Georgina's mother killed her husband and Georgina's mother shot three men and finally to Georgina murdered her mother. I was devastated by her treachery.

The scandal died down as fast as it had flared up, but for a while I was the school celebrity. Melissa's betrayal of my confidence had thrust me overnight into the spotlight, which I have always enjoyed without shame. Insult me but never ignore me, has been a useful motto, and I rather revelled in being famous for fifteen minutes. On the other hand I refused to discuss the subject with any of the other girls or to speak to Melissa, and, one by one, they soon got bored.

The atmosphere surrounding me never returned to normal, but I went on with my business of ducking and diving round the school rules and generally alleviating its monotony. At one extreme there were girls who courted my acquaintance for the novelty of associating with the daughter of a hanged murderess and at the other were those who learnt that it was de rigueur not to know me. 'Twas ever thus and ever will be, and now it doesn't affect me. I am who I am, and it is to neither my credit nor my disadvantage that my foundations were so unstable.

I grew older, I became more daring, and my jolly japes gave way to misdemeanours of less puerile intent. I flaunted my love of lipstick by daubing slogans in it all over the school. I sneaked out to make friends with a group of boys in the village, and I smuggled them in to school in the evening and out again before night patrol by monitors or teachers. It was all innocent fun. Just to be in the presence of boys was light relief, and there was never any proposal or suggestion of sex. It was fortunate that the school grounds abutted the main A34 road from Wilmslow on its way south and was well screened by rhododendron bushes. For those of us versed in the finer points of espionage by television's Napoleon Solo and Ilya Kuryakin in *The Man From UNCLE*, smuggling lads on and off the premises was simple.

In spite of the distraction of such escapades, I was still restless. O-levels appeared on the horizon, and I knew that once I got on board the academic treadmill, I would be increasingly pressurized to stay there. To me this was a blind alley, blocking my way to the future that I had determined was going to be mine. My appetite for glamour had been whetted by television and magazines, and my thirst for worldly experience had been far from quenched by the thrill of smuggling a few uninspiring boys into the common room for nothing more than the hell of it.

I told Phyllis and Peter I was leaving school. To my surprise, they accepted my decision. I suppose they had long abandoned their ambitions for me. Resigned to my independent spirit, they went along with my single-minded resolve to be a model, though not with their blessing.

My parents still saw me as a child, I suppose, but what parent does not? During the school holidays they had never discouraged me from going out in a group with friends. Had they been aware that instead of spending the evening at the youth club, as I had told them, we were in fact cooped up in barns and garages with bottles of cheap cider and the local male talent, they would have had apoplexy. However, I was still a virgin with little idea of what sex was all about. I suppose by Ruth's standards, I was a late developer. Development was just around the corner.

As Ruth moved with trepidation to her big city, London, so I ventured with surface confidence to mine. I enrolled on a grooming course at the Lucie Clayton Model Agency in Manchester. The principal was Sue Gresham, an elegant, beautifully spoken woman, who was kindness itself. Her second in command was a Bolton lass called Pamela Holt. She had abandoned her natural Lancashire accent and spoke with more marbles than Audrey Hepburn in *My Fair Lady*. She terrified me at first but later proved to be one of the most genuine people in the modelling game and established herself in her own right, having left Clayton's, as the undisputed queen of model agency in northern England. Not too long ago she sold out, but her name still epitomizes style across the fashion world.

Midway through the course, with the encouragement of those who were there specifically to advise on such things as hair and deportment, there was an in-house photo session. As a result of this I decided to go blonde. When I returned to Warrington that evening the look on Phyllis's face was one of abject horror. In her eyes, my bleached hair was just another Ruth Ellisism, a further manifestation of my gradual cloning. But it was nothing of the kind.

Long blonde hair suited me, and photographers all agreed that my look was right for the time. That is how I presented myself for the end-of-course photo session, which was carefully analysed, and graded by the course assessors. It was only after I started work on this book that I learnt that my co-writer, Rod Taylor, was often one of them. Whether he sat in on my passing out, neither he nor I remembers.

I was about to have my first taste of the glamour that is never far removed from the world of modelling. Warrington to me was what Brixton had been to Ruth: acceptable as somewhere to sleep but to be escaped from at all other times. Ruth found the London drinking clubs, and I discovered the discos of Manchester. The music throbbed loud and long into the night, but there was always someone prepared to give me a lift home in exchange for a virginal kiss at the front door. In one such disco, the Time and Place in Fennel Street, a man with a strong Belfast accent came up to me and asked my name. I told him Georgie, and he looked at me as though I were lying or trying to make fun of him. He asked me again, and when I repeated it he said: 'My name's George, too.'

'There's a coincidence,' I said quite disinterestedly. 'I'm Georgie Lawton.'

'I'm George Best. Come and have a drink.'

I had honestly never heard of him, but there was something about him that I could not help but like. His voice was lilting, his eyes twinkling, and his general demeanour suggested mystery and mischief. I knew my precious virginity was under threat. From that moment George cast his spell on me, and I was mesmerized like a rabbit caught in car headlights. He shared a flat in Prestwich with another Manchester United player, David Sadler if my memory serves me correctly, and it was there that he drove me in his Sunbeam Alpine sports car to deflower me without a hint of a struggle. George Best was to become, and to some extent remain, one of the most influential persons in my life. There are few loves that never die, and even fewer that never fade. I am lucky to have experienced this emotion twice in my life, albeit twenty years apart.

CHAPTER TEN

Countdown to Murder

Once Ruth had moved in with Desmond Cussen it did not take long for the first fireworks to explode. She no longer worked at a club, which meant that David's supply of free alcohol had run dry. He spent more and more time in Hampstead at the Findlaters, which only served to infuriate Ruth. Desmond put pressure on her to break with Blakely once and for all, but by this time, as she admitted in court, she was in love with David and not with Desmond, although she slept with both of them. Behind Desmond's back, she invited David round to Goodwood Court whenever Cussen was away, and she also used me as an excuse to get away. She told Desmond on more than one occasion that she was going north to see me as she was concerned for my welfare. Of course she never came within 180 miles of Warrington. She and Blakely checked into a small London hotel called the Rodney. She could not live without him.

It was Christmas night, 1954, when trouble flared in a major way. Ruth arranged a gathering of a few chosen friends to have a small party at the flat. They included Jacqueline Dyer and her beau, but David was not included as he had gone to Penn to spend Christmas with his mother and stepfather. Ruth, presumably with her tongue firmly in her cheek, had given both her men identical silver cigarette cases for Christmas. She was living very dangerously. That night Desmond had gone to another party first with some business colleagues but was expected back mid-evening. Ruth put Andy to bed, and she, Mrs Dyer and a couple of other guests went off to a club for pre-party drinks. They left Andy alone in the flat but attached a note to the front door for the benefit of other guests who might arrive. On it they gave the telephone number of the club to which they had gone.

Down in Penn, Christmas Day for David Blakely had been similar to most other days. The Cooks went to visit neighbours so, at lunchtime, David went to the Crown and got himself drunk. He had a late Christmas lunch with the family and carried on drinking at home right through the afternoon. He grew bored and drove himself to London on the pretext of delivering a present that he had bought for Andy, a toy revolver. He arrived at the flat drunk, read the note and went to phone Ruth at the club. She knew instantly that he was highly inebriated and apologized to her companions as she left, saying that she would be right back.

Ruth found David in an ugly mood outside the front door, and a fierce slanging match got under way. She took him into the flat, where both levelled strongly worded accusations of infidelity at the other, while simultaneously swearing their devotion. David accused Ruth of sleeping with Desmond, and she blamed him of doing the same with Carole Findlater. The shouting rose to screaming pitch and wakened a terrified Andy. They carried on regardless, hurling obscene invective across the room, she calling him a ponce and he calling her a tart. Both were quite right, of course, but it destroyed any hopes of a party.

Ruth managed to hustle David out of the flat and, as usual, showed no qualms about leaving her frightened son alone. She got him down to his car, where the quarrel continued. He refused to leave without her, so she agreed to go with him to the Findlaters' flat, for which he had a key. Ant and Carole had gone to Bournemouth to stay with friends for the holiday period.

Desmond, in the meantime, unknown to either Ruth or David, had pulled up close by in his own car. He observed David to be very drunk and later stated that he was frightened for Ruth's safety when he saw her getting into the car with David at the wheel. Whatever his motivation, the feckless Cussen followed them all the way to Hampstead, and assured that they had arrived safely he meekly turned round and went back to his own place. He had guests to attend to but no hostess to help him. He also had the unenviable job of trying to offer some reassurance to Andy that his mother was safe and well.

The following morning Ruth returned to Desmond's flat where he confronted her, telling her that he had followed them all the way to Hampstead so there was no point in her lying to him. Her imagination clicked into overdrive, and she blurted out a story that David had blackmailed her into spending the night with him by threatening to commit suicide. She claimed she was left with no choice. Desmond, whether through gullibility or to avoid a fight, swallowed the excuse. At all events he was desperate that she should not leave him.

Following such a tumultuous row, Ruth and David must have spent their passion in bed for both went about Boxing Day almost as though it had never happened. Ruth placated Desmond and spent the day in the country with him and Andy. David, who by all the laws of nature should have been laid up with a monumental hangover, drove down to Brand's Hatch, where he met up with Ant Findlater. The Emperor had been entered for its first competitive race in an event named the Kent Cup. David drove into a commendable second place.

David and Ruth had numerous telephone conversations over the next few days, and he picked her up to take her out on New Year's Eve. If she had any real belief that David's talk of marriage had any serious intent, it must surely have been dispelled by the events of the day. He suggested they go to the Crown at Penn for a drink, where he had taken her a couple of times before. It was as close as she ever got to his other life in Buckinghamshire. When they were approaching the pub,

David spotted his mother going inside, so he drove on to the Red Lion, further down the road. They then drove back to the Crown where David told Ruth to wait in the car. He went in, saw his mother was still there and took a drink out to Ruth. He would not allow her in the pub where he would be forced to make the introduction long desired by Ruth. She must have been deeply hurt that he was so ashamed of her.

They drove back to London in uncomfortable silence, broken only by the same accusations that always ignited their tempers. This time it was the married woman in Penn that Ruth threw at David, and a couple of punches that David packed in return.

Their every encounter was now stormy. Ruth consulted the specialist who had treated my father at Warlingham Park Hospital, and he put her on tranquillizers. She was wilting under the stress of juggling two men, and David was suffering the same strain from his involvement with two women. Friends on both sides later claimed that both Ruth and David were simultaneously whingeing about each other. She put it about that she wanted to break the relationship, but he would not let her; he told the same story in reverse. The Findlaters encouraged David to act rather than merely talk, and Desmond was pushing Ruth from his end. If there is any truth in those claims, it did not alter their sexual hunger for each other. How well I understand my mother's dilemma. On the day I married my second husband, Peter, I was pregnant with George Best's child. Neither Peter nor George knew, but that is another story.

The date of 8 January 1955 is an important one in the Ruth Ellis saga. That night she and David checked into the Rodney Hotel for another tryst, which spawned a blazing argument, provoking complaints to the management from other guests about the noise. It became violent, and blows, scratches, kicks and spitting were exchanged. It is said that Blakely taunted her over his woman friend in Penn, and Ruth was particularly vulnerable as her friend and fellow hostess Vicki Martin had died in a car crash just two days previously. They fought for much of the night, interrupting the slanging-match only for coitus. The next morning David went off to Penn, saying he had a business meeting. He promised to ring Ruth during the afternoon.

She expected his call, but it never came. She waited all night and the following morning, but still he did not ring. She was resigned to the affair being over. In what she saw as a final gesture of defiance, she sent a telegram to David at Silicon Pistons. It read: HAVEN'T YOU GOT THE GUTS TO SAY GOODBYE TO MY FACE = RUTH

The telegram reduced Blakely to a quivering wreck, not out of dread of losing Ruth but for fear that people at work might talk and their gossip reach the ears of his mother, Humphrey Cook and his other mistress. He repaired to the Crown for a much needed intake of alcoholic fortification. The decline in his affairs brought out the coward in him that was such a part of his make-up. He refused to face the evidence before him. One phone call to Ruth would have kept her quiet, and he could probably have laughed off the incident. Instead he opted to get drunk and worry himself sick over what Ruth might do next. He went running to the Findlaters who again coaxed him to have nothing more to do with her. He did not heed their advice, and before Ruth could make her next move he went sheepishly back to her with grovelling apologies and more talk of marriage.

Ruth got her decree nisi on 14 January, so she felt the time was right to turn the screw. The decree would be absolute in only six weeks so, as far as she was concerned, the only impediment to a legal wedding was removed. Blakely must have been blind, if he could not see himself being backed into a corner.

That whole month of January was punctuated by violence and hysteria. The chronological sequence is not of special importance, but all three central characters were involved. Ruth and David continued to meet at the Rodney Hotel. One night they were going to a dance together and met at the hotel beforehand. Sooner rather than later the barbs came out, and Blakely settled the argument in the only way he knew how, by hitting her. The dress she was to wear for the dance was strapless, and before they could leave he had to apply thick make-up to her arms and shoulder areas to cover the archipelago of bruises that he had inflicted.

On another occasion Blakely made a call for help to Ant Findlater, screaming that Ruth had attempted to knife him during a fight at Goodwood Court. Findlater and garage owner Clive Gunnell went haring round to the flat, where they found the pair of them drunk and hysterical. In the scrap she had seized his car keys and hidden them. She had a severe black eye, and she had hurt her ankle. Gunnell treated her eye as best he could and attempted to restore some semblance of peace. Blakely found his car keys and tried to make his escape. Ruth's fury returned, and a scene ensued outside as she jumped from David's to Ant's car, while Blakely finally got away as Gunnell distracted her. He and Findlater took her to a nearby café for a calming coffee, where they reassured her, lying through their teeth, that they were on her side and thought Blakely a cad to treat her so diabolically.

Ruth returned to Goodwood Court, where Desmond did his best to console her. Blakely went to the Findlaters, and Carole dressed the wounds on his back that he maintained had been caused by a knife. As she rested with Desmond, Ruth's vivid imagination got the better of her, and she became wildly jealous at the thought of her lover being with Mrs Findlater. She asked, or rather instructed, Desmond to drive her up to Hampstead where she could spy on the house. Complaisant as ever, Desmond did as she wished, and the two of them sat in the car outside the Findlaters' flat until they saw Ant, Carole, David and Clive Gunnell emerge. They followed at a discreet distance as the foursome wended their way to the Magdala public house. Again they sat in the car until closing time, when once more they trailed them back to the flat. Why Cussen complied with this idiotic vigil is beyond comprehension. It did not end there. Blakely did not go inside the flat but jumped in his car and drove off at speed. They lost him and returned to Goodwood Court. The bee in Ruth's bonnet was stinging furiously, and she tried in vain by telephone to trace Blakely's whereabouts.

By now even Desmond Cussen might imaginably have had enough of such nonsense. But not a bit of it. He agreed to drive Ruth all the way out to Penn. She had convinced herself that David was in bed somewhere there with another woman. In an incandescent rage she hammered on the door of his flat, which was opened by his nanny. Ruth ranted and raved to the point that pyjama-clad Blakely ran out in fear of his life and sped off in his car. He drove round the country lanes and managed to lose his pursuers. They returned to Goodwood Court.

That was still not the end of this ridiculous tale. The next morning Ruth was in considerable pain from both her eye and her ankle, which she feared might be broken. The pain was obviously not sufficient to divert her from her quarry. Chauffeur Desmond was ordered to head the car towards Penn, after she had tried ringing David at Silicon Pistons and was told he was unavailable. On the way to Penn, Ruth spotted David's car in Gerrards Cross, parked outside a pub, the Bull, in which they had drunk together on many occasions. At last Cussen stopped acting like the toy poodle he was and insisted that Ruth stay in the car while he confronted Blakely. He totally lost his temper and challenged David to step outside and fight a man instead of a woman. Ever the coward, Blakely declined the invitation and brushed Cussen aside.

Ruth had left the car and stood in the doorway of the pub hurling abuse at David for the entertainment of the other customers. She knew exactly what to say. She threatened to confront his mother with all the facts of their affair, the black eye and the suspected broken ankle. In panic David made an apology to her, and, mumbling an excuse about a business meeting, he bolted for his car and screeched off towards London.

Rather than carry out her threat of going to David's mother, Cussen persuaded her that the apology should suffice. He then wanted to take her to hospital to have the ankle X-rayed. She did as he requested, and they drove to the Middlesex Hospital, London, where it was confirmed that the ankle was badly bruised but not broken. They went back to Goodwood Court. Later that same day a delivery of red carnations was made to the flat. Pinned to the bouquet was a note that said: 'Sorry darling, I love you. David.'

In between all the violence, Ruth announced to Desmond that she was going to look for a job, and she decided that she would stand a better chance of getting one if she could speak French. True to form, he fell for this and made contact with the French Institute to arrange for one of their senior teachers, Marie-Thérèse Harris, to give Ruth private lessons at the flat. These began on 17 January. The real reason why Ruth wanted to learn the language was that David had been offered a prestige drive with the Bristol team in the forthcoming Le Mans 24-hour race. He had promised to take her, and she wanted to surprise him with her sophistication and linguistic abilities. The lessons, like the rest of her life, were a disaster, as she had no powers of concentration and no flair for languages.

In an act of supreme or calculated carelessness, Ruth left a hotel bill from the Rodney in a waste bin at the flat. Desmond found it, and his suspicions about her nocturnal absences were confirmed. She had not been visiting me in Warrington. When Ruth next went away, Cussen drove past the hotel at night, saw Blakely's car and went back to his flat deflated and dejected. The status quo could not continue.

Ruth came to the same conclusion. One evening shortly after the carnations had temporarily soothed their differences, she suggested to David that they live together again in a flat of their own. She said she could borrow some money from a friend for the rent, which they would be able to repay when the Emperor was profitable. The prospect of getting Ruth out of Desmond's flat delighted David, and he went along with the idea. What she did not tell him was that she intended to borrow the money from Desmond.

Ruth told Desmond of her desire to live in a place of her own and justified it by saying it was grossly unfair that he should become embroiled in scene after scene whenever David was around. Desmond was obviously relieved by the news and unhesitatingly agreed to lend Ruth the necessary money. In return she promised to look after him, cook for him from time to time and bestow her favours as before. She did not tell him that Blakely would be co-habiting with her on a full-time basis, though he must have known.

She bought the London evening paper, *The Standard*, and answered an advertisement for a furnished one-room service flat in a large Kensington house at 44 Egerton Gardens. She met the resident housekeeper at the flats, Joan Winstanley, and arranged to take the room at a rental of six guineas per week. She signed the agreement as Mrs Ellis and explained that she would be living there with her husband. On 9 February she and David moved in as Mr and Mrs Ellis. Mrs Winstanley never knew David by any name other than Mr Ellis.

The whole set-up was distinctly odd. While David took on the alias of Mr Ellis he was busy telling friends in general and the Findlaters in particular that he was not in love with Ruth and wanted out of the entanglement. He told them he was scared of Ruth and that more than once she had menaced him with threats not only to involve his family but also to set on him some of the gangland heavies who were her friends from the clubs.

After the farce of the French lessons, Ruth's next whim was to become a model, not the type she had been at the Camera Club, but a respectable couture mannequin. To this end the ever obliging Desmond took her along to the Marjorie Molyneux School of Modelling, where he paid the enrolment fee for her to start a course in March. She also became pregnant. She said the child was fathered by David, but it could just as easily have been sired by Desmond. Once more David ignored the advice of Carole Findlater and accepted that the unborn child was his.

Neither the new domestic arrangements nor the pregnancy served to stem the fighting. Nor did Desmond Cussen merely sit back and wallow in his own misery. In yet another peculiar arrangement he would call at Egerton Gardens most mornings after Blakely had left to go to work in Penn. So madly in love was Cussen that he continued to ask Ruth to marry him, and her refusal to abandon the beast that he perceived Blakely to be hurt him deeply. Cussen was prepared to settle for Ruth by day only rather than not see her at all. She had been forced to admit to him that Blakely was living with her as her husband, and still he swallowed his pride. He never knew what colour he would find her in the mornings, black, blue or shades of yellow from the latest hammering. The whole triangular set-up was unpleasant and unhealthy.

Ruth and Blakely fought as much in public as they did

at the flat. Witnesses had seen them come to blows at the Steering Wheel Club and the Hyde Park Hotel. Their brawls were commonplace, and mutual acquaintances took evasive action to avoid being in the company of either of them if they were both under the same roof. David's affair with the married woman in Penn grew in its ardour, and he spent several nights away from Egerton Gardens, telling Ruth that he was staying at his Penn flat for the sake of appearances. His deception ignited a full-blown battle royal, and Ruth was rewarded with her customary bruises and another black eye.

With Cussen as her chauffeur, she embarked on another round of tailing David's every move. They followed him to work, to the Crown and to the married woman's house. In a foolish slip of the tongue Blakely had divulged her name and address to Ruth during one of his alcohol-induced outbursts. Ruth was hurt, and her wounds were festering. In the most outrageous exhibition of her disillusionment, she had Cussen drive her to the married woman's house. There they kept vigil all through the night and were rewarded when Blakely emerged at nine o'clock the following morning. He had hidden his car in the parking area at the back of the Crown but on seeing Desmond's car, he dove back into the house. After Desmond knocked on the door, a contrite and ashen-white David reappeared and pathetically proffered the explanation that he had stayed the night on the sofa following a late party.

Later that day Ruth went to apologize to the married woman for causing a fuss, and she was invited in for coffee. The woman gave a version of the previous night that conflicted with the one David had told her. At lunchtime they all, including his Penn mistress, found themselves in the Crown, where more trouble was brewing over a dance to be held that evening by the British Racing Drivers' Club at the Hyde Park Hotel. David had said he did not intend to go to the dance, so Ruth had accepted Desmond's invitation to partner him. In the pub David announced that he would be at the dance after all. Several drinks later Desmond and David remarkably shook hands, and Desmond drove Ruth back to London where she had an appointment at the hairdressers. The hand-shaking episode is hard to understand since all other evidence suggests that the enmity between the two men had reached fever pitch. Maybe, temporarily at least, they had both had enough of Ruth's depraved tantrums.

David's party at the dance included his mother and step-father, which accounts for his reluctance to admit he would be present. Desmond and Ruth arrived late, having first been to the Steering Wheel Club. All three had had plenty to drink, and, according to Robert Hancock's version of the evening, Ruth danced alternately with Blakely and Cussen. At the end of the night it was Cussen who drove her home, but the following morning it was Blakely who was lying beside her in bed. She had no recollection of his return to the flat and was surprised and angry to find him there. She was still sore about the woman in Penn and told him so in no uncertain terms. Of these 24 hours, Ruth said at her trial:

> The tables had been turned. I was jealous of him, whereas he, before, had been jealous of me. I had now given up my business – what he had wanted me to do – left all my friends behind connected with clubs and things, and it was my turn to be jealous of him. . . . I told him we were finished, and it was all done with. I asked him for the key of the flat back, but he would not give it to me.

They stayed apart for about a week, during which time Desmond managed to retrieve the key from Blakely at the Steering Wheel Club by knocking him down in order that Ruth could grab his key-ring and take back her key. When the week was up, she returned to Egerton Gardens one night to find David hovering outside, remorseful and asking her to allow him back. He swore blind that he had once and for all terminated the affair in Penn, pledged his eternal love to her, and, feebly, she consented to a reconciliation.

The harmony was short-lived. The very next day she had Desmond drive her to Penn for lunch at the Crown. Her motivation was twofold; firstly it was a beautiful spring day, and she fancied going out to the country, but, more to the point, she needed to check up on the truth of what David had told her. When they walked into the pub, they saw David standing with the married woman. Sheepishly he went over to Ruth, bought her a drink and then made his excuses and left. That night at Egerton Gardens David reaffirmed that he was no longer in any relationship with the woman and added that it was hardly his fault if she elected to patronize the Crown. He was in no position to banish her.

The undercurrent of all this swirled about for a few days before inevitably dragging them into one of their major confrontations. Ruth told him that she could take no more of his deceit, and he would have to get out of her life. His reaction was to punch her in the face with a clenched fist, then put his fingers around her throat and thump her hard in the stomach with the other hand. At her trial she suggested that the blow to her tummy might have been responsible for her miscarriage. Subsequently she wrote that she had had an abortion. Whichever is the true version, she lost the child on or about the 28th of March.

Notwithstanding his disgraceful treatment of her, Ruth did not kick him into touch, as she ought to have done. For the umpteenth time she gave in to his grovellings, and talk returned to the subject of marriage. It is likely that David was taken aback by the miscarriage or abortion, because Carole Findlater had never believed Ruth's pregnancy and had all but convinced David that the whole story was a fabrication, a ruse to trick him into marrying her. The pregnancy had been real, though, and all the trickery had been Mrs Findlater's in another bid to discredit Ruth.

Ant Findlater, together with Clive Gunnell and David, had quietly gone on refining the Emperor, and David entered the car for a race at Oulton Park in Cheshire for Saturday, 2 April. Though she was suffering from the aftermath of losing her baby, Ruth was genuinely thrilled to be asked to join the party for the journey north to the racetrack. In truth Blakely only asked her to stop her pestering him. The fine tuning needed to prepare the car had necessitated many hours of work at Gunnell's garage, much to Ruth's annoyance. She resented every moment he spent away from her until, in a rash gesture, he promised to marry her as soon as the race was over. Content with that promise, she left him in peace to finish his beloved car.

Her earlier nagging was shortly to backfire on her. She, Ant and David drove up to Chester together, where they checked into a hotel. Carole made her own way north, joining them all later. She was officially there to write a fashion article for the *Daily Mail*. On the Friday afternoon David took the Emperor out for a trial run round Oulton Park. All the hard work and their hopes and aspirations evaporated in one split second during that practice. The Emperor broke down beyond immediate repair and had to be withdrawn from the race the following day. David vented his frustration and wrath not on the car, not on himself or Ant, but on Ruth. He blamed her for having interrupted his work schedule so many times and spoke of her as a jinx on the Emperor. This was unfair and unfounded, but Blakely was the sort who had to have a scape-goat, and he always picked the weakest victim.

His venom must have subsided by the time they all decided to stay on in Chester and watch the Saturday racing. Ruth and David slept together in the hotel, and though she was still losing blood from the termination of her pregnancy, she somehow managed to satisfy her lover's lust. They stayed the Saturday night at the hotel, and then, on the Sunday, they attached a tow rope to the sad Emperor and made the return trip to London. David Blakely had seven days left to live.

CHAPTER ELEVEN

The Best Set

I did not deliberately set out to emulate Ruth Ellis. On the other hand we have much in common. Central to us both was a desire to avoid falling into any rut that was the lot of so many of our contemporaries: hers the women of the forties and fifties, mine those of the sixties and seventies.

From our earliest teens my mother and I were patent non-conformists. Both blessed with a pretty face and an attractive body, we equally determined to employ our assets for personal benefit. We had it, and we knew how to flaunt it. Neglect of school work was something that she and I both shared and came to regret at certain times, but we were able to compensate for any educational shortcomings with our palpable charms. So many men are vulnerable to and oblivious of blatant female exploitation. And so many others wear the boot firmly on the other foot and delight in using women for their own ends. Some men are flagrant misogynists who hide behind a façade of machismo; others simper from within an Oedipus complex and are numbered among life's inadequates. Ruth and I had our share of them all. Occasionally, though, a man comes along who defies categorization. Just such a man is George Best, footballer extraordinaire and lover supreme, a kind, generous man, an alcoholic and a former guest of Her

Majesty's prison service, for whom justice was as unfairly administered as it was for Ruth.

From the moment I lost my virginity to George, I fell hopelessly in love with him. It was more than a teenage crush but less than an obsession. Most of all it was fun, which is precisely what had attracted Ruth to the apparently elegant men of the world who frequented her clubs. George is the most good-humouredly phlegmatic man I have ever met. Nothing fazes him, though his global adulation was a heavy cross to bear. The hero worship that was part of his life at Old Trafford carried over into his private life, where he was unable to distinguish his friends from the inevitable hangers-on, ponces and undesirables. He took them all in his stride and treated everyone equally.

At Manchester United home matches I was privileged to sit in the director's box alongside Matt Busby and other sports luminaries of whom I had never heard. Old Trafford is an infectious place, and I cheered my support along with the rest of the fans, dying each time he hit the deck, feeling relief when he got back on his feet, marvelling at his skills and discovering the euphoric surge of adrenalin that comes with a goal. In Manchester he was an undisputed king, and I revelled in being his queen or, more truthfully, one of them, for girls threw themselves at him, and George was ever the opportunist. Men flocked around him as much as women. When I learnt of the coterie of sycophants that clung to racing driver Mike Hawthorne in Ruth's days, it brought back images of George in the Brown Bull pub in central Manchester. I do not think George ever bought a drink in there either for himself or for me. They were lined up on the bar, sometimes five or six deep, purchased by admirers who would have been hurt had their offer been refused. I was drinking under age, but I adored sweet Martinis and drank them like fizzy pop. If I tried to point out to George that some people were taking advantage of him, he would defend them and claim they were his friends.

When we first started to date, George was under contract to the *Daily Express*, which ran an on-going feature on him and Mike Summerbee of Manchester City, under the title the 'Best Set'. He introduced me to the features editor, and I was contracted for the fabulous sum of £4500 to be the third member of the 'Best Set' for a year. Top fashion photographer on the *Express*, Peter Jackson, took an instant liking to me, and I was plunged into the hectic whirl of fashion and social photographic modelling. My elevation to the 'Best Set' brought a full contract with the agency, and a glittering new world opened up for me. George and I struck up a sexy, playful friendship. I was little more than a child, and I worshipped him, often silently, as I was too overawed sometimes to speak. He was nearly always in good humour, facetious and simple in his tastes. I cannot recall him ever ordering anything other than steak Diane in a restaurant. But there was a serious side to George aside from his career. He was an avid solver of crossword puzzles, and I have yet to find anyone who can complete the most complex and difficult puzzles set by *The Times* or the *Telegraph* quicker than George Best. I remember thinking how clever he was, but he must have found something interesting in me beyond my body. In spite of my long silences, he wrote in his book, *The Good, the Bad and the Bubbly*, that I had a sympathy and wisdom beyond my years. I think he must be referring to the support I was able to lend him during the bad days, which for him were just around the corner.

Being one of the 'Best Set' was a dream opportunity for any aspiring model, but each day for me was dogged by an oppressive fear. I was working under the name Georgie Lawton, but with such constant press coverage and attention I was convinced that a journalist would uncover my origins and reveal my real name. I even thought it likely that Melissa or someone else from St Hilary's might see my photo in the *Express* and sell my secret to some greedy hack. I was petrified because I felt that being exposed as the daughter of Ruth Ellis would signal the end of my fledgling career. Amazingly this did not happen; even George had no idea, but now that I know him so very well, I am confident he would have protected me to the best of his ability. All this was in 1967. It was 1975 before a newspaper tracked me down, and then I took the easy way out and co-operated. Rather than deter clients from booking me, it upped my profile, and I was more in demand than ever. That, to be dealt with later, was not long before the bad days arrived for me also.

Death has followed and haunted me all my days, not just that of my mother, my father, my brother Andy and my best friend Kathy Anders. On a prestigious photographic assignment for the *Express*, Peter Jackson dressed me in the fashion of 1967 in a suit made of tin foil and high court shoes, both of which made walking a new skill to be mastered. The location was to be the top of the *Daily Express* building in Manchester, a fabulous all glass edifice several storeys high, which, although no longer used for newspaper production, is, thankfully, subject to a preservation order. The only way up was via an open fire-escape. The ordeal was compounded by a fairly strong wind, which made the tin-foil whistle. Peter wanted me in the foreground, with a panoramic view of the city skyline behind me. To get his shot, he moved further and further back until he was right on the unprotected edge. With a premonition that he was going to fall, I broke my pose, rushed forward and grabbed his arm, just as he was about to take the fatal step backwards. So wrapped up in taking the picture, he had no notion that he was so at risk. We took time out for the palpitations to subside, but not long afterwards I heard that he had fallen to his death from a high balcony in Tenerife.

In 1968 Granada Television produced *Nearest and Dearest*, a new situation comedy. Its stars were Jimmy Jewel and Hylda Baker, a squabbling brother and sister who had inherited a pickle factory. The producers came to the agency to select two girls to act as hostesses for the audience before the recording of each episode. I was chosen along with Pam McCarthy, a girl I knew quite well. Pam was extremely beautiful, tall and slender with short dark hair setting off a gorgeous face perched on a Modigliani neck. Working together each week, we socialized after the shows, enjoying a few laughs and drinks. At the end of the series she went off on holiday to Tenerife. The plane on which she was travelling turned right instead of left or left instead of right and flew straight into the side of Mount Teide. There were no survivors.

I turned as always for comfort and support in all adversity to George Best. He had opened a menswear shop in a previously down-market part of Manchester, which immediately moved up-market and became fashionable. The area, which covered no more than 500 square yards, became known as the Village. A little further down the street was the Village Barber, run by one of George's more worthwhile friends, Malcolm Wagner. Between the two there was a small vacant corner unit, which George suggested I should rent and from there run a business selling clothes I made myself. We called the shop Georgie Girl after the hit 1966 movie *Georgy Girl*, starring James Mason, Lynn Redgrave and Charlotte Rampling. George was at the zenith of his football career, as the whole world had watched his incredible contribution to United's victory over Benfica in the European Cup Final. The pressure was getting to him, and he sought refuge and anonymity in my corner shop, where he said I made 'the best brew in the north'.

Our whirlwind romance had matured into a firm friendship that still holds today. There was never any hope of it being permanent. To tie George down would be to try to cage a wild bird. His idea of the perfect wife was someone who would wait at home for him while he flew round the world doing whatever he liked. I made it quite clear that if anyone in my life was going to go jetting off it would be me. One night as we sat in a restaurant, the Isola Bella, in the city centre, George asked me what I most wanted out of life. I gave him the answer he least wanted to hear: 'Freedom'.

It is wonderful to have a friend like George, and that is surely the role Desmond Cussen should have played for Ruth. Instead of pursuing an unrequited love, he could have used his ten-year age advantage to protect her, not only from David Blakely but also from herself. In her greatest hour of need there was nobody to help her, and, as far as I can gather, she had not one single, on-going friendship of any real value. I count myself so much more fortunate than she was to have enjoyed a handful of true friends whose loyalty has never wavered no matter how erratic my behaviour, no matter how low I have sunk. I will always love George in my own way.

I saw him at intervals for years, sometimes intimately, other times not. He was unpredictable, which ensured he was never dull, always exciting. His attitude to money was rarely other than careless, and he was magnetically drawn into scandals. One such notorious scandal resulted from a dalliance with American beauty Marjorie Wallace, who had just been crowned Miss World. She had a well-publicized romance, an engagement no less, with racing driver Peter Revson, heir to the giant Revlon cosmetics empire. What George did and did not get up to I have no idea, but he ended up splashed across the front pages accused by Wallace of stealing cash and a fur coat from her. In the midst of all that, Revson was killed in a tragic accident.

The weekend of Revson's death, George and I had been to a couple of Manchester night-clubs, Oscar's and Slack Alice, when George decided he wanted to go gambling. I had never been in a casino before, and I sat goggle-eyed, drinking scotch and watching the play. George got lucky and won almost £5000, which he stuffed into plastic bags. I drove him home to the council house in Chorlton where he lived under the caring eye of landlady Mary Fullaway. By now George was very drunk and furious that I intended to return home to my Peter, my husband-to-be. He went berserk, the bags burst, and the cash went all over the place.

I drove home in a car strewn with money only to find Peter waiting outside. George had telephoned. I turned the car round, drove back to Mrs Fullaway's and stuffed every single bank note through the letterbox. The next day he told me I was the most honest person he had ever met.

He was a natural womanizer. He could no more be faithful than David Blakely. Even in 1994 he made the headlines for approaching a young woman he had never met before and saying, 'I love you.' He got her into bed and almost destroyed the most stable relationship he has ever had. He will not change as long as he remains an irresistible and fatal attraction for women.

I had no illusions. George and I were in London together, and we came into contact with a lovely girl, Angie, a model who was working as personal assistant to singer and actress Cher. That evening George and I went to Geales restaurant for dinner with footballer Rodney Marsh and his wife. In the middle of the meal George left the table to go to the toilet.

He did not return. It transpired he had climbed through the window of the gents' lavatory and vanished. I later found his car, and there on the passenger seat was Angie's model card. He was up to his old tricks.

On the other hand he could be ferociously possessive. At one time, after a particularly remunerative assignment, I treated myself to a brand new Mini 1275 GT. I was living with a man whom I would later marry. One night George was so furious when I told him I was going home to this man that he started to kick my car, my pride and joy. He went berserk. I must add that, though he beat up my car, George never once laid a finger on me.

There was a gentle, tender side to George too. When all hope of a reconciliation between him and Manchester United had evaporated, he signed a contract to join the American club, Tampa Bay Rowdies. About four weeks before he was scheduled to leave we shared a candlelit supper in my flat in Chorlton. He was nervous about the prospect of playing in the States and dreaded a repeat of what had happened to him in Britain: that they would build him up, place him on a pedestal only to shoot him down again. His confidence was fractured. We watched some black-and-white videos of Pele. George said, 'I will never be as good as that.' Pele has since been quoted as saying that George Best is the greatest footballer who ever lived.

Later that night I conceived. The day he left George rang me from Manchester airport. I suspected I was carrying his child, but I said nothing. His last words to me were: 'I will always love you, Georgie.'

I never heard from him for weeks and weeks, during which time ghastly morning sickness confirmed my suspicions of pregnancy. Peter, my second husband, was urging and pushing me to marry him. He believed the child in my womb was his, but I knew otherwise. Peter pestered and pestered me to marry him. I knew it was wrong, but I gave in and said yes. The day after the wedding, the very next day, George telephoned: 'Get yourself down to London. I've got two best seats for Frank Sinatra at the Albert Hall.'

I said, 'George, I got married yesterday.'

George swallowed hard. 'You silly cow,' he said, 'what've you done that for?'

I answered with, 'And where have you been all these last weeks and months?'

'I've been for a long drink,' was his reply.

He hung up, and I heard nothing further from him for several weeks, during which time I had an abortion. My marriage was already the disaster I had known it would be, and Peter had knocked me about a bit. Eventually George made contact. We met at the old, empty flat where we made good, if uncomfortable, conversation. He invited me back to his digs at Mrs Fullaway's, and in her front room I told him of the pregnancy and the abortion. I had seven or eight large sherries to pluck up the courage to tell him. All the colour drained from his face, and he fixed me with a stare that seemed to say that he would never forgive me. Then, like the little boy that is never far from his surface, he said,

'I would have been so proud if you had had my child.'

I guess George and I were just two vulnerable people who had a lot to live up to and a lot to live down. When the press did finally nail me as the daughter of Ruth Ellis, it was George Best who helped me turn the resultant publicity to my own advantage. When I made the decision to write this book, it was George, along with another old friend, Eddy Shah, who gave me good advice, and it was George who gave me carte blanche to write about all that we had shared. All he wanted in return was a signed copy. I was reminded of our first night of love in Prestwich, at the end of which he said to me, 'I was the first – I'll be the last.'

CHAPTER TWELVE

Seven Days to Live

Monday, 3 April 1955 was a grey, still day with spring showers that fell intermittently over London. Ruth Ellis was in bed, where she would remain for the next 48 hours. She was suffering from a chill and the after-effects of her termination had been aggravated by the trip north. She lay in the one-room flat heavily tranquillized on the drugs that had been prescribed by Dr Rees at Warlingham Park Hospital and was barely conscious that her young son Andy had come home for the Easter holiday. It was the first time Andy had seen the grotty flat at Egerton Gardens, and nobody had thought to tell him that he would have to sleep in the same room as his mother and whoever was sharing her bed. Andy's lot was a canvas camp-bed pushed up against a wall.

David Blakely and Ant Findlater were severely depressed by the débâcle at Oulton Park. Blakely's mood was filthy as he struggled to come to terms with the stark reality that there was no alternative but to try and sell the Emperor. He was cleaned out, and his principal source of income from Humphrey Cook had dried up. His dreams of success, fame and fortune were in tatters. Ant's mood was no less doleful as he, too, had dreamt of the money they would make when the Emperor

126

became a production-line car. As usual when those two were in the doldrums, they got drunk.

Carole Findlater inwardly rejoiced in their failure. She had harboured a bitter resentment of the Emperor ever since Ant had relinquished his job with Aston Martin, even though she had grudgingly acquiesced in his resignation. She was busy writing her article for the *Mail* on the fashions of the Cheshire Set at the race meeting.

Desmond Cussen, who should by rights have been thoroughly sickened by all the ludicrous spy missions and harebrained chases along the country lanes of Buckinghamshire, was still ready to dance attendance on Ruth. Indeed it was he who had collected Andy from school and delivered him to the flat. Ruth's feelings were so obviously with Blakely that Cussen should have put himself at as great a distance as possible from her. Instead he stuck like chewing-gum to the sole of her shoe.

Matters had got worse while Ruth and David had been in Chester, and Desmond had been faced with a crisis that was totally Ruth's responsibility. He had been in Wales on tobacco business and returned to Goodwood Court on the Saturday. There waiting for him was a telegram from Andy's school saying that he had broken up and did not know where to go. Not only had Ruth forgotten or given no thought to Andy's school holidays, but she had also failed to notify the school that she had changed her address. It was only when Desmond telephoned Egerton Gardens that he learnt from Mrs Winstanley that Ruth had travelled north 'to watch her husband motor racing'. The school actually let Andy stay with them until the Monday, when Desmond drove to Aylesbury to fetch him home.

David Blakely did not get back to the flat until the small hours of Tuesday morning, when his original foul mood, further depressed by the effects of excess alcohol, had turned pitch black. He collapsed in a stupor. The following morning, notwithstanding the presence of Andy, David laid into Ruth with a torrent of verbal abuse. He was convinced that she had jinxed the Emperor. He threw in her face the fact that she had told him before they went to Oulton Park that he would never have any luck because of the way he treated her. He accused her of being a witch, a sorceress who had ruined his chances.

Andy told me later that he had felt like a caged animal. He wanted to run away, but there was nowhere to go. He did not even know the area round Egerton Gardens in the way that he was familiar with Knightsbridge, near the Little Club, and Marylebone by Goodwood Court. The poor child was shown no consideration by the warring factions. Only 'Uncle' Desmond, as Andy called him, ever acknowledged his existence and considered him. Andy went out for an aimless wander.

Ruth hit back at David and released feelings that she had kept bottled up since Chester. Apparently, just as they were about to leave the north with David's Vanguard towing the damaged Emperor, David had asked Ruth for £5.00 as he was not able to pay the hotel bill in full. She gave it to him without question but was surprised to see, as she came down the hotel staircase to join him at the desk, that he was paying the whole bill by cheque. She felt he had conned her out of the cash. It was a cheap lie, and it hurt her. If he had said he was short of money, she would have given him £5.00 willingly. She was upset that he had resorted to deception, and it fuelled her already well-primed fears that she could neither trust him nor believe a word he said.

After David stormed out, and Andy had gone walkabout, Desmond turned up. He was livid about her negligence towards Andy but even more angry that Mrs Winstanley had told him she had gone north with 'her husband'. After all Desmond was paying the rent on the flat. He was sore and with justification. Mrs Winstanley was the innocent party, but she, in turn, was reprimanded by Ruth, who had left a note telling her that if Mr Cussen should ring, she had gone away for the weekend to visit her daughter, me, in Warrington. While in Chester, of course, she was no more than 25 miles away from Warrington, but she never came any nearer. Mrs Winstanley found the note too late and in any case did not appreciate its subtleties. Though she had often seen Cussen visiting in the mornings, she neither knew him nor especially warmed to him. She found him surly, whereas David, whom she believed to be Mr Ellis, always engaged her with his charm.

The day passed, tempers subsided all round, and Ruth recovered from both the chill and the vaginal bleeding. Throwing aside her mistrust of David, she consoled herself that all would be well after their marriage, when all the rowing, complicity, acrimony, acts of violence and stresses and strains would disappear. The Wednesday, 6 April, gave her no cause to doubt her optimism. Even the sun was shining.

While events were simmering in Kensington, Knightsbridge and Hampstead, on 6 April 1955 Winston Churchill resigned as prime minister and was replaced by Sir Anthony Eden. A general election was looming, which was one of the main reasons why Churchill had opted to stand down. Eden was not only a younger man but also married to Churchill's niece, and the grand old man was anxious to keep government in the family. If I appear to digress, forgive me, but that forthcoming general election played an important role subsequently in the fate of Ruth Ellis.

The Wednesday was an important day in David's life. He had been selected to drive again for the Bristol works team in the Le Mans 24-hour race scheduled for 9 June. The team had assembled for each member to be photographed officially, and that day he returned to the flat with an enlargement of his portrait, which he gave to Ruth. He had signed it: 'To Ruth with all my love, David'. When this photograph was produced as evidence in court, it was the only time during her trial that Ruth betrayed any emotion. She cried, but when the judge offered her the option of sitting rather than standing in the witness box to complete her evidence she told him she preferred to stand. She very quickly recovered her composure.

David was proud of his photo and elated to be a Bristol driver. He and Ruth stayed in that evening, and, according to her testimony, things went so well that David even broached the subject of marriage again. Ruth said in evidence that they were both very happy, despite David's decision to sell the Emperor. She urged him not to take such drastic action and was clearly carrying some guilt. David told her that he would need to find £400 immediately if the car were to be saved. He even, with no hint of shame or wounded pride, suggested she might borrow the money from Desmond Cussen.

The following morning, the Thursday, David went off to work. As soon as he had gone, Ruth's irrationality returned with a vengeance and kick-started her suspicions and jealousies. She rang Desmond and asked him to pick her up in his car and take her to Beaconsfield. The motive behind this latest daft mission was to find the shop of the photographer who had enlarged the portrait of David. She needed to know if another enlargement had been made at the same time, and if so then she would know that he had given that one to his married woman in Penn.

This was sheer madness. As it happened, they never did find the photographers and after several gins in a Beaconsfield pub she dropped the idea. Desmond left Ruth in Beaconsfield for a short time while he went to the Crown at Penn to look for David. He found him there, but the two men did not speak, such was the open hostility between them. However, if that were the case, why had Desmond bothered driving to Penn at all? He had no reason for going other than to see David, so why find him and ignore him?

Ruth returned to Egerton Gardens and waited there for David. They had booked tickets for the theatre that evening. He telephoned her from a call-box on Western Avenue, telling her that he was stuck in traffic and did not know what time he would be home. She believed he was telling the truth because she could hear cars and the unmistakable sound of traffic in the background. He returned too late for the theatre so they went to a local cinema instead. In her evidence Ruth said: 'All through the cinema, which was rather annoying, he was telling me he loved me and all kinds of things. . . . He seemed very attentive to me.' After the film the couple discussed their plans for the forthcoming Easter weekend, which included an outing for Andy, drinks in Hampstead with the Findlaters and a visit to a motor-racing circuit on Easter Monday.

The following morning, Good Friday, 8 April 1955, they awoke in fine spirits, each at peace with the other and with no hint of a raised voice. David left the flat at around ten o'clock, and in court Ruth's description of how they parted was as being 'on the very best of terms'. She understood that he was meeting up with Ant Findlater to discuss the options open to them for the Emperor, but that he would be back that night. First thing on the Saturday morning they would set off with Andy for their day out.

That was Ruth's version of Good Friday morning. The Findlaters painted a different picture. They said they met up with David that lunchtime in the Magdala public house in Hampstead. They found him in a state of anxiety and depression, which he put down to Ruth's unpredictable and irrational outbursts. He told Ant and Carole that he had woken with a throbbing hangover, and Andy, ten years old and full of energy, had made much noise and been thoroughly disobedient both to Ruth and to himself. He also complained that he was physically, mentally and sexually exhausted. Rather than he and Ruth parting that morning 'on the very best of terms', the Findlaters claimed David told them that he and Ruth had parted following a verbal tirade of traded insults and accusations. In view of subsequent events, the Findlaters' version seems more plausible.

David, according to Ant and Carole, said that he could not take any more of Ruth Ellis, and all he wanted was to get away from her. He told them that he was expected back at Egerton Gardens that night, but he had no desire to go there. He expressed his fears that if he went home to Penn, Ruth would go looking for him and cause another disturbing scene in the sleepy village, compounding the embarrassment already inflicted on his mother and stepfather. Carole Findlater accused David of being spineless and pointed out that if he were simply to leave Ruth, there was not a thing she could do about it. It was then that Carole proposed David spend the whole Easter weekend with them at their flat and added that if Ruth tried to cause any trouble they would handle it. While Carole was no less than scornful of David's weakness, Ant was more sympathetic and encouraged his friend to take up their offer. He agreed with Carole that between them they could handle whatever reaction Ruth might have.

While these plans were being formulated, Desmond had picked up Ruth and Andy, at Ruth's specific request, and taken them to Goodwood Court for lunch. After that the three of them went to see a science-fiction film in the West End before Desmond drove them back to Egerton Gardens in the early evening. Ruth's aim was to settle Andy in bed before David's return at 8.00 pm. Then, with Andy tucked up for the night, she and David would be free to go out drinking. She dolled herself up in readiness, poured herself a drink and waited. She poured another drink and another and waited some more. Her waiting was in vain. At around 9.30 pm she telephoned the Findlaters only to be told they were out. The phone was answered by the nanny who cared for their daughter and, when pressed by Ruth, informed her that she had no idea whether David was with them or not.

At around half past ten she rang again, and Ant picked up the receiver. He lied to her that David was not with them. She was not fully convinced by Ant, conscious that his voice sounded rather 'cocky'. Nonetheless she was genuinely worried for David and told Ant so. She had a feeling that they were making a laughing stock of her, lying to her and probably working on David to turn him against marrying her. She rang the Findlater home repeatedly over the next couple of hours to the point that Ant began to lift the receiver and put it straight down again without speaking. This incited Ruth's anger and, at the other end, put the fear of God into David who was terrified at what she might do. Ruth, now convinced beyond a shadow of doubt that David had sought asylum in the house of her avowed enemies, was doubly frustrated that there was no reply when she tried to ring Desmond at Goodwood Court. She was well oiled with alcohol and at her wits' end.

It was after midnight when she finally made contact with Desmond Cussen. Though he had been drinking with friends all evening he went round immediately to Egerton Gardens. Ruth persuaded him to drive her to Hampstead, so, without a thought for Andy who was fast asleep, they set off on yet another David hunt. Outside the Findlater flat in Tanza Road, they soon spotted David's Vanguard parked close by, thus confirming Ruth's worst fears and inflaming her violent temper. She rushed up the stone steps and rang the doorbell repeatedly and at length. Nobody came to the door. Carole had taken herself to bed with a sleeping pill, David was cowering on a sofa, and Ant was determined not to respond to the bell. He, like David, knew full well what sort of a mood she would be in, and the prospect of a face-to-face confrontation with her was most unattractive.

When she thought she heard a woman giggling, Ruth's imagination told her it was the young nanny and that David was likely as not in bed with her. In a fury she went and found a telephone kiosk, but once more the receiver was put down before she could speak. She walked back to the flat and started ringing the bell once again. Nobody came to the door. Her wrath had to have an outlet, so she collected a heavy rubber torch from Desmond's parked car and took out her venom on David's Vanguard. She said at her trial: 'I knew the Vanguard windows were only stuck in with rubber, so I pushed at one of them, and it came clean out from the rubber. It did not break it, just made a noise, and I did the same with two other windows.'

Desmond Cussen simply sat and watched. Even more bizarrely, at the trial he was never questioned about that night. In any event Ruth's actions had the desired effect, and Ant Findlater came to the door, but not before he had called the police. He stood his ground on the doorstep, denied vehemently that Blakely was in the house and kept her talking until a police car reached the scene. Ruth rounded on the police officers and ranted at them about the way she had been treated, while Ant tried to calm her down and give a coherent account. Desmond kept his head down. Ruth told the police that the Vanguard was partly hers anyway, since she had helped to pay for it, and the officers, having advised Ruth to go home, wrote it off as a domestic incident requiring no further action on their part. Before the police left, Findlater explained that David Blakely was not in the flat but that when he had seen him earlier that day he had expressed the wish, quite clearly and calmly, that he never wanted to see or speak to Ruth Ellis again.

Ant Findlater went back indoors, and Ruth licked her wounds. She was not the sort of woman, alas, who could lick them quietly, and she began shouting obscenities in the street. She was in a state of extreme emotional distress. Findlater again called the police and, forced to make a second visit, the officer who had tried gentle persuasion the first time round was more forceful the second.

At last Ruth rejoined Cussen in the car and allowed him to drive her home, where she sat up the rest of the night smoking, drinking a little and allowing her thoughts full rein to torture her. She was racked with the feeling that she had been wronged unjustly by the man to whom she had given her all. She reminded herself of all she had done for him, the free drinks, the money, the mothering and the sex. She was hurt deeper than she had believed possible when she confronted the stark reality that Blakely had jilted her and, without the guts to face her, run off to hide behind the Findlaters. It was a cowardly and cruel conspiracy. After all she had not only given up her job for him but also moved from the safety and comfort of Goodwood Court just to accommodate him in her bed.

The protective shield that the Findlaters built around David was still in place on the Saturday morning. Ruth telephoned at first light, her fury in no way attenuated by the passage of a few sleepless hours. Once again the receiver was taken off the hook and replaced at once. Leaving Andy to fend for himself, she took a taxi to Tanza Road, Hampstead. It was a bitterly cold morning, and she shivered in her vigil in the doorway of a house just down the road from no. 29. Round about ten o'clock that morning, she observed Ant leave the house, look up and down the road to check if the coast were clear and beckon to David who joined him to inspect the damage to the Vanguard. The two men climbed into the car and drove away.

Ruth had her proof. Most women I know can put up with many of the wrongs that men perpetrate against them, but the one thing that no woman can tolerate is being lied to. If only, and this is a story of if onlys, David had been man enough to face her and finish with her in a half decent manner, she would have had her say, possibly screamed and shouted, but at least she would have been able to release her pent-up emotions. As she stood there, huddled in a concealed doorway, she saw those who were conspiring against her make a run for it. She was utterly disgusted that her lover could treat her so shabbily, and she had every reason to feel such disgust.

Ruth logically assumed that David and Ant would head for Clive Gunnell's garage to fix the repairs to the windows. She calculated how long it would take them to get there and then made her way to the phone box, where she rang the garage. Using a false name, she asked to speak to Ant, who, as soon as he heard her voice, hung up on her. Not knowing which way to turn next, she hailed a taxi-cab and took herself to Desmond Cussen's flat. Ever the lapdog, Desmond telephoned the Gunnell garage, giving a false name but an authentic one from the world of motor racing, and asked to speak to Findlater. Ant recognized Desmond's voice and returned the receiver to its cradle.

With a little prompting from Desmond, Ruth was forced to divert her attention to Andy who had been left alone at Egerton Gardens. Together they went round there and prepared some lunch for him. After they had all eaten, Desmond and Ruth drove Andy to the London Zoo end of Regent's Park and left him with sufficient cash to spend the afternoon there as well as get himself back to the flat later. The two adults, although I employ the term lightly, then set off on the next round of Hunt the Blakely.

They found the Vanguard, duly repaired, outside the Magdala pub. Ruth decided she would go to Tanza Road and hide out discreetly to watch for David's return and check who was sharing his company. She had firmly convinced herself that David and the nanny, engineered and encouraged by the Findlaters, were a romantic item. Nothing could be further from the truth, but my mother, once she formulated such a notion, had immense powers of self-persuasion as to its veracity.

Desmond, moronic to the end, said he would wait for her in the car near the Magdala. What his own rationale was for continuing the pantomime is hard to establish, but it is just remotely possible that already he was toying with the idea of exterminating his adversary and rival. Why else, the night before, would he have sat with such pathetic passivity and watched Ruth use his torch to damage the windows of Blakely's car? Was he perhaps premeditating a murder? Maybe he could sense that this time there was no reconciling the warring couple, and he wanted to be on hand to ensure that his intuition was correct. Whatever the real reason for spending his Easter driving a half demented woman up and down to Hampstead at all hours of the day or night only he knew, and he has never disclosed the truth from that day to this.

When Ruth reached Tanza Road she had some opportunistic good fortune. At a house not more than a few doors from Ant's and Carole's place, workmen were toing and froing. She began talking to a couple of them, and they told her it was for sale. With a piece of quick thinking she posed as a potential purchaser and was introduced to the owner who lived on the premises. The woman invited Ruth to take tea with her, and, as luck would have it, she served it in the room of the house that afforded the most perfect view of the entrance to the Findlaters. She saw them all return from the Magdala: Ant, Carole, David and the nanny with baby Francesca in her arms. After tea Ruth resumed her position in the same doorway that she had used during the previous night. From there she saw them all, baby included, come out of the flat once more, get into the Vanguard and disappear down Parliament Hill.

Ruth was not able to pursue them on foot, and Desmond was some streets away, driving round and round and up and down wondering where she was. By the time they eventually met up, David and company could have been anywhere. Ruth unburdened her conviction that David had been paired off with the nanny to Desmond as he drove them back to Egerton Gardens. Andy was already home and was hurriedly fed supper and put early to bed. There was no television in the flat, no distraction of any interest to a boy of his age, and it appears that he was constantly sent to bed at the ludicrously early hour of seven in the evening. I know what response my ten year olds would have offered if that had been their bedtime.

With Andy bedded down for the night, incredible though it may seem, Desmond and Ruth headed back to Hampstead.

Desmond may have made this trip unwillingly, but I do not think that is accurate. I believe he was already arming Ruth with motives to finish with Blakely once and for all. He was stirring the poisonous brew with which he hoped to see David removed from the frame.

Much has been written about how Ruth was consumed by jealousy, and how David left her because he had made impossible and imprudent promises of marriage, which he had neither the intention nor the means of fulfilling. As I see it, the jealousy was at its most fervent in Desmond Cussen. His role hitherto had been as doormat, chauffeur, money supplier and object of ridicule. In return he had got to sleep with Ruth spasmodically and little else. I can understand, I hope, how he must have felt, but I can never condone how he allowed Ruth to go, indeed led her, into such a potentially harmful situation that day. He knew they were not on her side and had good reason to accept that Ruth was being truthful about their unwillingness to help her reach Blakely when his own attempts to make telephone contact with the Gunnell garage were thwarted by the simple expedient of putting down the telephone.

As Desmond and Ruth motored to Hampstead, a small and intimate party was getting under way in the Findlater flat, Carole's idea to help David and Ant overcome the disappointments that the failure of the Emperor had brought. She invited over a few mutual friends in an attempt to cheer the men up.

With her mind blown by hallucinatory misconceptions and her emotions in tatters from the non-stop rejection and refusals to respond to her desperate telephone pleas, Ruth popped tranquillizers in serious excess of the dosage prescribed by Dr Rees. Whether she did this behind Desmond's back or with his connivance we shall never know, but he must have been aware that her behaviour was absurd, even by Ruth's standards, and her irrationality exorbitant. Aside from David Blakely himself and the Findlaters, Desmond Cussen was the only human being in a position to avert the forthcoming tragedy. Either wilfully or out of an insane stupidity while the balance of his own mind was disturbed, he did nothing that can possibly exonerate him from the guilt that ought to have placed him in the dock alongside my mother. During this entire week she had no contact with her own family other than 10-year-old Andy.

When asked at her Old Bailey trial why she had kept these obdurate vigils outside the Tanza Road flat she answered: 'Like a typically jealous woman I thought there was something going on which I should know about. In the afternoon I stood in a doorway two houses away from the Findlaters' flat and was invited into the house to tea.' Of the second Saturday stake-out she added: 'The window was open, and there seemed to be a lot of noise coming from there . . . I heard David's voice . . . I heard somebody giggling a lot. I thought it was somebody I knew but . . .' For some reason best known to Mr Melford Stevenson, her QC, she was not permitted to complete her sentence.

Everything Ruth saw that Saturday night she misinterpreted. Towards ten o'clock she saw David, Ant and a woman she presumed to be the nanny leave the flat. She was hiding in close enough proximity to hear David say to the woman: 'Let me put my arm round you for support.' The woman was not the nanny but a party guest. The three of them went off in the car. Ruth said in evidence that she had to leave her post for a brief while. She gave no reason for this, but she probably felt the call of nature. When she resumed her position, the car was back in its parking place so she knew she had missed the return.

The next incident that Ruth described later in court occurred, according to her, just after half past midnight. As she watched the house the blind in the front room on the floor beneath the Findlaters' living-room was lowered, and the light was turned out. The light in the hall was switched off also. Ruth wrongly thought it was the nanny's bedroom, and, letting her thoughts run riot, she pictured David climbing into bed with the young girl. In fact, the nanny's bedroom was at the rear of the flat but she had made up her mind, and that was that. The party continued in the rest of the flat and she made her desolate way back by taxi to Egerton Gardens where Andy was asleep and alone.

During research for their book, Laurence Marks and Tony van den Bergh spoke with Mrs Winstanley, the housekeeper at Egerton Gardens. She told them how she had looked into the Ellis flat on this Saturday night to ensure that Andy was all right. She noticed something different about the room but could not immediately put her finger on precisely what it was. Then it dawned on her that David's photograph, the one in his racing overalls, had been either removed or destroyed. She attached no real significance to it at the time, and content that Andy was sleeping soundly, she left the room.

All the evidence that Ruth offered at the trial about the events of that Saturday night and Sunday morning is blurred by confusions, non-sequiturs and contradictory statements, which suggests her memory was gravely affected by the drugs she had taken. For the second night running, once she was back at Egerton Gardens, she did not go to bed. Through all the hours of darkness she sat alone, chain-smoking and racked with that abominable sensation that jealousy and rejection cause in the deepest pit of one's stomach. When the sleeping capital city once more awakened, it was Easter Sunday, Ruth's last day of freedom, and David's last day of life. She began the morning with yet another phone call to the Findlaters' number. She told of this call in her evidence:

'I thought if David was sleeping in the lounge, and the divan is next to the phone, he would be the first to pick it up. . . . I waited a long time before it was answered and then Anthony answered the phone. . . . I think I said: "I hope you are having an enjoyable holiday, because you have ruined mine."'

Ruth contended that she still expected David to call her, which was delusion considering he had made no contact with her for more than 48 hours. She persuaded herself so on many counts, mostly the combined result of no sleep, drugs and alcohol. Andy was left to amuse himself while she mooched and paced around the confines of the flat, reminding Andy, as he later told me, of the animals he had seen at the zoo the previous day. Her expectation that David would call was based on their prior arrangement to go motor racing on Easter Monday, and, however he felt about her, she convinced herself that he would not let down Andy, who was supposed to accompany them. In truth, if David Blakely had any feelings at all for the boy he kept them securely locked away. Other than giving him the toy revolver for a Christmas present, Andy could recall no other displays of care or affection from David.

David did not call. Ant Findlater subsequently revealed that when Ruth made her Sunday-morning call, the entire Tanza Road household was asleep. Ruth had been correct in her supposition that David would be on the divan in the lounge but it had been agreed between the conspirators that under no circumstances was David to answer the phone. The reason why it was so long before her call was answered was that Ant, who had been unanimously appointed telephonist, had to get out of his marital bed, don his dressing gown and make his way to the lounge. When he heard her tone of voice, he instantly cut off the connection. Findlater also was able to clarify Ruth's false interpretation of the blind being drawn in the room below their living-room. That room was not even part of the Findlater complex. It was occupied by their landlord. If David had only picked up the telephone it might well have saved his life.

Sunday lunchtime was spent by all participants in the story in relative orthodoxy, except for the fact that Ruth's judgement and self-control were impaired and subject to random fluctuations of cohesion. Desmond collected her and Andy shortly before lunch, and the three of them went to Goodwood Court for a bite to eat. All her usual flamboyance was absent as she was unable to concentrate on anything other than her own despair. What they did during the afternoon remains unclear. In evidence Ruth said that she had completely forgotten. Cussen was not even questioned about it, but I guess that he plied her with Pernod, consoled her in a fatherly manner and sowed the seeds of annihilation in her addled brain. I cannot prove it, but then no one can disprove it either.

Meanwhile, up in Hampstead, the occupants of 29 Tanza Road had gradually surfaced, attacked their respective hang-

140

overs with Alka Seltzer or fried breakfast and braced themselves for another day of cat and mouse. Carole and Ant told David that the worst was surely over and that he had weathered the storm. After the one early-morning phone call they felt Ruth to be a spent force who had surely given up her crazed intrusions of their privacy. The three of them went to the Magdala at lunchtime, where they met up with Clive Gunnell and made arrangements that he, Clive, should spend the evening at the Tanza Road flat and that David would pick him up from his home later. The afternoon was spent on Hampstead Heath, where the Easter fairground was in full swing. By the time they arrived back at the flat, most of the day had passed without interruption from Ruth.

There is one uncorroborated report, to which I can attach no credulity, that suggests Desmond Cussen took Ruth to Epping Forest for target practice. Andy, who was with them all day, dismissed the notion as ridiculous and was adamant to me that no such thing had happened. He was equally certain that, just before they all left Goodwood Court in the early evening, he saw Desmond take one of his guns from the drawer where he kept them, oil it and place it in mother's handbag. He was 10½ and not prone to invention. When he originally told Muriel and, years later, me about this, he stated it plainly and without embellishment.

During those lost hours of the Sunday afternoon that Ruth claimed not to remember, Desmond kept her well topped up with Pernod and demonstrated how to use the gun. It was a .38 Smith and Wesson black revolver. Once he was satisfied that she could handle the weapon, he loaded it with six bullets and put it in the handbag. He also made her promise that, were she to use it, she would not incriminate him in any way, in consideration for which he swore his promise that, whatever the outcome, he would always look after Andy and take care of his education. At some time in the region of half past seven, they all three went to Egerton Gardens, and Andy was put to bed. At the same hour, David and Carole Findlater went in David's Vanguard to collect Clive Gunnell, his record player and some records from his home in nearby South Hill Park. They drove back to Tanza Road and settled down to a mildly boozy evening of music and chat, just a small, intimate gathering.

Once Andy was settled, Ruth and Desmond went out and left him alone in the flat, as he had been every night since his homecoming. Desmond was anxious to maintain Ruth's intoxication at a high level so they went to a club for drinks, she imbibing more of the lethal Pernod to add to all that she had drunk over the last three days and nights. She was embarking on her third evening without going to bed. She knew neither where she was nor what she was doing, her body and mind working only on automatic pilot and both aching from being discarded by David Blakely and his smart Hampstead accessories.

At approximately nine o'clock that evening Carole smoked her one remaining cigarette and asked her former lover, David, to nip out to the Magdala and buy some more for her. David agreed willingly enough and suggested that Clive Gunnell accompany him, so that they could replenish the depleted stocks of beer at the same time. Although the pub was no more than a quarter of a mile from the flat, they opted to be lazy and take the Vanguard. They went into the pub and ordered drinks from the landlord, one Mr Colson, who knew them both well and had, earlier that day, cashed a cheque for Blakely.

Ruth, meanwhile, alternated between being morose and hopping mad, her anger burning. She and Cussen set off again to Hampstead to see what was going on in enemy territory. It was to be the last time. When they reached Tanza Road and could see no sign of David's vehicle, their first thought was to check out the Magdala. Sure enough, parked outside the pub on the same side of the road and facing down the hill was the grey-green Vanguard. Ruth left Cussen's car and went to peer through one of the pub's stained-glass windows. She was just in time to see David, at the off-sales counter, buy the beer and cigarettes. As he and Gunnell drained their glasses and collected their purchases to take back to Tanza Road, Ruth was outside and ready for them.

For her it was now or never, and she felt the loaded gun in her bag. She was wearing her glasses, something she rarely did in public places; glasses that she needed to counter her acute myopia. Gunnell was the first to emerge, walking towards the car and round to the passenger door. Blakely followed him armed with some of the beer, which caused him to fumble for his car keys. From the darkness Ruth spat out his name: 'David!'

If he heard her, he elected to ignore her, trying to reach the sanctuary of his car. She opened her bag slowly and deliberately and pulled out the gun. She called his name a second time, which caused him to turn and see her facing him, revolver in hand and pointing directly at him. As he tried to make the car his cover, she fired two shots. David Blakely's last word was 'Clive'. Ruth screamed: 'Get out of the way, Clive!'

As David started to run, a third shot felled him. She fired a fourth shot and then moved in on the body and fired into his back from a range of two or three inches. Out of five bullets fired, four had hit their target, and the resting-place of the fifth was never discovered. Eye-witness reports say that Ruth then lifted the gun to her own head and tried to kill herself with the last remaining bullet. Either the gun jammed or her nerve broke at the last moment. She took the gun away from her head and squeezed the trigger again. The final bullet hit the pavement or the road or a wall, hitting a Mrs Gladys Yule in the thumb, an innocent stroller on her way to the Magdala with her banker husband for a quiet drink, who was right in the flight path of the ricochet. As her unfaithful lover lay slumped and dying with blood pouring from the wounds in his body, Ruth turned to Clive Gunnell and said, 'Go and call the police.' Desmond Cussen was nowhere to be seen.

CHAPTER THIRTEEN

Me, Georgie: In the Lap of Luxury

How I wish my mother had been able to foresee the virulence of the consequences of her actions; that forty years on I, her daughter, am still obliged to turn a blind eye to the pointings and murmurings that I know are saying to someone who does not know: 'That's Ruth Ellis's daughter, you know. She looks just like her.' My grandmother suffered the most, I suppose, at least in the days, weeks and months that followed the shooting, but it is pitiful Andy, my illegitimate half brother, who came off the worst as the years passed by. Her pulling that trigger was selfish and inexcusable, equally so was the venomous Desmond Cussen who pushed her into it when she was out of her mind with drugs, drink and lack of sleep.

Almost my entire modelling career was lived in abject fear of being found out. Odd as it may seem, I felt a great deal safer once I moved to London. For the first time in my life I realized how small Warrington and Manchester were in comparison with the sprawl of the Metropolis. I arrived, in pursuit of my musician boyfriend Nicky, with my head in the clouds and in the full expectancy that the very brightest of lights would be mine for the asking. I saw the bright lights all right, but I was swiftly brought down to earth when I discovered how much money it cost to enjoy them. We were a pair of hopeful kids, and Nicky's earnings from Streatham Locarno were swallowed up by the rent.

I have always been industrious, and when needs will as needs must I simply get on with it. I found myself with three jobs: I worked in a smart London shoe shop by day as a junior sales assistant; in the evening I served in an Italian restaurant; and first thing every morning, no matter how long the midnight oil had burned, I dutifully carried out my chores as a cleaner at the Cat's Whisker in Streatham. This was hardly the glamour that I had come to London to enjoy, and I shared with Ruth the frustration of knowing that it was there for me if only I knew how to grasp it. My three job stint was the equivalent of her waitressing and posing nude for the Camera Club when she first arrived.

A couple of nights a week Nicky played with the band at a smart ballroom just by Piccadilly Circus. On Saturday nights I used to go with him to watch, and over the weeks I got to know the ballroom manager reasonably well. One particular night we all went to the BBC to record a heat of *Come Dancing*. It turned out they were one judge short. The manager asked me if I would make up the numbers on the panel, and I readily agreed. On the panel with me was Lionel Blair, choreographer, dancer and television star, and he chatted to me throughout the proceedings. He told me he was soon to produce a major extravaganza in New York and suggested I audition to be one of his 'Ladies', as he billed his dancers in those days. I confessed immediately to having had no formal dance training, but he said if I could move in tempo and look a million dollars it would be no handicap to my getting the job, as the dance element was minimal.

I auditioned and was duly selected by Lionel who partnered me through the required steps and quite literally swept me off my feet. He decided to launch me, and before I could blink I was dressed in a very low-cut, white evening gown and photographed for the William Hickey column of the *Daily Express* as 'the face of the future'. Warrington was not ready for this, and Phyllis and Peter had letters of complaint from a few clients who thought it inappropriate that Georgie

Lawton should be publicly exposed in such a state of undress.

With this national exposure in the newspaper, all my old fears swarmed back with a vengeance. If they find out who I am, I told myself, Lionel Blair will drop me, and my burning excitement at the prospect of New York cooled. Then I realized I was pregnant. It was a calamity. The dates for Lionel's rehearsals were imminent, and by the time the show was to be staged I would be somewhat larger than the trim figure he had booked. I went running home to Warrington and, though I was terrified of their reaction, told the Lawtons of my plight. I need not have feared. They were as wonderful as they always have been and calmly arranged for me to have a private abortion in Warrington General Hospital.

I woke up after the operation in excruciating pain and later I learnt the reason. The job had been badly bodged, and later that day I passed the remains of what I presumed to be the foetus. The pain eased, and the first rehearsal was only two days away. I had to get to London and, against all medical orders and to the horror of Phyllis, I discharged myself from the hospital.

I went to the first day of rehearsals, vacillating between mere pain and occasional pangs of agony, wearing at least four pairs of knickers. How I got through that day I will never understand, but somehow I managed. In the evening Nicky and I went to a restaurant in Chelsea's King's Road for a meal. Suddenly the pressure inside me intensified, and the pain grew unbearable. I just made it to the toilets, where it was revealed that I had been expecting twins. I was rushed to hospital where I was given blood transfusions, kept under close observation for several days and told that I had ruined my chances of ever having children in the future. I never got to New York, and my first chance of stardom was destroyed along with the embryos that Nicky and I had created.

Our marriage was doomed, just as I had been warned by my adoptive parents, but although Nicky and I split up, he still had a significant role to play in my life. However, for the next year I was destined really to taste the good life that accompanies stardom and lots of money.

After the abortion and loss of the lucrative contract with Lionel Blair, I might easily have followed in the call-girl footsteps of Ruth in the need to subsist in London, had I not impulsively, and with cheek I reflect on with amazement, breezed into a building where I had no appointment and no right to be. It came about following a short convalescence back home in Warrington, just as Ruth had made a short-lived return to her own parents' home after the termination of her pregnancy by the wealthy club member who deserted her. Unlike Ruth, however, I spent what few pounds I had and went for a brief holiday to Spain, where I ended up staying six months. As soon as I felt up to it, I headed for the station with little more money than the price of a single train ticket to London and a great tan. My intention was resolute. I was going to be a film star, and no two ways about it. I was conscious that I looked the part and thought it would be a relatively simple matter to knock on a couple of Wardour Street doors, and meet one or two casting directors who would be overjoyed to find the new Julie Christie or Susan Hampshire standing before them.

It does not work like that, as I was soon to find out the hard way. I knocked on doors all right, but they remained firmly secured against my advances. I found that becoming a film star was not the piece of cake I had naively imagined. Someone told me that EMI were currently the biggest British film producers. I decided to change my strategy. No more tapping on doors for the regulation polite rebuttal; I had had my fill of those. This time, looking the star to the best of my ability, I sauntered up to EMI's headquarters in Golden Square, and, with a swell of confidence and a smile like a clenched fist, I strode past the uniformed security officer and took the lift to the top floor. I had no idea of the layout of the building nor who was who, but, once inside, the top floor seemed as good a place as any from which to explore. The corridor in which I found myself was luxuriously carpeted, and I walked along hoping I might find a door with a sign on it saying Casting Director. Needless to say there was no such door, but I selected a pair of double doors that looked important and opened them.

Inside several men were sitting round an impressive table. I had stumbled into a board meeting. A sudden silence descended, before someone came over to me as I stood in the doorway and asked what I was doing and what I wanted. I told him I wanted to see a casting director, and he, incredulous but kindly, took me to another room where he asked me to wait. When he returned he told me that his name was Jack McGraw, and I subsequently learnt that he was head of EMI's film division. He asked me a few questions, including how I had gained access to the building, and he shook his head disbelievingly but with a warm twinkle in his eye. After a while, another man came into the room, and I was introduced to him as David Niven Jr. He also was taken aback by the ease with which I had secured the interview now in progress.

During the course of conversation, Jack McGraw drew from me the information that I was from the north and that I had absolutely no money and nowhere to stay. In a fatherly and kindly way he advised me to go home to Warrington, and he even gave me the money for a taxi and the train fare out of his own pocket. Before I left, however, he took my name and address and promised to write to me if he could do anything to advance my ambitions.

Feeling quite smug and pleased with myself, I did as he advised and took the next train home to wait. I did not have to stay there long for Jack was true to his word. Within days a letter arrived from him with another train ticket enclosed for me to return to London, where I would take a screen test at Elstree Studios. I was off like a shot and duly reported to Golden Square, where this time I signed in officially and was escorted to Mr McGraw's office. I thanked him profusely for arranging the test, and he told me where and when it would be shot. Next he asked me if I had anywhere to stay, and when I told him I had nowhere, he handed me a set of keys. He said: 'This is Terry Stamp's flat, but he's away on location so you can stay there for a few days.' I was speechless. Terence Stamp was my idol, a dream guy and, even though he was not going to be there, just to stay in his flat had me quaking at the knees.

I was sent up to Elstree, where I and a handful of other

hopefuls of both sexes were looked at by make-up and sized up by wardrobe. At lunch we all went to the canteen, where our conversation was giggly and quite loud. For some reason and in response to something someone had said, I shouted: 'Knickers!' A man with an Irish accent sitting just behind me said: 'That's fantastic! Say it again.' So I did, and he turned away laughing his head off. I asked if anyone knew who the strange chap was and was told it was Richard Harris. What a shock it turned out to be when the moment for my screen test finally arrived, and I learnt I was to play a love scene on a bed, in which my only lines appeared to be 'I love you, I love you, I love you'. The man opposite whom I was to play was no less than Richard Harris himself, at the studios for his starring role in *Cromwell*.

We completed the scene with Richard unable to suppress his laughter but nevertheless showing some degree of passion. I could tell he enjoyed the kissing and all because his body responded, but I never expected to see him again. After I had changed back into my own clothes I was given a message, hand-written, which asked me to go to the main front entrance of the studios. When I got there Richard's Rolls-Royce was waiting, and I was whisked, not unwillingly, to his magnificent residence in the Boltons, in the very smartest part of Kensington.

The opulence of Richard's home was outside anything that I had ever experienced, and I was, quite literally, swept off my feet. There were Filipino servants running round to cater for Richard's every whim, and over a few drinks he played me some music including his own fantastic recording of Jimmy Webb's 'MacArthur Park'. Even Richard does not know what the words mean. I had been right about the passion of the afternoon on the set, and we made love without a second thought. Richard asked me if I would accompany him to Paris, the city of my dreams and, ironically, the city of my mother's dreams. I readily agreed. My dreams of Paris were about to be fulfilled, unlike Ruth's; when Blakely promised to take her there he lied and said all the planes were full, when the truth was that he did not have the money to pay for tickets.

Richard told me he was having problems with his then

wife Elizabeth, most of which revolved around money, but, as it was none of my business, I showed little interest in his matrimonial affairs and set my sights on the adventure ahead. Although I had no idea at the time, this was just the beginning of an intense twelve months with Richard Harris, who ranks in my estimation alongside George Best as the cleverest of all the men with whom I have ever been involved. Richard was more serious than George and used his brain power more effectively than George ever did, and the age difference between us meant that Richard became more of a father figure to me as our relationship took its course.

The Rolls came to pick us up and took us to Heathrow, and we flew to Paris. I felt like a schoolgirl but tried to act with controlled maturity as I wallowed in the attention that is the lot of an international film star. In Paris we went directly to the fabulous Hotel George V, situated just around the corner from the Avenue des Champs Elysées and the Place de l'Etoile. There we checked into a magnificent suite and moved hastily to the magnificent, enormous bed, where the romance that is the essence of Paris carried us off into its own special ecstasy.

That evening, my first time abroad, let alone in the city of lovers, we attended a state film première, the most glittering and glitzy affair imaginable. Press photographers swarmed round us like hornets with Richard casually explaining me away as the daughter of a Swiss baroness friend. The film was *Cromwell*, and I clearly recall Richard turning to me during the screening and whispering that he would have given a better performance if he had not been drunk during the shooting. Richard had taken me to Vicky Tiel, a friend of his who owned one of the most exclusive fashion shops in Paris. There he bought me a simply exquisite gown, and I felt able to hold my head high with pride alongside him and in the company of a host of starlets, including the divinely beautiful Romy Schneider who was in our party.

Afterwards, we all dined at Maxim's, and I became wildly jealous when Richard spent more time than I considered reasonable talking to Romy to the exclusion of me. She was so gorgeous and so mature, and I sat there wishing that I, too, were 38 years old like she was. Romy's husband, like me, sat

Above: Ruth's oldest brother
Julian arriving at Holloway
Prison with flowers for his
younger sister. Ruth refused to
see him during the last days of
her life and denied him access
to her in the condemned cell.
(Popperfoto)

Right: During the moments
after Ruth's execution, two
men in the crowd threw torn
newspapers in the air and
shouted: 'Another murder.'
(Syndication International)

Above: Ruth, *right*, with David Blakely, enjoying a day out at the races, a welcome break from the violence and hysteria that punctuated most of their relationship.
(Syndication International)

On track: David Blakely, *above*, and David Beard, *left*, indulging themselves in one of their favourite sports.
(Blakely photo: Popperfoto; Beard photo: John L. E. Gaisford)

Right: No. 44 Egerton Gardens, where Ruth and David lived together. Landlady Joan Winstanley never knew David by any other name than Mr Ellis.
(Popperfoto)

Above: A lucky charm ornament given by Ruth Ellis to David Blakely. She was always generous with her men, but this charm was not lucky for Blakely. (Syndication International)

Above: Clive Gunnell, who owned the garage where David and Ant Findlater worked on the Emperor, and where they repaired the damage Ruth had inflicted on Blakely's car. Outside the Magdala on the night of the killing, Ruth was to scream at him: 'Get out of the way, Clive', as she pointed the gun at his companion, her lover, David Blakely. (Syndication International)

Right: Gladys Yule, the innocent victim and subsequent witness for the prosecution, who was shot in the thumb by a stray bullet from Ruth's gun as she walked into the Magdala for a quiet drink with her banker husband. (Syndication International)

Left: Carole and Anthony Findlater's flat at 29 Tanza Road, Hampstead, where David was a regular visitor, and where he hid out from Ruth before the murder over the Easter bank holiday weekend. (Syndication International)

Below: The Magdala Tavern, Hampstead, where the fatal shooting took place that fateful Easter of 1955. (Popperfoto)

Above: Arthur and Bertha Neilson, with Ruth's brother Granville and his wife, leave home to visit Ruth for the last time, their efforts to gain a reprieve for her having failed. Ruth was hanged the next day. (Hulton Deutsch Collection Limited)

Right: Mrs van der Elst (in black), the famous campaigner against capital punishment, raises her hand outside Holloway Prison on the morning of my mother's execution as if to say, 'Enough.' She attended every execution she could to petition the Home Secretary to abolish the death penalty. (Pepperfoto)

Left: Jacqueline Dyer, who worked with Ruth at the Little Club. A staunch friend and almost a daily visitor at Holloway, she helped rouse public distaste for Ruth's sentence and subsequent execution. (Syndication International)

Above: The front page of the *Daily Mirror* for 14 July 1955, the day after the hanging. Ruth's death touched a nerve nationwide and was partly responsible for the eventual abolition of the death penalty in Britain. (Syndication International)

Left: Crowds gathered outside Holloway Prison on the day Ruth was hanged. (Syndication International)

Above: At the première of *Dance With a Stranger*, the film made about my mother's life, which starred Miranda Richardson, *left*, and Rupert Everett. In death, by proxy, Ruth was given the starring role she had so much wanted in life. (Rex Features)

Right: When Holloway Prison was demolished and rebuilt, my mother's remains were taken from the prison grounds and removed to a small church graveyard in Amersham, Buckinghamshire. In a forlorn attempt to preserve her anonymity, her headstone reads: Ruth Hornby, using my grandparents' original surname. (Syndication International)

RUTH
HORNBY
1926 ~ 1955

quietly and never said a word. I do not know if he had the same pangs of jealousy that put me off the delicious food or maybe he was accustomed to his wife flirting with other stars. Romy and Richard had just completed a film together, *Bloomfield*, in which Richard not only starred but also directed, so it was hardly surprising they had much about which to talk. A few days later I went with them both to a preview of *Bloomfield* with the producers and the cameraman present. After the viewing I congratulated them on what I felt would be a great success, and they looked at me as if to say: 'What the hell do you know, child?'

The whole of my year with Richard Harris was lived in the lap of luxury. My screen test for EMI was totally forgotten, and I do not even know the result. Richard kept saying he would cast me in one of his films, but it never came to pass. We flitted between three homes: the Boltons, the suite at the George V and a wonderful house in Normandy that belonged to Vicky Tiel. It was there, in Normandy, that Richard was at his most relaxed, taking long walks along the beaches and the rivers. He drank less in Normandy than when he was under the spotlights and feeling the pressures of the capital cities. Life in the hurly burly of those cities was always star-studded.

One night in London we went to Tramps, the most coveted of all the clubs, and were drinking in the company of the owner, Johnny Gold. We were at a large circular table that we were sharing with Peter Sellers and Britt Ekland, and American trumpet star Herb Alpert. We all ordered steaks to eat, and, with champagne flowing like water, a good time was being had by all. On an impulse I turned to look behind me and locked eyes, there is no other way to describe it, with Richard Burton who was accompanied by a woman whom I recognized as Suzy Hunt, the wife of racing driver James Hunt. We stared transfixed for a few seconds, before I looked away again. Fortunately Richard Harris had not noticed this. After a while I excused myself and went to the ladies' room. When I came out, Richard Burton was waiting for me. He said: 'You are one of the most beautiful women I have ever seen. Do not be used by men. Trust me.'

I went weak in the legs. He was easily one of the most charismatic men I have ever encountered, and it was not hard to understand why women of all ages fell in worship at his feet. The sound of his voice was enough to set the pulse racing. Nothing ever came of it, but after that night we saw each other in the clubs quite often and always managed to steal a muted conversation behind the backs of Suzy and Richard Harris. I felt that to embark on an affair, even a casual one, with Burton would be like diving into a pool of bindweed from which there could be no way out without devastating hurt.

Richard Harris loved to play the star. One night we went to a Blood, Sweat and Tears concert at Bruno Coquatrix's famous Olympia Music Hall in Paris. Afterwards we went off to Maxim's, and Richard sandwiched himself between Françoise Hardy on one side and the ubiquitous Romy Schneider on the other. He was in his element. Though I was always jealous of Romy, she did nothing wrong towards me, and I was deeply saddened when, years later, I read of her premature death from cancer.

When Richard was attentive he oozed his southern Irish charm. He was warm and generous and would lavish praise on my appearance. His chauffeur, Reggie, told me one story that filled me with delight. One night I was absolutely tired out and could not wait to get a good night's sleep after a succession of nights on the town. I retired to the suite at the George V, but Richard was still raring to go, so he and Reggie went off together, with my blessing, to the Crazy Horse. That night, Brigitte Bardot was in the famous nightclub, surrounded as was normal for BB by an army of young men. On this particular night she decided to make a play for Richard, but, according to Reggie the chauffeur, Richard looked her full in the face and said: 'Back in my hotel, I have a girl who would knock you into a cocked hat.' With that he turned away. Imagine, Richard Harris turned down Brigitte Bardot because of me!

In spite of such incidents and all the passion, Richard never told me directly that he loved me. He did declare that he was growing increasingly fond of me. He knew all about my ongoing relationship with George Best, and he, southern Irish, would mock George's northern Irish accent to torment me. He used to say to me with the saddest of looks in his eyes: 'He's the one you really love.' I am sure he was troubled by the difference in our ages. His birthday was the day before my own, but he was almost 40 years old, and I was coming up 19. He was always making references to George like: 'He's still your man.' It was because of George, I am convinced, that we eventually grew apart.

I was with Richard when news of his divorce came through. Elizabeth went off to marry Rex Harrison, and Richard, with his caustic wit, said to me: 'She's only married him so she won't have to change the initials on the luggage.'

I doubt Richard will ever know the full extent of the influence that he had on me. He taught me so very much and encouraged me in my development and in whatever I tried to turn my hand to. I took to painting when we were in Normandy, and he praised my efforts. One day a helicopter came to whisk him away for a meeting about a film he had contracted to make with Sean Connery. While he was absent, I took a rowing boat up the river and painted. When he returned he flattered my efforts and made me feel good. Whenever he went away, he always came back with presents. One was particularly poignant, not for the gift itself, a book that Richard fancied turning into a film, but for the inscription that he wrote to me inside. It read: 'Come September, and every September, I will remember her swinging under the willow tree.'

When he inscribed those words Richard did not know of my history, so the 'swinging under the willow tree' was not a sick joke but rather Richard the poet expressing his emotions. I did not tell him who my mother was until the very last day of our relationship, by which time we had quite simply drifted apart, and there was no way forward together. For Richard, the obstacle was always going to be George Best and for me? I think I was too young to know what or whom I really wanted. Richard advised me to go home to the Lawtons in Warrington, with whom I had hardly communicated save for one phone call made from L'Hôtel in Paris, when Richard and I were in occupation of Greta Garbo's incredible suite with its satin bed raised on a dais and waterfalls cascading down the walls. Richard felt I should return home and sort myself out before it became too late. The Rolls came to collect me from the Boltons and took me to Euston station to catch the train north. As the car purred outside, I told him about my mother, and for once Richard was lost for words. I am delighted to say we have kept in touch for almost 25 years, and he occupies a very special place in my heart.

His advice to me was sound, but headstrong idiot that I can be, I chose to ignore it and instead of going to Euston I told the chauffeur to take me to Liverpool Street station. There, I bought a single ticket to Norwich where my ex-husband Nicky was living. I moved back in with him and, to cut a long interval very short indeed, got pregnant and gave birth to my first child, Scott. I wanted that baby so very much after the abortions and doctors' predictions that I would never be able to have children. Scott was, from the outset and continues to be, a source of great delight. He is the first grandchild of Ruth Ellis, a stigma with which he has had to cope, and with which he has coped admirably.

Nicky was playing in the resident band at a Norwich nightclub cum discotheque called Legs, and, both before and after Scotty's birth, I worked there too as a disc jockey. Though Nicky and I were Scott's natural parents, our relationship was in no way restored to that of man and wife. To both of us it was just a convenience, and it was only a matter of time as to when I would return to the north, George Best and the model agency.

Before that happened, though, I became very friendly with regular visitors to Legs who were part of the Lotus motor-racing team, whose headquarters were close by on the outskirts of Norwich. One of these was the great Stirling Moss, a true gentleman in every sense of the word. It soon became clear to me why my mother had found the inner circle of the world of motor racing so attractive and exciting. There is no doubt that those talented daredevils who risk their necks at high speed are a charismatic breed unto themselves. It is very seductive, and when I watch events on television these days and see the scores of gorgeous bimbos hovering around the pits, I picture my mother as one of them. The roar of the engines, the smell of the grease, the sweat and the scent of danger give the sport a unique lure, and the social scene that runs in tandem is vastly different to that which accompanies, for example, footballers. Those who race motor cars are extremely cliquey, fiercely dedicated and tend, or certainly did in those days when the risks of death were possibly greater, to live life in the full knowledge that it might be a short one.

It was through Stirling Moss, whose kindness extended to looking after Scott while I was disc jockeying, that I came to meet Emerson Fittipaldi. He spoke little English at the time, and Stirling, with a nudge and a wink, suggested I help him with the language. Though I was his 'English teacher' for no more than three or four weeks, Emerson and I went about his studies with fervour, and we both enjoyed some wild, wild nights. Our pleasures came to a natural end when Emerson was no longer required to visit Norwich, and shortly afterwards, I packed my bags, and Scott and I headed back north, to George and my short-lived second marriage to Peter, which I have written about in a previous chapter.

I already had left a trail of men in my wake and felt no continuity in my life other than George Best and my baby. From what little I knew of my mother's life I began to see the parallels between us and the omens foreshadowing my future.

CHAPTER FOURTEEN

Ruth Ellis, Murderess

While all around her was screaming and panic, both outside and inside the Magdala, Ruth stood quietly, staring blankly and still holding the revolver. Clive Gunnell shouted for the landlord to call the police and an ambulance. He and several customers had heard the shots but assumed they were the sound of a car backfiring. An off-duty police constable, Alan Thompson, who had been drinking at the bar, took immediate charge. He made his way through the hysterical crowd that had gathered outside and headed deliberately towards Ruth. It was a brave move for she gripped the gun tightly in her shaking hands, and he was not to know that all the bullets were spent. As he drew close to her, she asked in a small voice: 'Will you call the police?' Equally quietly he told her that he was the police, and he took the gun away from her and placed it in his own pocket with no concern for fingerprints. I suppose this was reasonable given that there was a body, eye witnesses and no immediate suspicion that anyone else was involved in the shooting. It was an odds-on bet, however, that Desmond Cussen had handled the weapon himself within the previous few hours.

Not so calm and collected was old Mrs Yule whose hand was gushing blood from the base of her thumb. Her husband was not prepared to wait for the emergency services and hailed a passing taxi, only for the driver to be reluctant to allow her into his cab in case her blood stained his floor and seats. The result was that the injured woman was conveyed to hospital with her arm held at full length out of the cab window. As it transpired, Ruth could not have hit a less agreeable passer-by; not that anyone would be thrilled to receive a bullet while out for a peaceful stroll on a Sunday evening. Mrs Yule, however, was an avid supporter of the lobby to retain hanging, and when, over the course of the ensuing weeks, the groundswell of support for Ruth's reprieve gathered momentum, she wrote a letter to the London *Evening Standard*:

DON'T LET US TURN RUTH ELLIS INTO A NATIONAL HEROINE. I STOOD PETRIFIED AND WATCHED HER KILL DAVID BLAKELY IN COLD BLOOD, EVEN PUTTING TWO FURTHER BULLETS INTO HIM AS HE LAY BLEEDING TO DEATH ON THE GROUND.... THESE HYSTERICAL PEOPLE, GETTING UP PETITIONS FOR A REPRIEVE AND THEN RUSHING TO SIGN THEM. DO THEY REALIZE THAT RUTH ELLIS SHOT DAVID BLAKELY TO THE DANGER OF THE PUBLIC?

She had a point, of course. There was no way she could know, as I believe to be the truth, that my mother had no real notion of what she was doing, and the apparent cold-hearted composure that she showed in the wake of the killing was the usual reaction of shock. A friend of mine, fool that he was, once drove a motor car having drunk a great amount of alcohol. He had a serious accident, fortunately with no other party involved, and he remembers with total clarity that the shock of the accident sobered him immediately. That was in pre-breathalyser days, and when the police interviewed him, he was so lucid in that shock-induced sobriety that he was not even asked if he had been drinking.

In what must have seemed an eternity but was, in recorded fact, only a few minutes, an ambulance, police cars and officers from Hampstead police station arrived. David Blakely was taken to New End hospital but was pronounced dead on arrival. His body was removed to Hampstead mortuary. Ruth was driven to Hampstead police station. PC Thompson had already formally cautioned her, and on arrival at the station, the caution was repeated by the duty sergeant. Then she was given a cup of tea and told to wait.

Clive Gunnell, dazed and incredulous, had returned to Tanza Road to break the news to the Findlaters. Police at the Magdala took statements from all and sundry, and the pub's one claim to fame was established. Today there is a plaque on the wall commemorating the event.

CID officers, before interviewing Ruth, went to inspect the body at the mortuary, so it was a full hour and a half that Ruth was left with her own thoughts. She knew she had killed David, and she wanted to die with him, without a thought for anybody else: Bertha whose grief for her daughter could never be assuaged, no matter how many tears were shed over the years that followed; Andy, oblivious and asleep at Egerton Gardens before the police took him round to Muriel's house; Muriel herself who feels she has borne the brunt of the ongoing social resentment over forty years; and me.

It is ironic that my mother had made an appointment with Leon Simmons of Victor Mishcon's firm of solicitors for the Tuesday, the first day after the bank holiday. The express purpose was to discuss my welfare, and Mr Simmons was surprised when Ruth, who had always been reliable in his experience, did not show up for the meeting. He had not heard of the murder, and neither had many other people. Ruth had to wait to hit the headlines because there was a national newspaper strike at the time of the shooting, and, though David Blakely was shot on 10 April, word of it did not reach the news-stands until the strike was resolved. The morning editions of 21 April all blazed with the story, which the Fleet Street hacks had been forced to sit on in frustration.

Three CID officers, led by Detective-Superintendent Leonard Crawford from Hampstead's 'S' Division, began their interview with Ruth just prior to midnight. As she sat before them, frail and vulnerable, her first response to a question was to say: 'I am guilty. I am rather confused.' She was ever the mistress of understatement. She stumbled on: 'It all started

158

about two years ago. When I met David. At the Little Club. In Knightsbridge.' She spoke haltingly. Det.-Supt Crawford, hardly able to believe his ears, inquired if she would care to make a written statement. She agreed that she would, and a uniformed officer joined the CID officers with the requisite forms.

The statement Ruth made and signed has been fully reproduced in every work on her of which I am aware and was read out fully during her trial, but I feel it is important in understanding how her mind was functioning, without regard for anyone except Cussen, to reproduce that statement once more in these pages. It went as follows:

About two years ago I met David Blakely when I was manageress of the Little Club, Knightsbridge; my flat was above that. I had known him for about a fortnight when he started to live with me, and has done so continuously until last year, when he went away to Le Mans for about three weeks, motor racing. He came back to me and remained living with me until Good Friday morning.

He left me about ten o'clock a.m. and promised to be back by 8 p.m. to take me out. I waited until half past nine, and he had not phoned, although he always had done in the past. I was rather worried at that stage as he had had trouble with his racing car and had been drinking.

I rang some friends of his named Findlater at Hampstead, but they told me he was not there, although David had told me he was visiting them. I was speaking to Findlater, and I asked if David was all right. He laughed and said: 'Oh yes, he's all right.' I did not believe he was not there, and I took a taxi to Hampstead, where I saw David's car outside Findlater's flat at 28 Tanza Road. I then telephoned from near by, and when my voice was recognized they hung up on me.

I went to the flat and continually rang the doorbell, but they would not answer. I became very furious and went to David's car, which was still standing there, and pushed in three of the side windows. The noise I made must have aroused the Findlaters, as the police came along and spoke to me. Mr

Findlater came out of his flat, and the police also spoke to him.

David did not come home on Saturday, and at nine o'clock this morning [Sunday] I phoned the Findlaters again, and Mr Findlater answered. I said to him: 'I hope you are having an enjoyable holiday,' and was about to say: 'because you have ruined mine,' and he banged the receiver down.

I waited all day today [Sunday] for David to phone, but he did not do so. About eight o'clock this evening I put my son Andrea to bed. I then took a gun which I had hidden, and put it in my handbag. This gun was given to me about three years ago in a club by a man whose name I do not remember. It was security for money, but I accepted it as a curiosity. I did not know it was loaded when it was given to me, but I knew next morning when I looked at it. When I put the gun in my bag I intended to find David and shoot him.

I took a taxi to Tanza Road, and as I arrived, David's car drove away from Findlaters' address. I dismissed the taxi and walked back down the road to the nearest pub, where I saw David's car outside. I waited outside until he came out with a friend I know as Clive. David went to his car door to open it. I was a little way away from him. He turned and saw me and then turned away from me, and I took the gun from my bag, and I shot him. He turned round and ran a few steps round the car. I thought I had missed him so I fired again. He was still running, and I fired the third shot. I don't remember firing any more, but I must have done. I remember then he was lying on the footway, and I was standing beside him. He was bleeding badly, and it seemed ages before an ambulance came.

I remember a man came up, and I said: 'Will you call the police and an ambulance?'

He said: 'I am a policeman.'

I said: 'Please take this gun and arrest me.'

This statement has been read over to me, and it is true.

Though no more than a couple of hours had elapsed since the shooting, Ruth was already signing her own death-warrant. Much of the statement is a lie, especially the reference to the taxi rides to Hampstead and the total fabrication of how she came to be in possession of the gun in the first place. In the entire statement there is no mention of Desmond Cussen, which substantiates the submission that a deal had been struck between them that she was prepared to honour. I believe, as I have previously stated, that, in consideration of Desmond's supplying the gun, of him transporting her to Hampstead and agreeing to care for Andy, she contracted to keep his name out of all possible repercussions to using the gun, and devise a fictitious, ultimately implausible story of how she came to possess it.

Even a junior policeman on the beat could have seen through parts of her statement, and the CID officers remained far from convinced that she was telling the whole truth. Nonetheless, the statement stood and, as she had been cautioned, was used in evidence against her.

Marks and van den Bergh accurately observe that if she had gone to Hampstead by taxi, whoever had been the driver would have boasted later to his mates that he had taken Ruth Ellis to the murder location. Her looks were distinctive, and Easter Sunday was quiet. A fare the distance of Kensington to Hampstead with a pretty blonde for a passenger would have stuck in the memory, which would have been jogged by the mass of publicity. No cab driver remembered any such fare.

Police were round at the Findlaters' flat, no. 29 Tanza Road (and not 28 as Ruth said in her signed statement), interviewing everyone and fitting into place a few pieces of what already appeared to be a simple jigsaw. Unknown to each other, Ruth had tried to condemn Ant Findlater as a false, untrustworthy friend to both David and herself, the man who motivated the shooting, and he, in turn, was manufacturing his evidence, which would paint her as a cold, callous killer.

On the afternoon of Easter Monday, Ant Findlater accompanied police officers to the mortuary, where he formally identified the body of David Blakely. A special bank holiday sitting of the magistrates' court was convened, and Ruth was remanded in custody for nine days. She was then escorted to Holloway prison, which was to be her address for the remainder of her life.

The post-mortem examination of David's body carried out that morning revealed that a couple of the bullets had merely grazed his skin, but two, those fired from point-blank range, were responsible for the injuries that killed him. The official cause of death was given as shock and haemorrhage. Forensic officers took a bullet that had been removed from his body and various other samples for their case requirements. A quantity of amyl nitrate tablets had been found in his possession, which, it was later suggested, David had needed to enhance his substandard sexual performance. Several of his former lovers stepped forward over the weeks and months to denounce his prowess as a bedmate.

The behaviour of Desmond Cussen was strange. According to Muriel, it was he who broke the news to the family, telephoning Bertha and Arthur Neilson who, ironically, had been living for some months in Ferncroft Avenue, Hampstead, less than a mile from both Tanza Road and the Magdala, where so much had unfolded without their knowledge. Cussen told them that the heat would be on, and, with Andy safe with Muriel, he drove my grandparents to catch a train for Hemel Hempstead, where they took refuge with Granville.

Before that, however, Cussen had taken himself to Hampstead police station to volunteer a statement that contradicted Ruth's account of Good Friday night. He told the police that she had not travelled by taxi that evening, but that he had driven her by car. He stressed, and this is probably the reason for his visit to the police, that he had been with her on the previous day, the Sunday, but having taken her and Andy back to Egerton Gardens, he had not seen her again after half past seven in the evening.

All the principal players, Ruth included, were busy weaving their tangled webs of lies to suit themselves. Quite why Desmond should hustle my grandparents away so quickly is suspicious. I would have expected Bertha's first reaction to have been a request to go to Holloway and see her locked-up daughter. It could be that Cussen was afraid Ruth might confide the truth to her mother in a breakdown reaction and be suddenly filled with remorse, a distinct possibility to someone as used to her vicissitudes as Desmond.

For all but Ruth it was a hectic day. She was left alone in a police cell for much of the time, fed twice and given tea and cigarettes. A formal charge of murder was read out to her, and she was cautioned yet again. Her only response to the charge was, 'Thanks'. Her appearance before the special magistrates' court was brief and her journey to Holloway swift. There, as a remand prisoner, she was put through the standard, impersonal reception formalities. All she asked for was a Bible and a photograph of David. Ruth Ellis became prisoner 9656 of HM Prison, Holloway, London N7.

Having spent two nights in two different cells, alcohol and drugs free, Ruth turned her attention on Tuesday, 12 April, to dealing with her priorities. She had slept, if only under sedation, and she was more *compos mentis* than she had been at any time over the holiday weekend. She had strengthened her resolve to die for her crime and to be reunited with her lover. Today their graves, since her body was transferred from the precincts of Holloway to Amersham, are only a few miles apart.

There is no evidence of which I am aware that her thoughts had yet strayed to her own family, but some time on that Tuesday, on prison notepaper, she wrote a letter to the woman whom she had hoped would one day be her mother-in-law, any expectation of which was cruelly extinguished from Good Friday onwards. She wrote to David Blakely's mother:

DEAR MRS COOK,
NO DOUGHT THESE LAST FEW DAYS HAVE BEEN A SHOCK TO YOU. PLEASE TRY TO BELIEVE ME, WHEN I SAY, HOW DEEPLY SORRY I AM TO HAVE CAUSED YOU THIS UNPLEASANTNESS.

NO DOUGHT YOU WILL KNOW ALL KINDS OF STORIES, REGARDING DAVID AND I. PLEASE DO FORGIVE HIM FOR DECIEVING YOU, HAS REGARDING MYSELF.

DAVID AND I HAVE SPENT MANY HAPPY TIMES TOGETHER.

THURSDAY 7TH APRIL, DAVID ARRIVED HOME AT 7.15 P.M., HE GAVE ME THE LATEST PHOTOGRAPH HE HAD, A FEW DAYS HENCE HAD TAKEN, HE TOLD ME HE HAD GIVEN YOU ONE.

FRIDAY MORNING AT 10 O'CLOCK HE LEFT AND PROMISED TO RETURN AT 8 O'CLOCK, BUT NEVER DID. THE TWO PEOPLE I BLAME FOR DAVID'S DEATH, AND MY OWN, ARE THE FINLAYTERS. NO DOUGHT YOU WILL NOT UNDERSTAND THIS BUT <u>PERHAPS</u> BEFORE I HANG YOU WILL KNOW WHAT I MEAN.

PLEASE EXCUSE MY WRITING, BUT THE PEN IS SHOCKING.

I IMPLORE YOU TO TRY TO FORGIVE DAVID FOR LIVING WITH ME, BUT WE WERE VERY MUCH IN LOVE WITH ONE AND OTHER UNFORTUNATELY DAVID WAS NOT SATISFIED WITH ONE WOMAN IN HIS LIFE.

I HAVE FORGIVEN DAVID, I ONLY WISH I COULD HAVE FOUND IT IN MY HEART, TO HAVE FORGIVEN WHEN HE WAS ALIVE.

ONCE AGAIN, I SAY I AM VERY SORRY TO HAVE CAUSED YOU THIS MISERY AND HEARTACHE.

I SHALL DIE LOVING YOUR SON, AND YOU SHOULD FEEL CONTENT THAT HIS DEATH HAS BEEN REPAID.

GOODBYE.

RUTH ELLIS

I print that letter as my mother wrote it, spelling mistakes and all. It reveals to me an insight into the depth of her love for David, and how firmly she had set her sights on being his wife. When David gave her the photograph, he could not have had the slightest idea how much she would read into the gesture nor how much it meant to her. It was, I think, in her eyes tantamount to presenting her with an engagement ring, which would account for the way in which she reacted to the rejection less than 26 hours later, and one more example of David's insensibility to the feelings of a woman. Assuming he had it in mind to jilt Ruth, to reject her, over Easter, it was extremely misguided of him to present her with a photograph signed 'To Ruth with all my love, David'. He, ever self-centred and ineffectual, had toyed with her emotions without a thought for her dreams and beliefs, her trust and sacrifice, which he had encouraged and exploited only to dash them against the rocks of his safe harbour in Hampstead.

The letter also confirms Ruth's conviction that the Findlaters were the orchestrators of her downfall. To extend the previous metaphor, she saw them as the coastguards who gave shelter to David's ship, while leaving her without a sail to drown in the open, tempestuous sea. Her mind was full of imaginings, all-consuming pictures that gnawed at her brain. When she underlined the word *perhaps* in the letter, it is to indicate that she had decided publicly to pronounce, either through the newspapers or from the witness box, on her version of the tragedy that Ant and Carole Findlater had perpetrated by their influence on Blakely.

I, Georgie, of all people understand how hatred can distort events. I have blamed X or Y when the real culprit was either myself or Z. It is easy to see 40 years on, that Ruth misdirected her energies. Certainly the Findlaters played their unpleasant part, but the real guilty party in the whole scenario in Hampstead is, in fact, Blakely himself, Cussen an equal first. If Ruth had been able to bear the truth and not delude herself further about David, she might have realized that she could construct a defence to her charge that would have endeared her to any jury in any court in the land. She elected without hesitation to reject that opportunity. She stuck to her belief that Ant and Carole were going to rue the day they plotted to oust her from David's life. When the two of them walked away from the Old Bailey without the slightest tarnish on their exemplary characters, her spirit was broken, her goal unattained.

Ruth was resigned to her own death to atone for David's from the moment she shot him. She maintained that resignation for thirteen weeks and one day. With her execution little more than a day away, for the first time she dropped her Findlater fixation and turned the spotlight on Desmond Cussen. Unfortunately, her target could not be found.

Those thirteen and a bit weeks, the rest of Ruth's life, were to be a palace of varieties, in which the star turns included baffled policemen, desperate close family, newspaper vultures, frustrated solicitors, inept barristers, do-gooders and ne'er-do-wells, hysterical and indifferent politicians, uncomprehending foreigners, ghouls and nutters, friends impotent to influence, cowering cowards, moralists, compassionate clergymen, merciless retributionists and a voracious global public ready and willing to swallow up each new revelation and develement that was grubbed up and served for their daily consumption. As stories go, this one was destined to run and run.

CHAPTER FIFTEEN

Prisoner 9656

When I think of my mother, or anyone else for that matter, incarcerated in one of those dingy and dismal prisons that the Victorians built, a shiver runs down my spine. I am always put in mind of the words of Oscar Wilde who, when imprisoned in Reading gaol, wrote of: 'That little tent of blue which prisoners call the sky'.

Ruth seems to have abandoned her own existence from the very moment she committed her crime. She offered no indication of any other ambition than to make her own peace with God and atone for her evil with her own death. Was she mad? I suspect she trod a fine line between sanity and insanity, which today might be recognized as a split personality. Having said that, I do not believe she was in any way clinically mad prior to that Easter weekend.

I am often asked the question: 'What made her do it?' I honestly believe that only a woman can come close to understanding why, since there are essential fundamental differences in the make-up of the sexes, which produce different responses. Women have an in-built capacity to be conciliatory towards men and remain the natural homemakers and the centrepiece of family life.

Ruth Ellis was a very feminine woman. She delighted in looking good, being flattered and treated like a lady. When, after so much mistreatment going back to Andy's father, my father, Maurie Conley and a whole string of other absolute pigs, she fell head over heels in love, it was a tough throw of the dice that the recipient of her love was another pig, reincarnated in the form of David Blakely. There are no two ways about it, she was in love with him as she had never been in love with a man before; a pattern that I was to repeat myself with David Beard more than thirty years later. Sadly, we are rarely able to control the dictates of the heart.

If a woman accepts that a relationship is over, and that she is no longer in love with a man, it is easy for her to shrug and walk away, to set her sights on a new beginning. When she seeks revenge on him, however, it is invariably because she is still in love with him. An act of vengeance is a last-ditch way of saying, 'Look how much you have hurt me; look how much I love you.' All women require in that circumstance is a chance to express their feelings and be heard; so many men are lousy listeners. When the ears are muffled, it becomes impossible for the woman to communicate, and the natural consequence is an eruption of violence, as the avenger tries in desperation to assert herself in the only way left open to her. The only man who could have put me in that position was David Beard, and the only man who did create that dilemma for Ruth was David Blakely.

Ruth Ellis was the model prisoner. She was tranquil, obedient and co-operative; but she was also introverted, hardly surprising considering how her life had been turned upside down over just a few days. It was outside the prison walls that all the dramas and agonies were taking place. Though there were no newspapers on the streets, Fleet Street was quick to realize that a hot story was about to unfold. Editors briefed their news desks and armed them with unlimited funds to buy the story.

Ace crime reporter Duggie Howell of the *Sunday People* was first out of the starting-blocks, and he tracked down Mrs Winstanley, the housekeeper at the flats in Egerton Gardens. She was his first lead, and, though she was in no position to act on Ruth's behalf, she listened to what Howell had to say and confirmed to him her view that Ruth had no money. He had pointed out that her legal costs would be extremely high, but the *Sunday People* would cover all those costs if they could buy Ruth's exclusive story. Howell suggested that a friend of his, John Bickford of Cardew-Smith and Ross should act for Ruth.

John Bickford went to Holloway that evening but did not see my mother as she was under sedation. He met her the next day, ironically at about the same time she should have been keeping her appointment with Victor Mishcon and Leon Simmons to discuss my welfare. Baffled by Ruth's non-appearance, the first her solicitors heard of the murder was when they received a phone call from John Bickford asking if they had any objection to his handling the case. They were shocked by what he told them but invited him to go ahead as they were not themselves criminal lawyers.

One of Ruth's first visitors in Holloway was Jacqueline Dyer, her hostess colleague from the Little Club days. Robert Hancock interviewed Mrs Dyer for his book and learnt that during the short visit Ruth expressed more concern for David than for herself and asked her to go and see David's body and return to tell her how he looked. She was most concerned that David 'was being properly looked after'. Mrs Dyer was later able to satisfy Ruth on this point, having found David in a chapel of rest in Kensington, properly laid out in a coffin lined with white satin.

John Bickford had read the statement that Ruth had signed at Hampstead police station and was not convinced by her story. His suspicions were further aroused when she asked him to visit Desmond Cussen and tell him that she had told the police she had come into possession of the murder weapon as security on a loan. Bickford was further shocked when Ruth told him that she intended to plead guilty, and, wherever David was, she wanted to be with him. She had anaesthetized herself to the powerful logic of all his efforts to persuade her to fight for her life, even to the argument that she at least owed it to Andy and myself to do so.

When not receiving visitors, Ruth sat in her cell and quietly read the Bible, rediscovering the faith that she had allowed to lapse. Within the immediate family, it was Granville,

Ruth's brother, who took charge and tried to steady everyone. Muriel was given the task of not just taking care of Andy but also keeping the truth from him. My grandmother Bertha and my aunt Elizabeth were both reeling from shock, uncomprehending and dumbfounded.

John Bickford was not to be put off by Ruth's casual lack of concern for her own fate, and set about uncovering all the facts of the case. Following up what few leads she had given him, he proceeded to interview a great number of people, and, piece by piece, he constructed a case based on all that he knew. He did a very thorough job, but Ruth stuck rigidly to her account of how she came to have the gun. To John Bickford and indeed to all her other visitors she expressed her consistent desire that the Findlaters be exposed for their wrongdoings. To this end she agreed to tell her story through the *Sunday People*.

When the strike that had brought the newspaper industry to a standstill was resolved, the first editions that followed hit the news-stands on the morning of Thursday, 21 April. All the tabloids featured the story on their front pages. At last she was a star as her picture and the details of her life and crime were wired around the world. She had made a second brief appearance in Hampstead magistrates' court on the Monday, 18 April, which resulted in her being remanded in custody for seven more days. Reporters who attended that hearing wrote of her glamorous appearance. She had sat in the dock wearing a grey tweed two-piece suit with black piping, set off by a white silk handkerchief embroidered with forget-me-nots. On her feet she had a pair of patent black high-heeled shoes.

John Bickford spent the next few days preparing his case and briefing a barrister, Sebag Shaw, to represent her the next Monday, 25 April. At this stage, her legal advisers nursed a quiet confidence that, even if they failed to have the charge reduced to manslaughter, they would at least wring a recommendation for mercy out of a jury. For her next court appearance Ruth dressed herself in an elegant black-and-white two-piece and a silk blouse. She knew the eyes and ears of the world were upon her, and she was concerned to present her image as she wished it to be seen.

For the first time the more juicy details of the story were revealed in court. Journalists crammed into the press box were foaming at the mouth with each new revelation. As the evidence unfurled, they knew the story was bigger than any of them had imagined. The following day, the headlines reflected their excitement with lines like: MODEL SHOT LOVER – COURT TOLD and MODEL SHOT CAR ACE IN THE BACK.

The bare bones of the allegations were given for the prosecution by a Mr J. Claxton who first disclosed the love triangle of Ruth, David and Desmond. Some of the facts he gave were incorrect, such as saying how Ruth and David had first met at the Little Club, and that she had told Desmond Cussen how she had twice been married and twice divorced. For the first time the name Findlater was mentioned in court as Mr Claxton outlined the events of the January evening when David had summoned Ant and Clive Gunnell to rescue him from Ruth's clutches, when she had confiscated his car keys. He told how she and Blakely had lived together as man and wife, truncated to the bare minimum the events of the Easter weekend and then read out in court the statement that Ruth had signed at the police station.

Ruth sat through these committal proceedings without registering a great deal of interest. She sat up with a start, though, when Desmond Cussen was called as a police witness. She put her glasses on as if she could not believe he was there, and she visibly fumed with anger as he spoke of his role as her chauffeur on her missions to Hampstead and of how he had sat in his car and watched her push in the windows of Blakely's car. He said nothing that was of the minutest help to Ruth, but what he did say was food and drink to the voracious journalists who could hardly wait to ring through their copy. It was of course, full of flowery exaggeration, elevating Ruth to model status and Blakely to racing ace, all the hyperbole that makes a good story even better.

The hearing was almost interrupted when my father, George Ellis, turned up at the courthouse extremely drunk. He started shouting, saying that he wanted the proceedings to be halted so that he might give evidence himself. He was only just prevented from bursting into the courtroom itself. In fact he was diverted from such potentially damaging behaviour by one of John Bickford's staff, who prevailed upon him to retire to a pub with a reporter from the *Sunday Pictorial* who signed him up to tell his story. His version of events, incidentally, was not published until after his death. He refused to sign his agreement to publication when whoever sent him the proofs for approval carelessly and stupidly left an inter-office memo attached that contained details of his drunkenness and his occupation with the editor's handwritten comment: 'I suggest we expose this bastard.'

Other witnesses who appeared that day included PC Thompson, the off-duty copper who had disarmed Ruth, Ant Findlater and Clive Gunnell and Mrs Winstanley. In the public gallery sat Maurie Conley and other friends and acquaintances. Desmond Cussen was the last witness for the crown, and it is reported that he left the witness-box and the court without a glance in Ruth's direction. Sebag Shaw formally entered her plea of not guilty to the murder charge and reserved her defence. She was committed by the magistrates for trial at the Central Criminal Court and driven back to Holloway prison.

During this period of remand Ruth received scores of letters from past acquaintances as well as frequent visitors. Desmond became a regular visitor and plied her with flowers on an almost daily basis, no doubt as part of his insurance policy that she would not change her story and incriminate him. She was coaxed by her advisers to allow them to plead a defence of insanity, but she resolutely refused. She remained steadfast in her determination to pay for her crime according to the law of the land. Neither her lawyers nor her family could make any headway in breaking down her stubborn resistance to presenting the most obvious and plausible case for her defence.

Granville, in a letter published after the execution, wrote that she said to him: 'I'm not worried, and I've no regrets as to what lies ahead for me. The children are provided for, and you are all right at home. I won't let them plead insanity for me. I'm not crazy, I know exactly what will happen. They are going to hang me.'

My grandmother Bertha, who sold her own story after the execution to the *Sunday Dispatch*, told Godfrey Winn that

Ruth had said to her: 'I was sane when I did it, and I won't go to prison for ten years or more and come out old and finished.'

Ruth made one more brief appearance in court, this time at the Old Bailey on 11 May, when she was represented by Mr Melford Stevenson QC, and in a three-minute hearing he successfully applied for more time to prepare the case and make further inquiries. The trial was put back to the June sessions.

Most of the murder inquiry, especially that conducted by the police, was remarkably slipshod by the standards we have come to expect. Marie-Thérèse Harris, who had laboured in vain to teach my mother French, read of the murder in the papers, and it jogged her memory. On one of her visits to Goodwood Court for Ruth's lesson, she recalled how she had casually remarked to Andy that she had problems where she lived with pigeons. Andy's response was that she needed a gun, and he calmly opened the drawer of a writing desk to reveal two such weapons.

As an honourable citizen Mrs Harris telephoned the police and gave them the information, with the result that officers were sent to interview Cussen. He wormed his way out of a difficult situation by producing an air pistol that used caps and a starting-gun that fired only blank cartridges. He naturally denied that he had ever supplied Ruth with a gun. The police removed the two pistols and showed them to Mrs Harris. She was unable to identify either as the guns she had seen. Incredibly, they did not show her the murder weapon for identification.

Equally incredible is that on no occasion did the police interview Andy to corroborate Mrs Harris's story. I know the family wished to protect him from the murder and its aftermath, but he was bound to find out about it sooner or later, and the evidence that he had to offer was crucial, especially his recollection of how he had seen Cussen place the gun in mother's handbag.

John Bickford, ever thorough and concerned, busied himself all over town interviewing anyone he could find who could shed new light on the case. He knew Ruth was not telling the truth about the source of the gun but did not understand the reason behind her lies. He was not helped by her; each time he saw her, she was preoccupied with being reassured that the Findlaters would be thoroughly grilled in cross-examination and exposed for the tyrants she believed them to be. Ant Findlater was to appear as a witness, and, on a just-in-case basis, Bickford served a subpoena on Carole Findlater, much to Ruth's delight.

In the forensic labs, police scientists were not able to make a positive confirmation that the oil on the murder weapon was the same as that on the guns taken from Goodwood Court. They could only say that it was of a similar type, and, with that, Desmond Cussen was ever after left in peace.

Those acting on behalf of the Director of Public Prosecutions arranged for a psychiatrist to interview my mother and prepare a detailed assessment of her mental state, to be offered in evidence. He was Dr Duncan Whittaker, and he spent some time with Ruth early in June – the exact dates are at variance in the assorted reports but of no importance. What is of great importance is that Dr Rees, the psychiatrist who had treated her at Warlingham Park Hospital and whose medication she was taking at the time of the shooting, was not interviewed either by the police or the team of defence lawyers. It is, I suppose, remotely possible that they were unaware of his existence, but the drugs that he had prescribed were there to be found, either in her possession or back at the flat in Egerton Gardens. At no time did it ever emerge in court that she was being treated for depression. What a difference this might have made. Dr Rees was subsequently quoted as saying he had been surprised not to have been called to give evidence. If that were so, why did he not voluntarily establish contact with her legal representatives?

In the meantime, with a plea of insanity ruled out by the defendant herself, the three barristers briefed to construct some sort of defence on Ruth's behalf were poring over their books. They were desperately trying to find a precedent in case history in which jealousy had been established as an admissible mitigation. Their search was in vain, but it was the only footing they had on which to build a defence. They pressed on along this untrodden furrow, consoled by the belief that a jury was unlikely to be anything other than merciful when Blakely's provocation was outlined to them.

Ruth, although not oblivious to all the efforts being made on her behalf, was more concerned with other matters. In particular, her vendetta against the Findlaters had grown out of all proportion and consumed her thoughts as much as her desire to die and join David. But before that could happen, there was the Old Bailey trial to look forward to. Her preparations for this did not involve issues of defence or legalities; her concern was how she would present herself and be seen centre stage by the eyes of the world. It was at this point, to the horror of all her team of lawyers, that her hair was dyed to the tarty, platinum blonde she most favoured, which made her look like the brassy moll of the drinking and night clubs rather than the broken and wronged, classy model that John Bickford wished to portray. Ruth Ellis, femme fatale, was ready for her first and only starring role, and she was not going to be seen as anything less glamorous than Marilyn Monroe, Brigitte Bardot or any of the other blonde bombshells of her day. This was Ruth's big show, for which the rest of her life had been only a rehearsal. Her dreams of the security of a house and family had vanished, and all that remained for her was a solo virtuoso performance before a transfixed, international audience.

CHAPTER SIXTEEN

The Trial

My mother had to wait almost six weeks between her arraignment at the London Central Criminal Court and the commencement of her trial. In between there was a general election, actor Jack Warner went into rehearsal for what was to be the first of 367 episodes of *Dixon of Dock Green*, and, on 9 June, a tragedy of horrendous proportions shocked the world of motor racing. In the Le Mans 24-hour race, the very one in which David Blakely had been booked to drive for the works team of Bristol Motors, 82 spectators were killed by flying metallic debris that flew into the crowd during a track accident.

All the sports writers for the continental press, without exception, blamed Blakely's hero, Mike Hawthorne, for what happened. Hawthorne had pulled over his Jaguar into the pits, clearly indicating, Hawthorne protested, his intention to make the turn. Observers claimed that he gave no such signal. Behind the Hawthorne car, British driver Lance Macklin jammed on the brakes of his Austin Healey. On Macklin's tail was French driver Pierre Levegh in a Mercedes, which hit the Austin Healey, flew up into the air and hurtled into the crowd. The full extent of the disaster must not have been immediately apparent because the officials allowed the race to continue;

Hawthorne rejoined the track from the pits and drove on to be declared the winner. It was there at Le Mans that Ruth should have been with David; this was one of the reasons for her half-hearted attempt to learn French. This plan, a promised trip to Paris, even though David knew he could never afford to take her there, and all that might have been, preoccupied Ruth in Holloway.

In London, *Kismet*, *The Boy Friend* and *Salad Days* were packing in audiences to the West End theatres, but the hottest ticket in town was for the 20th of June at the Old Bailey, where Ruth was top of the bill. Admission to the general public was by ticket only, and the touts were having a field day. Ruth was not the first person accused of murder to draw a capacity crowd. The street ticket sellers had done good business with the trials of John Christie of 10 Rillington Place fame and the fiasco of Derek ('Let him have it') Bentley and Christopher Craig, which resulted in Bentley being unjustly sent to the gallows.

Ruth felt well prepared for her trial. On the day before it was scheduled to begin she met with John Bickford and her three learned counsel, Melford Stevenson, Sebag Shaw and Peter Rawlinson, in Holloway. She communicated her priorities, which were to ensure that the Findlaters be given a thorough questioning in order to show, beyond a shadow of a doubt, that Ant and Carole jointly conspired to separate her from David, that they had deliberately and repeatedly lied to her over David's whereabouts over the Easter weekend, and that they had, from the outset, intended to ostracize her from David's friends. After her legal team left Holloway, her only other preparations for the next day concerned her hair, make-up and wardrobe selection.

The atmosphere in Number One Court at the Old Bailey, quite an imposing room even when empty, was electric as expectant voyeurs craned their necks to take in the scene. There, assembled before their eyes, were the counsel appearing on behalf of the crown, led by Mr Christmas Humphreys with Mr Mervyn Griffith-Jones and Miss Jean Southworth in support. Adjacent to them were the three defence counsel. Behind all those bewigged gentlemen and lady were the representatives of the Director of Public Prosecutions and Ruth's solicitors from Messrs Cardew-Smith and Ross. The press box was packed to the gills as was the public gallery. The area in this court known as the 'City Lands', or the posh seats, rows of green leather benches similar to those in the House of Commons, were jammed with the 'lucky' ticket holders, some of whom were reported to have paid more than £30.00 for the privilege of being there. Only the judge's bench, the witness-box, the jury benches and the dock were empty. Murmurs of excitement buzzed in many languages. Extra seating accommodation had been arranged for the international press corps who had converged on London for the show.

On the usher's command, there was an instant silence as the whole house stood for His Lordship, Mr Justice Havers, resplendent in scarlet robes and white wig, and flanked by his attendants who wore the traditional jet-black knee breeches and collars of white lace. The judge exchanged bows with his fellow professionals before taking his place in his huge chair, behind which a symbolic sword of justice was attached to the wall. This was the signal for the farce to begin.

The prisoner, Ruth Ellis – my mother – was led up the tiled staircase from the cells below and into the vast wooden dock. The only difference between her own arrival and a typical Marlene Dietrich entrance was that Dietrich would have walked down a staircase. Ruth smiled. Her hair was immaculate in the brassy Hollywood style that she favoured. From her vast collection of clothes that she had accumulated from the profits of hostessing, she had selected a smart, well-cut black suit, ostentatiously trimmed with astrakhan, the whole outfit set off with a white silk blouse. There was no question about who was the star of the show. Ruth looked positively stunning, every inch the opposite of how her legal advisers had hoped she would present herself. Among the breathy whispers that greeted her arrival from the public gallery, the word 'tart' was distinctly heard by at least two reporters. Others merely gasped, speechless. My grandparents and my aunt and uncle were all in the court but too numbed by the occasion and too shocked to find their family in such difficulty and under the public gaze to have any accurate recall of the first few minutes.

Ruth was accompanied in the dock by a wardress from Holloway, and the two women exchanged gentle smiles. The warm-up act was the clerk of the court who began the proceedings: 'Ruth Ellis, you are charged that on 10 April last you murdered David Moffatt Drummond Blakely. How say you, are you guilty or not guilty?' Ruth entered her plea of not guilty. Then, as in any variety performance, the opening act of acrobats and clowns came on, and the ten gentlemen and two ladies representing the British public were duly enpannelled and sworn in as the jury.

Mr Christmas Humphreys then presented the case on behalf of the crown. He, like his eminent judicial father, Sir Travers Humphreys, was a skilled advocate, and he addressed the members of the jury in simple but effective language. He it was who coined the phrase 'the alternative lover' to describe Desmond Cussen as he told how Ruth had had simultaneous love affairs with both David and Desmond. His description of the murder was brief and to the point, and he read extracts from the statement that Ruth had signed at the police station on the night of the murder. Mr Humphreys, in all fairness, made it abundantly clear to the jury that in no way were they to concern themselves with questions and issues of morality. He stressed that adultery and sexual misconduct were not part of the agenda other than as a help to understand her frame of mind when 'she did what it cannot be denied in fact that she did'.

After a mere half a dozen paragraphs and the extract from the statement in which Ruth had said: 'When I put the gun in my bag, I intended to find David and shoot him,' the jury's collective mind must have been all but made up, and the verdict signed sealed and delivered. To hammer home his case, Mr Humphreys described how Ruth, a hostess, had lived with Blakely and then moved to Goodwood Court to live with Cussen but continued to see Blakely. He told of the incident when Ant Findlater had been called with Clive Gunnell to rescue David because 'Blakely was trying to leave her, and she was trying to stop him going.'

Ruth sat impassively as the case against her unfolded eloquently and, by and large, accurately from the mouth of her prosecutor. He concluded his opening address as follows:

> Members of the jury, there in its stark simplicity is the case
> for the crown, and whatever be the background and whatever
> may have been in her mind when she took that gun, if you
> have no doubt that she took that gun with the sole purpose of
> finding and shooting David Blakely and that she shot him dead,
> in my submission to you, subject to His Lordship's ruling in
> law, the only verdict is wilful murder.

It is obvious to me and, I suspect, to any lay person of
reasonable intelligence, that Ruth's only chance thereafter was
to establish that she was out of her mind on drugs and drink
and emotionally disturbed, not only when she shot Blakely but
also when she made and signed her original statement. Insanity
can be temporary as we all know. Mr Humphreys, respected
orator that he was, had avoided any reference to drugs or
Pernod while delivering his catalogue of events. He had avoided
any reference to how a skinny, frail young woman might have
come by a Smith and Wesson revolver. He had painted a
black, one-sided case from which it would have required a far
better performer than Melford Stevenson to recover.

The first two prosecution witnesses were police officers
who gave technical evidence. Next up was Joan Winstanley
who corroborated the fact that Ruth and David had lived
together at Egerton Gardens as Mr and Mrs Ellis. She answered
a couple of harmless questions from Mr Humphreys who then
sat down. Whether Mr Stevenson had fallen asleep or what, I
have no idea, but he declined to cross-examine Mrs Winstanley,
thereby passing up the first opportunity to establish that David
had been prone to knocking my mother about and leaving her
visibly bruised. As it was, Mrs Winstanley simply stood down
from the witness-box, making way for Desmond Edward
Cussen who was called to follow her.

I hope he was quaking in his boots as he took his oath.
He should have been, knowing his own guilt and that he was
about to commit perjury on a grand scale. In mostly monosyl-
labic answers, Cussen attested to his involvement with Ruth,
that he had been her lover, that she had lived with him for

some time and that he knew she continued to see Blakely. He confirmed that he drove her to Tanza Road on the evening of Good Friday, that she had pushed in the windows of David's car and that he had spent most of Easter Sunday with her and Andy. He said that he had not seen Ruth after 7.30 that evening.

Mr Melford Stevenson rose to his shaky feet for the first time. He established with Cussen's positive responses that he, Cussen, had been in love with Ruth and had begged her to marry him, but that she repeatedly went back to Blakely. Stevenson started to make headway when he asked if Cussen had ever seen bruising on Ruth's body, and Cussen affirmed that he had, on about six occasions. When asked if he had ever taken Ruth to hospital for treatment, he admitted that he had once taken her to the Middlesex when she was very badly bruised. With that he let Cussen go, his cross-examination, incredibly, over. Never did he ask Desmond Cussen if he knew the cause of the bruising, nor once attempt to show that David Blakely was a woman beater, or to ask Cussen if he had ever seen Blakely hit her.

Not one of those obvious questions was posed. Surely Mr Stevenson must have realized that he had to discredit the character of the deceased in order to stand any chance of a reprieve for Ruth. If pushed, who can say whether or not Cussen would have broken under pressure in the witness-box? He had the potential to be the most valuable witness in the presentation of the entire defence. As it was, he must have been delighted to be released without having had to face one single difficult or probing question. At one point during the brief mention of the bruising, Mr Stevenson even said to Cussen: 'I do not want to press you for details . . .' How extraordinary! Why did he not want to press him for details? If the end result had not been the death of my mother, I would cast Mr Melford Stevenson as principal light comedian in this extravaganza. As it is, I cast him as the fool.

It was the last time Desmond and Ruth would ever set eyes on each other, and Desmond walked out into the sunshine and freedom that he so ill deserved. He had given her no support whatsoever, and I trust he lived out his days in his own disgust and shame. Instead of his tedious one-syllable responses to Mr Humphreys he could at least have paved the way for Melford Stevenson by tarnishing and blackening the reputation of his rival, David Blakely. Anyway, that was that, and Cussen was written out of the script from that moment.

What Ruth must have thought as she watched and listened to the charade, I cannot imagine, but it could be nothing compared to what she must have thought when the next prosecution witness took the stand. As Ant Findlater took the oath in his full name, Anthony Seaton Findlater, Ruth licked her lips in anticipation. This was to be the crucial interrogation when the world at large would discover the truth about the despicable antics and devious machinations of her arch enemies.

The evidence that Ant Findlater gave during routine examination by Christmas Humphreys stuck to the basic facts. Again the January incident was raised, when he and Gunnell went to Goodwood Court following Blakely's plea for help. Findlater said: 'Blakely asked if I could assist him to leave her. This was said in her presence. I cannot remember her exact words, but she was rather sarcastic about him needing some help to leave her.' I bet she was sarcastic. How feeble to require two big men to help him escape a tiny woman.

The examination of Ant Findlater was not a protracted affair, and after he had given his very short and largely correct version of the highlights of the Easter weekend, it was the turn of Melford Stevenson to cross-examine. Ruth waited with bated breath. She waited, and she waited. Firstly he asked some innocuous questions about Ant's business relationship with Blakely, before touching on the incident when Ruth attacked the car windows, including the irrelevant question of how many windows she had actually damaged. Then he asked his first pertinent question:

'Was it quite plain when you spoke to her on the telephone that she was in a desperate state of emotion?'

'No,' Ant replied.

'What?' Stevenson inquired in a tone of disbelief.

'I said no,' Ant reiterated.

'Do you mean she was quite calm? Do you really mean that?'

'It was just a telephone conversation. She rang me up, as she had done hundreds of times, and asked if I knew where David was. It was just a telephone conversation.'

'I know it was just a telephone conversation. Just bear in mind what she said, and the way she said it, and the fact that she afterwards pushed out those windows. Did you observe no indication of her being a very desperate woman at that time?'

'No.'

'Never mind about the word desperate.' Mr Stevenson was quite clearly becoming desperate himself. He went on: 'Was it obvious to you that she was in a state of considerable emotional disturbance?'

'Well,' replied Findlater, 'I did not get that impression over the phone. She might have been.'

So, with Ant Findlater's statement, Stevenson let the matter drop. He asked a couple more idiotic questions and then sat down. He did not raise the question of a conspiracy between Ant, Carole and David. Nor pose any of the questions that Ruth had instructed him to ask. For her sitting impotently in the dock the man and woman whom she blamed for David's death had got off lightly and not been exposed in the way that her desire for revenge and justice as she saw it required.

When asked by Mr Stevenson about the Findlater nanny, Ant could not recall walking down Tanza Road with Blakely and the nanny, nor could he remember Blakely saying: 'Let me put my arm around you for support.' Mr Stevenson's feeble attempts to establish a motive of jealousy were negated by Ant's comments and quickly shot down in flames when Christmas Humphreys briefly re-examined him, concluding with:

'Was there any incident with a young woman outside the house that you can remember?'

'No,' replied Ant, and that was his final utterance in court.

From that moment on, according to my grandmother, Ruth perceptibly lost her spirit and most of her interest in the proceedings. Her singular goal, her revenge, had been to disclose the skulduggery of Ant and Carole Findlater to the eyes and ears of the assembled court. She had watched with receding belief and mounting anger as the golden opportunity was squandered. She appeared to pay scant attention when Clive Gunnell gave his evidence, adding nothing of any value to her cause. He in turn was followed by the arresting officer and PC Thompson, the off-duty policeman. Then came the vindictive Mrs Yule with her damaged thumb, a police pathologist who confirmed the number of bullets that had hit Blakely and the very close range from which one of them had been fired and, finally, the CID officer to whom Ruth had made her initial statement. Mr Melford Stevenson declined to cross-examine any single one of them. It is impossible for me to come to terms with any plausible rationale behind his tacit acceptance of the statements of the prosecution witnesses.

The CID officer who took Ruth's statement, Detective Chief Inspector Leslie Davies, was asked by Mr Humphreys if he had formed any impression of her emotional condition at that time. Davies replied:

'I did. I was most impressed by the fact that she seemed very composed.' Davies then read her entire signed statement. The defence team did not cross-examine. I am left wondering what the wonder Queen's Counsel of recent years, George Carman, would have made out of this parade of soft and occasionally hostile witnesses? Mincemeat, I suspect. Though it can only be a hypothesis, I am convinced the outcome would have been markedly different had a lawyer of his calibre been assigned her case.

Proceedings had moved with unprecedented rapidity. It was immediately after the recession for lunch when Mr Melford Stevenson rose to open the case for the defence. The stage was set for him to follow his hitherto miserable performance with a rousing, spirited plea on behalf of a woman who had been tortured both physically and mentally by a man who was derided by even some of his closest friends.

He addressed the jury, inviting them to consider that the emotional disturbance of Ruth Ellis at the time of the shooting was sufficient to unseat her judgement and inhibit and cut off those behavioural sensors that ordinarily control our conduct. If, he submitted, the members of the jury could accept her state of mind to be such, then they were open to say that the offence of which she was guilty was not murder but manslaughter.

He also stressed to the jury that he would call an expert witness to testify to the effect of jealousy upon the female mind. After this address, he called Ruth to the witness stand.

In fairness to Melford Stevenson it was an odd and off-balanced situation. His client had far from told him the whole truth. He was fighting to have her charge reduced to the lesser one of manslaughter, which she did not want on account of the fact that it would have carried the lengthy prison sentence she felt unable to face. This dichotomy did nothing to help him in what was always going to be an uphill struggle. The case, to most observers, was open and closed before he ever spoke.

To begin with Mr Stevenson solicited from Ruth the basic facts about how her relationship with David had begun and progressed to living together with the promise of marriage. Several incidents were referred to, including the abortion, her affair with Cussen and the fact that she withdrew from contesting her divorce from my father in order that she would be free to marry David. The subject of violence was skirted, and Ruth surrendered the chance to give a true impression of just what a cowardly woman-beater David Blakely had been. Mr Stevenson asked her how the violence had manifested itself. She replied with her usual capacity for understatement:

'He only used to hit me with his fists and hands, but I bruise very easily.'

Ruth was questioned about the incident that necessitated her treatment at the Middlesex Hospital, and the card Blakely had attached to the flowers he sent her in the wake of the incident was produced, as an exhibit. She was asked to read aloud the message on the card, which said: 'Sorry, darling. I love you. David.' The effect of this was, of course, to show Blakely as a man of remorse, which, as far as I can gather, is not true. The married woman in Penn was referred to. The reason I do not know her name is mainly because Mr Stevenson began this reference by saying: 'I do not want to mention names . . .'

Ruth's pregnancy was mentioned, but not the fact that David thumped her in the stomach just days before she lost the baby, and then they moved on to the events of the fatal week following the Oulton Park race meeting. She told her version of the telephone calls to Tanza Road, saying that Ant Findlater's tone had been 'cocky', and she did not believe he was telling her the truth when he denied David's presence in their flat. At no time during my mother's time in the witness-box was it suggested that she was taking medication for depression, nor that she had been on a Pernod-drinking binge for several days. She stuck rigidly to her story of how she acquired the gun and how she took a taxi to Hampstead on the final trip. She kept her word to Desmond Cussen. He was never mentioned other than to establish she had lived with him for a while and that he had driven her to Penn and Hampstead on occasion.

As Mr Stevenson led her gently up to the final act, he asked her, with reference to the evening of Easter Sunday:

'At what time did you put the child [Andy] to bed?'

'At about 7.30.'

'Was there still no message from Blakely?'

'No.'

Mr Justice Havers then interrupted to clarify that Ruth had by then returned to her own flat. Mr Stevenson, in all innocence, continued his line of questioning but unfortunately and quite unknown to him, my mother was about to sign her own death warrant. He asked:

'And what did you do next?'

'I put my son to bed,' Ruth answered.

'Yes. Go on.'

'I was very upset,' she continued, 'and I had a peculiar idea I wanted to kill him.'

'You had what?' The hapless Mr Stevenson could scarce believe his ears.

'I had an idea I wanted to kill him,' she repeated. At this Mr Stevenson threw in the towel.

The cross-examination of Ruth by Mr Christmas Humphreys consisted of just one question and answer, which went like this:

'Mrs Ellis, when you fired that revolver at close range into the body of David Blakely, what did you intend to do?'

Without a moment's hesitation she replied: 'It is obvious that when I shot him I intended to kill him.'

As Ruth stepped down from the witness-box, the jury knew nothing of her background whatsoever. She had deliberately suppressed her hardships, her early poverty, the fact that Andy was illegitimate, her hostessing and call-girl activities, the entire gamut of circumstances that might have incited some degree of sympathetic consideration from the twelve members of the jury.

It was in an atmosphere of anticlimax that the only other defence witness, psychiatrist Dr Duncan Whittaker, who had interviewed my mother in Holloway Prison, took the stand. He waxed eloquent about the 'primitive reactions of women in the grip of jealousy' – and how 'they are more prone to hysterical reactions than men.' He did make one point that had my mother nodding in agreement, again according to my grandmother. He said: 'I believe that if Mrs Ellis had been given a chance to blow Blakely up on the telephone, the emotional tension she had would have been released, and the incident could not have occurred.'

I have to ask myself why Carole Findlater was not called, and such a point put to her. An attempt should have been made to prove that Ruth was deliberately fobbed off with a pack of lies all over the Easter weekend and that she became more and more hysterically out of control as her every phone call was refused. It is all history now, just one more set of if onlys.

As I have said earlier, the defence of diminished responsibility did not, in 1955, exist in English law. Mr Stevenson was lamely trying to secure his case for a charge of murder to be reduced to manslaughter on the grounds of jealousy, provoked by cruelty and mental torture. He was batting on a very sticky wicket as Mr Justice Havers pointed out. He asked Mr Stevenson:

'Does your proposition come to this, putting it in its simplest form? If a man associates with a woman, and he then leaves her suddenly, and does not communicate with her, and she is a jealous woman, emotionally disturbed, and goes out and shoots him, that is sufficient ground for the jury to reduce the crime of murder to manslaughter?'

Mr Stevenson made no direct answer, and His Lordship was left to ponder his own question overnight. The court adjourned until the following morning. One of the most sensational murder trials of the century had exhausted the evidence put by both sides in just one day. The entire case for the prosecution had lasted one hour and fifty minutes and not much more for the defence. I trust the audience, especially those who paid a high price for their tickets, went away content that they had had value for money.

No doubt they all retired to various pubs for a gossip and a drink, while my mother was driven back to Holloway to ruminate on how the Findlaters and Desmond Cussen had been let off so lightly. More than that, if she cared to, she could have pondered on why Dr Whittaker, who had only seen her for a few hours, was called as a witness instead of Dr Rees, who had treated her for years? Moreover, the doctor who terminated her pregnancy just before the murder should have been traced and called. The entire process seems in retrospect to be a one-sided fiasco with my mother contributing as much to the distortion as anyone else. Her pride was her downfall, together with a wish to die and be with David, a desire that must border on insanity.

When it had been Christmas Humphreys' turn to probe Dr Whittaker he virtually destroyed all the valiant efforts of the defence with just two salient quesions. The first:

'In your view, at the time of the killing, was she mentally capable of forming the intent to kill?'

'Yes.'

'In your view, was she at the time, within the meaning of the English law, sane or insane?'

'Sane.'

As Kenneth Wolstenholme said when England won the World Cup at football: 'They think it's all over. It is now!'

Ruth and her team had scored so many own goals there was no way back. The referee, Mr Justice Havers, blew the whistle first thing the next morning. He had slept on the case and reached his conclusion. I do not believe he had any choice, based on the evidence placed before him. I do not believe, also, that there is any human sin other than cruelty towards another human being. The harm that David Blakely inflicted upon my mother had been but peripherally touched upon and thinly portrayed. Thereafter it had been glossed over by a parade of almost irrelevant trivia that had nothing to do with Ruth's state of mind, nor with that which had driven her to exterminate her perfidious lover. I conclude that the defence counsel were jointly and severally blinkered to the real issues and failed to pursue those whom time has deemed worthy of castigation. Not for the first time do I concede that my mother herself was as much to blame as anyone else.

The second day began with the jury being absent from court while His Lordship made a judicial ruling to the advocates on both sides. It is worth repeating. He said:

> I feel constrained to rule that there is not sufficient material, even on a view of the evidence most favourable to the accused, for a reasonable jury to form the view that a reasonable person so provoked could be driven, through transport of passion and loss of self-control, to the degree and method and continuance of violence which produced the death, and consequently it is my duty as a judge, and as a matter of law, to direct the jury that the evidence in this case does not support a verdict of manslaughter on the grounds of provocation.

With that ruling Mr Stevenson accepted that there was no point in his making any closing submission for the defence. The jury was recalled, and Mr Stevenson told them as much. Mr Humphreys also added that, in the circumstances, he, too, had nothing to say. Mr Justice Havers summed up, and at 11.52 a.m. the jury retired. They took a mere 23 minutes to reach their verdict. At 12.15 p.m. they returned to their places, and the foreman, on behalf of his colleagues, returned the verdict that they found my mother guilty of the murder of David Blakely. When asked if she had anything to say before the passing of sentence, she remained silent. Mr Justice Havers then donned the traditional black cap and said:

> Ruth Ellis, the jury have convicted you of murder. In my view, it was the only verdict possible. The sentence of the court upon you is that you be taken hence to a lawful prison, and thence to a place of execution, and that you there be hanged by the

neck until you be dead, and that your body be buried within the precincts of the prison within which you shall last have been confined before your execution, and may the Lord have mercy upon your soul.

Almost simultaneously, Ruth said: 'Thanks,' and the court chaplain intoned: 'Amen.'

The jury had added to its corporate verdict no recommendation for mercy. My blinkered and misguided mother smiled. My grandfather and my grandmother, together with Muriel and Granville, wept openly, and Ruth's true friend Jacqueline Dyer sobbed inconsolably, repeating over and over: 'I can't believe it, I can't believe it.' The press left to file their copy, the professionals disrobed, and the public once more retired to the pubs. The whole trial was over and done with in less than a day and a half.

It fell to my grandfather, Arthur the musician – he who had been stymied at each turn in his life, he who had been eaten up by so much frustration that he hit out against those whom he loved, he whom my grandmother had berated for all family misfortunes – it fell to him to go to the cells below Number One court and see his daughter. He was allowed to spend a whole hour with her. Though he was overcome with emotion, Ruth was fully collected. She was resigned to her fate and assured him that she felt justice had been done, restating the 'old eye for an eye' doctrine and her desire to meet her maker having paid for her mortal sins at the hands of her fellow men. My grandfather could make neither head nor tail of her logic. As would any other normal human being, he returned to his family confused, the horrified father of a daughter condemned to have her neck judicially broken at the gallows.

CHAPTER SEVENTEEN

Me, Georgie: Playgirl

I t was a long time after Richard Harris that I embarked on another committed or at least semi-settled relationship with a man. I had immersed myself in work and play, something that would have been unthinkable had it not been for Phyllis and Peter Lawton, who were prepared to take the lion's share of raising Scott. I had a variety of jobs, but by far the most fun was my stint as a bunny girl at London's Playboy Club on Park Lane, just up the road from the Dorchester Hotel.

The Playboy was in its heyday and attracted super-rich business men from all over the world, drawn either by the gambling or the luscious array of bunny flesh. To qualify as a bunny girl required stringent tests, which had been laid down originally by Hugh Hefner and implemented this side of the Atlantic by the head of the British operation, Victor Lownes.

I passed with flying colours in every department bar one. I failed the maths test, which will come as no surprise to those exasperated teachers at St Hilary's who had laboured in vain to instruct me in the most basic skills of arithmetic. I remain to this day quite hopeless with figures and statistics other than the vital ones. My hopes of joining the Playboy empire were only kept alive by bunny mother Donna Reid, who had made up her own mind that she liked me and wanted me as a member of her team. She broke all the rules and helped me, secretly, retake the maths test, which I sailed through with ease.

To begin with, life as one of Hef's famous bunnies was fun but very hard work. The discipline was fierce with costume inspections and hard and fast rules about fraternizing with the punters, no bad thing since everyone, girls and punters alike, knew exactly where they stood and how far they could go. Flirtation was good for business, but anything more was not encouraged and carried the penalty of instant dismissal. It was very different from the places that Ruth had worked, where a boss like Maurie Conley expected his girls to satisfy the lusts of his customers. Hugh Hefner created an elitism, and bunny girls were cast as the great untouchables, thank God, for many of his punters were greasy lechers, with whom an assignation would have been repugnant. On the other hand the club was also frequented by the highly eligible rich and famous, some of whom could and did charm the pants off my scantily clad colleagues.

We had lots and lots of laughs, but in the end dipping and bobbing in the uncomfortable outfits became wearisome in its repetition, and my spirit, as has always been the case, longed to return to the north. I have nothing against London and nothing against England. I am proud of my country, even if I do carry a tinge of bitterness about what the laws of this green and pleasant land did to my mother. However, as long as I remain in England, I am more comfortable and at home in Lancashire and Cheshire than in the capital. I say as long as I am here because I have resolved that, if I have any choice in the matter, I hope not to die here. Since Richard Harris introduced me to her myriad delights, my heart has belonged to Paris, and that is where I plan to end my days.

When I returned to Manchester luckily I was able to pick up my modelling career as if I had never been away. Assignments came thick and fast, and soon several of the top photographers were asking for me and constructing their shoots around my availability schedule. Pamela Holt, whom

I had first met at Lucie Clayton's, had broken away and set up her own agency and, go-getter that she was, had soared to premier place in the aggressively competitive world of model agencies.

With my star in the ascendant, I enjoyed a wide circle of good friends, and life was one gregarious round of photo-calls, parties and clubs. George Best was never far away, except when he staged his famous disappearing acts, and I dated all sorts of men, while making sure that I spent adequate time with Scott at weekends or whenever else I could.

Then, out of the blue, my worst fear was realized in Wendy Henry and Noel Botham, who introduced themselves to me as reporters for the *News of the World*. I wanted the floor to open up and consume me on the spot. My cover was blown wide open. I felt like a stick of dynamite had been attached to my ankle, and these two people were about to light the fuse and glory in my destruction. As all this confusion surged through my brain, I somehow managed to steady myself and gather my thoughts to allow me to make sense and order out of the emotional jumble. It seemed to me I had two choices of action: either I could be hostile, in which case they would doubtless do a hatchet job on me; or I could co-operate in the hope that they would treat me sympathetically. I opted, wisely as it transpired, to take the latter course of action, thereby beginning a relationship with the press that continues to be relatively good. They still treat me fairly and kindly even if, occasionally, they are intrusive.

So it was that I found myself photographed by Terry O'Neill, who did me up to look like Ruth, and emblazoned across the front page of the *News of the World* under the headline: MY AGONY BY THE DAUGHTER OF RUTH ELLIS. They ran the story over two consecutive Sundays and, I have to admit, told it as accurately as I told it to them, though they dramatized here and there, as one would expect. The article began: 'They hanged my mother, and now I want to tell the world what it's like to grow up with the shadow of the gallows always in the background.' I did not want to tell the world at all, I simply felt I had no option. The peg on which they based the article was an announcement that a film was going to be made about my mother's life, with Angie Bowie playing Ruth.

I was sufficiently indignant to suggest that if anyone was going to portray my mother on film it should be me; at any rate certainly not Angie Bowie, whose credentials for the role seemed to me to be non-existent. As it happened, that film was never produced, and it was not until 1985 that a version of my mother's life was made for the big screen when Goldcrest produced *Dance With a Stranger* with Miranda Richardson portraying Ruth Ellis.

Muriel co-operated with the makers of the movie, but she was bitterly disappointed with the end result. What emerged was a good film but a muddled account of the events, which evoked no sympathy at all and failed to take a viewpoint. It has always struck me as odd that the screenplay was entrusted to Shelagh Delaney. Ruth's story was a London story through and through, and Miss Delaney, rightly acclaimed for *A Taste of Honey*, was a Salford lass with roots and attitudes vastly different from those required to understand my mother's mind.

The director was the highly talented Mike Newell, who had learnt his craft in Manchester at Granada, where he had started as a graduate trainee. It was through him that I was invited to the première in Leicester Square, where I spent much of the evening being wryly amused at the reluctance of Miss Richardson to allow photographers the opportunity of getting a picture of her and me together. It was the picture they all wanted.

The *News of the World* article quoted me as saying: 'The shadow of Ruth Ellis will be with me for ever. But I know I will never hate her. I feel in a sense that I am searching for the happiness which she never found. To live my life for both of us.' I think that is more or less accurate, although there was still a long procession of men ahead of me before I found Mr Right. His name was, and still is, Eric James Enston.

I was in one of Manchester's great character pubs, Goblets, just off Deansgate, which, like so many buildings of merit, has since been converted into something that the Prince of Wales might call a carbuncle. On that particular evening a friend of mine, one of the city's ubiquitous personalities, by the name of Richard Davis, was there having a drink with a man whose looks turned me into butter. It was Richard who introduced me to Eric. I think we would have begun our affair there and then in the bar if we could have done. I did not know it at the time, but Eric's mates nicknamed him Omar since he bore an uncanny physical resemblance to Egyptian actor Omar Sharif, and, with me still seeing myself in the Julie Christie mould, we could have made *Dr Zhivago* in Goblets.

Eric was not just handsome. He was suave and beautifully spoken with great charm and perfect manners. That we would be lovers was inevitable, but I tried, in the beginning, to keep him a secret from the wealthy man with whom I was involved at the time. It did not take him long to become suspicious, and there was no alternative but to make a clean break and admit my affair with Eric. This so very much parallels Ruth's decision to leave the comfort of Desmond Cussen's home for the far less desirable amenities of the flat in Egerton Gardens where she lived with David Blakely.

As I was making this difficult decision, my problems were compounded by Scott whose behaviour was at times irrational. On reflection I can see that his actions were as much a cry for my attention as Andy's occasional bursts of malice had been for Ruth's. Scott got up to all kinds of mischief. One day, I found he had smeared the suede-covered walls of my lover's penthouse with chocolate for no apparent reason; on another occasion, he was playing with the cigarette lighter in the back of the Rolls. He knew he was forbidden to do that, but do it he did, and the first I was aware of it was when he set fire to the carpet.

My lover was patience personified, much more so than I was. We took Scott with us from time to time when we went away but he always found some way, like appearing in hotel lobbies in his pyjamas, of causing embarrassment. I suppose it was his way of getting back at me for giving so much of my life and time to another man. I am happy to say that Scott has turned out very well indeed in the end, and we are great friends today.

Life with Eric began in Sale in a semi-detached house that he owned, which had been divided into two flats. We were both seriously in lust, and I would have lived with him in a tin hut if that was all that was available. I found him intensely charismatic, not only because of his looks and charm but also for his quick sense of humour, his tenderness and a deep sexuality that most women found irresistible.

This was my man. We were not married, but we both wanted to start a family as soon as possible – perhaps with hindsight I wanted children more than he did. Anyway, we were having a great deal of fun trying to make a baby. Eric was always ready for sex at any hour of the day or night. He was exhausting but exciting, and his virility never ceased to astound me. In spite of this non-stop merry-go-round of hyper-sexual activity, nothing was happening in the conception department. I poured out my frustrations to Phyllis, my adoptive mother, who loved Eric and wanted to help. She had read of the pioneering work of Oldham-based Dr Patrick Steptoe who had been much publicized for his research into fertility and test-tube babies. Phyllis paid for me to have a private consultation with Dr Steptoe who put me on a course of Chlomide, a fertility drug. It did the trick, and within weeks I was pregnant.

I had no complications, and the child in my womb grew so that all could see from my bump that I was in the family way. Eric proposed that we marry, and I accepted. We decided on a quiet wedding and set the date for 13 December 1980. By now we were living in a small house in Fog Lane, Didsbury, so we decided to ask only a handful of close friends and drew up a list that came to a total of thirteen people. We booked our time at the Register Office in Manchester, and Pamela Holt agreed to help me, while Eric called on Richard Davis to be his best man on the day. It never crossed our minds that any outsiders would be remotely interested in our wedding, but as Eric and I pulled up for our appointment with the registrar, an army of reporters and photographers awaited us outside. I said quietly to Eric, 'You don't have to go through with this today, you know. We can do it some other time.'

'No,' he said, 'today's the day.'

I wore a dress that I had made for myself on Grandma Bertha's sewing machine and a little hat that I had concocted of cardboard and covered with the same material as my dress. I also produced a handbag from the cardboard and glued on more of the fabric to cover it. Though I say so myself, it all looked very effective, but thank goodness it was a dry day, otherwise my hat and bag would have disintegrated into a soggy heap with trickles of glue running everywhere. Fortuitously, I was carrying a large bouquet of flowers that, having composed myself to face the barrage of cameras, I used to cover my decidedly conspicuous bump.

We emerged as Mr and Mrs Eric Enston, and faced the cameras for a second time, before our little party went back to our new home for eats and drinks. Eric and I had hardly any money between us, so Phyllis and Peter (where would I ever have been without them?) paid for the reception. Scottie's birthday was also 13 December so we had a combined celebration. I had made him his own chocolate cake covered in smarties. The following morning we woke to find ourselves splashed across the tabloids with predictable headlines like RUTH ELLIS DAUGHTER WEDS. It was my third marriage, but they kindly made no play of that, and, for which I am ever appreciative, none of the photographs suggested my pregnancy.

My beautiful daughter Laura arrived to complete our happiness. She had the most voracious appetite of any of my children, and as I was breastfeeding her I was in constant demand. Eric was working flat out for a property company, and I used to glow with pride each morning as he left home in his three-piece pinstripe suit. He managed to come home at lunchtime for his sandwiches, or at least that was the excuse that he made at the office. One of Eric's great attributes was his skill as a DIY craftsman, and he made our home truly beautiful, although he did have a tendency to flit from job to job leaving holes and unfinished work here and there.

After three months or so I went back on Dr Steptoe's drugs and conceived again. The result was our second daughter, Emma. Everything was going well until Eric was made redundant. Using his redundancy payment, he set up his own business, with some help from a friend who was managing director of a huge electrical company, selling discount appliances direct to the general public. He decided to operate from home, which meant that my neat and tidy house – tidy that is apart from nappies and the usual paraphernalia that goes with two babies – was suddenly cluttered with washing-machines, refrigerators, cookers and boxes of this that and the other household appliance.

Eric worked all hours, and often there were queues of cars all the way down the road to take advantage of his unbeatable prices. He must have been selling them far too cheaply because, notwithstanding the time he put in, we never seemed to have any money. Life for me was one long round, without any respite, of babies, washing, cooking and making love. There was no let-up in this latter activity, and I again became pregnant. We already had two girls. Scott was living with us for much of the time, and we were financially stretched to the limit. I gave birth to our son, James, who has inherited his father's looks and is now a very handsome young man.

It is hard to pinpoint exactly when things started to go wrong, but unconsciously we began slowly but surely to fall apart. A combination of shortage of money, three children in three years plus Scott, business and personal stresses and permanent tiredness, bordering on exhaustion, forced us to face the reality that we had taken on too much too soon. We began to lead partially separate lives. Eric had temporarily lost his sense of purpose. The proud man in the three-piece suit was a changed person following his redundancy. I was not privy to the full extent of his difficulties, which is a pity because a problem shared can indeed be a problem halved.

We were on a slippery slope, and it soon reached the stage where we hardly saw each other at all. I was booking babysitters with increasing frequency as I fought for my sanity by escaping from the house. Our rows intensified in their bitterness. Life as we were living it grew intolerable. I reached for the bottle from time to time, but my responsibilities to the children somehow held me in check. Had it not been for them, I would have sauntered down my mother's path and mixed the heady cocktail of alcohol and valium that drove her to murder. How well I understood her during this period. The slide from bad to worse left me beyond consolation, and my girlfriends began to despair of me. Eric and I were equally deranged in each other's presence and would lash out at each other at the slightest provocation. He was spending his evenings at Manchester's Playboy Club, yet another of life's ironies.

I was sinking rapidly, all my usual buoyancy failing to keep me afloat in our storm-lashed marriage. I almost touched the bottom but found one last gasp of air to stop me drowning. I stared at myself in the mirror. I told myself not to let a man destroy me as David Blakely had so brutally ruined my mother. I resolved to pick myself up and try to start again. Encouraged by those friends who perceived a glimmer of hope, one last vestige of the real me, I went for an interview for a job with Chanel on their perfume counter in Kendal's department store in Manchester. They took me on, and I managed to work around the children with the help of casual babysitters. Eric did not take kindly to this, and, rather than encourage me, he berated me unfairly for neglecting the children and putting myself first. He had no concept that without this job I would have been destroyed beyond restoration.

Evenings out remained a rarity, since my day job tired me out, and I had my three little ones and one big one to attend to as soon as I returned home. One evening, though, a girlfriend persuaded me that I needed a break and coaxed me out of my self-imposed social exile. Needless to say I met a new man. I was ready to do so by then because, much as I had loved Eric, all hope of happiness with him had come to an end.

Tony Neary was the former England rugby captain, a tall man who was wholesome but very sexy. We struck up an instant friendship that was pure and chaste. Though there was a strong and immediate sexual chemistry between us, it remained dormant. We were both married, and I happened to know Linda, Tony's wife. Tony and I were never lovers in a physical way, but we were certainly in love with each other. The times we spent together were fun, our behaviour jokey and often stupid, laughing and giggling with gay abandon. To laugh again was such a tonic, better than all the alcohol or valium. Tony reminded me that life is there to be enjoyed. We became entwined in each other's lives, sharing the burden of commitments and laughing in the face of the pseudo-respectability behind which we sheltered. One day, sitting in his car he asked me: 'Do you think we will ever make love?'

'I shouldn't think so,' I replied, and we never did.

Once I wrote a fantasy letter to Tony, which, of course, I never gave him. It was merely me expressing in fiction my desperation to be loved. Unfortunately, Eric found this letter and went berserk. While our life under the same roof was grim for both of us, Eric remained possessive and given to outbursts of jealousy. There was no possibility that I could explain away the letter in any way that he would have understood. If I told Eric once, I told him a hundred times that my friendship with Tony was platonic. He refused to believe me. Tony and I discussed the situation, but we felt we had a balanced, mutually advantageous arrangement, the balance of which, if we even once consummated our relationship, could be thrown totally out of kilter. It was a risk neither of us wished to take, and, for my part, I do not think I could have lived with the guilt because I had tremendous respect for Linda Neary, a highly intelligent and beautiful woman who featured in the Coca-Cola adverts at the time of 'I'd Like to Teach the World to Sing'.

Once Eric got hold of the wrong end of a stick, he was immovable. He would not believe that we were not romping in naked passion behind his back, and he put the cat well and truly among the pigeons by writing to Linda and telling her what he thought was going on. All hell broke loose with Tony storming round to our house, Eric making himself scarce and me locked in the middle of an all-round misunderstanding of an innocent but, for my sanity, vital relationship.

I was not prepared to surrender Tony, who had become the focal point of my bid to keep my life in some sort of perspective and who was offering me the nearest thing to normalcy available at the time. With Eric having disturbed a hornet's nest with his letter to Linda, I did not exactly run away, but I did feel an overwhelming need to have a little bit of space and, to that end, I embarked on a one-day escapade to London, unfettered by anything or anyone. All I took with me was my House of Fraser credit card – credit limit £200 – and a desire to have a day to myself, free to go walkabout without constraint and in absolute anonymity. It worked. I was able to talk to myself in a rational way, and I had a thoroughly good meander around Knightsbridge, sweeping my current problems under some of Harrods' most expensive carpets.

I must state that I had not just swanned off without making provision for the welfare of the children, but for that one day it was therapeutic not to be at their every beck and call and to pass each hour for and on behalf of myself exclusively. The day fair flew by, and by the time I arrived at Euston for my return journey north, only the last and tediously slow train was left for me to catch. It lurched its cumbersome way up the west side of England, making eternal stops in the middle of nowhere and with no refreshment facilities on board. I do wish those who draw up the schedules of inter-city trains had to travel on them, especially second class in the late hours of the evening with a grumpy guard offering no information as to why we have been diverted via Northampton and why we are running fifty minutes late. I wonder if I will live long enough to see Britain have a rail system that works and of which we can be proud?

The result of this journey was that I trudged up the path to our home and put the key in the door at just after one o'clock in the morning. Eric, stewing in his irrational jealousy, had put two and two together and made seven and a half, and as I stepped through the door, I was met by a flying drawer, which broke my arm. It was probably the same flying drawer I had thrown at him on a previous occasion. Eric was remorseful for reacting that night, but I was in plaster for weeks; so much for the therapy of my awayday.

Tony Neary will always hold a place in my heart as a first-class athlete, a man in every sense of the word and a gentle, loving, faithful soul who was my source of inspiration to survive at a time when my need was at its greatest. In the end, I believe, he and Linda parted, and the last I heard of him was that he had gone to live in South Africa. Wherever he is, I wish him well and thank him for all we endured and enjoyed together: the walking, the talking, the driving, the laughing and, yes, the loving.

There was worse to come. I look back and wonder how Eric and I, two people of reasonable intelligence, could behave as we did when we had such a perfect family. Equally, I am forced to wonder how my mother could have turned her back so selfishly on both Andy and myself without, seemingly, a second thought for what might become of us or what stigmas her behaviour might bring to be the cross we would have to carry throughout our own lives. It was the children, Laura, Emma and James, who were to be the focus of the battles that remained to be fought.

When I think back on my time with Eric Enston, and once again I have to say that we now have a civilized, valuable friendship, and we sun ourselves in the reflections of our three superb children, I have a feeling that we both set out with the same objectives: we wanted each other completely, and we wished to raise a family together; our aims had simple beginnings but fell apart through quirks of fate and immature intolerances on both sides. Wise men say, only fools rush in, but our foolishness, considered in the cold light of almost ten years of hindsight, was not caused by rushing in but, rather, by a build-up of pressures, financial and personal, that we were ill-equipped to handle.

Anyone who has been through matrimonial breakdown will understand what I am about to say next: once the lawyers get involved, the acrimony will increase, and any chances of reconciliation will vanish. The only ones with anything to gain from divorce proceedings are the members of the legal profession who prefer to count their time in pounds at the expense of the distraught participants in the action. That certainly obtained once Eric and I got into battle over the children.

Prior to the fat-cat lawyers licking their greedy lips, Eric and I had been living in the same house, each of us keeping to a defined area, out of bounds to the other. That really is no way to live, and in the end it was Eric who left me. What followed was a nightmare of litigation and a tug-of-war over the children. I am no fighter when the stakes involve hurting my children, and, in the end, Eric was awarded custody of Laura, Emma and James. There was an overflow of vitriol, which, I am overjoyed to say, has subsided, and Eric has done a fine job in raising the children, in spite of another failed marriage along the way.

Just weeks after Eric left me, and when I was at last out of the frying pan, I jumped into the fire. I met David Beard.

CHAPTER EIGHTEEN

Condemned to Death

On the afternoon of Tuesday, 21 June 1955 my mother was transported from the Central Criminal Court back to Holloway Prison, where she was shown to her new quarters, known as the condemned unit. There she would live out her days under 24-hour guard to await Albert Pierrepoint and his bag of tools.

The condemned cell at Holloway was a double one, 15 feet wide by 14 feet deep and decorated pink and brown. It had an extra large window, fitted with one-way glass so that the occupants could not be seen from the outside. It was sparsely furnished with a bed, three chairs, a table and a wardrobe pushed up against the side wall. Unknown to the prisoner, the wardrobe was on castors and concealed the door that led directly to the execution chamber. The trapdoors lay no more than 15 feet away from right-hand side of the bed as the condemned slept. To the other side of the cell was a bathroom constructed from a single cell and containing bath, WC and wash basin. The bathroom in turn connected to the next single cell, which was partitioned by glass and used by the prisoner to meet visitors and legal representatives. No visitors were allowed in the condemned cell itself. Furthermore, no flowers were allowed in the unit at all, so Ruth instructed that the many bouquets sent to her by friends and well-wishers be used to decorate the prison chapel.

She took to her new setting with much the same composure that she had demonstrated since the shooting, though inwardly she still fumed with anger that the Findlaters had escaped the trap that she thought she had so carefully laid. The next morning her solicitor, John Bickford, went to visit her and take new instructions. A more altruistic practitioner of the law she could not have found, and he must have been taken aback, to put it mildly, when she informed him that she would not appeal against her sentence. Acting in her best interests but against her wishes, Mr Bickford began work assembling all the data and relevant material to back a plea for a reprieve. Ruth received several visitors, Desmond Cussen not among them, who all sought to reassure her that she would be reprieved. Instead of showing gratitude for such support Ruth grew short-tempered with them, saying that she was quite content to die and she did not seek a reprieve. On the other hand the family, marshalled by Granville, and with rock solid support from my grandparents and Ruth's other brothers and sisters, urged Mr Bickford to press on with whatever was required to ensure a reprieve.

Her fate was in the hands of just one man, the Home Secretary of the day, Major Gwilym Lloyd-George. Between the shooting of David Blakely and Ruth's being sentenced to death there had been a general election on 26 May. In the weeks leading up to the election it had been widely predicted by the national press that the Labour party, led by Clement Attlee, would win power and defeat the Conservatives, led by Sir Anthony Eden who had become Prime Minister just a few weeks earlier on 6 April following the retirement of Winston Churchill. If the papers had been correct, and Labour had won the election, it is probable that my mother's life or death would have been decided by a less bovine Home Secretary than the Establishment-bred upper-class and out-of-touch Major.

Between visitors Ruth occupied her hours reading her Bible, doing jigsaw puzzles and making animals and shapes from fabrics that my grandmother took to the prison for her. Granville was her most frequent visitor, urging her to fight for her life. His pleas were falling on stony ground, and, during one visit, she managed to slip a note into his hand, unseen by the wardress. It was a request for him to obtain for her some lethal poison so that she might take her own life and save the hangman the trouble. In consultation with my grandfather, they opted to destroy the note and ignore her request.

Press and public debate over the forthcoming hanging gathered rapid momentum, and the lobby for a reprieve garnered some big supporting names who wrote letters to the papers and encouraged others to embark on similar courses of action. The campaign to force Lloyd-George to grant a reprieve was a powerful one. All over the country ordinary people were organizing petitions to demand that this mother of two young children should be spared. John Bickford issued, through the press, details of how a petition should be worded and the address to which they should be sent. Ruth Ellis was never off the front pages, although she was not permitted to see any newspapers.

Her old friend Jacqueline Dyer, almost a daily visitor, took time out to seek her own local MP, George Rogers, who took up the cause with gusto and brought his powerful voice to join those already raised by such respected pillars of society as Sidney Silverman MP, Anthony Greenwood MP, crime writer Raymond Chandler and Emanuel Shinwell MP who wrote: 'I say that Ruth Ellis should not hang.'

Sir Beverley Baxter MP added his opinion, writing to the *Evening Standard*: 'If this woman hangs, then the shame of it will be upon us all.' The Methodist leader, Donald Soper, wrote that the hanging would be: 'degrading, retrograde and un-Christian'. Of course the pro-hanging enthusiasts had their say as well and among their number penning letters to the press were Ludovic Kennedy, writer Dennis Wheatley and Mrs Gladys Yule, still nursing her wounded thumb.

By far the most eloquent plea against the execution was voiced in the *Daily Mirror* by the legendary journalist William Connor, writing under his famous pseudonym, Cassandra. His article has been much quoted and fired the debate to an incandescent degree. It is available for all to read in the academic and journalistic books that have been written on the subject. I will just pick out a few sentences, which give an indication of the flavour and tone of the piece:

Pity comes hard after such dreadful deeds. Compassion weeps but is silent.

Yet had I the power I would save her. This was a murder of love and hate. The one as fierce as the other – the storm of tenderness matching the fury of revenge. . . .

By the ingrained horror that most people have at the prospect of a woman shortly to be dragged to the scaffold, it is inevitable that millions of people will be increasingly drawn towards the shortening shadow of the hideous event to come. . . .

This ghastly business, this obscene ritual which we, who claim to be the most civilised people in the world, have never succeeded in getting rid of, is witnessed by many people – some of whom have the decency to want to vomit. . . .

What we do to her – you and I – matters very much. And if we do it, and if we continue to do it to her sad successors, then we all bear the guilt of savagery untinged with mercy.

Powerful, heady stuff! There had been a free vote in the House of Commons in February of that year on a motion to suspend the death penalty for an experimental period of five years. It was defeated by 245 votes to 214. One of those who had voted in favour of the suspension was George Rogers, Labour member for North Kensington and, prodded by the tireless Mrs Dyer and inspired by Cassandra's article, he wrote to the Home Secretary asking that he grant a reprieve. The Home Secretary ignored his letter completely. George Rogers was undeterred and visited Ruth on several occasions. He it was who first penetrated her resolve to die without a struggle. He it was who forced her to see what effect her death would have on her children, particularly Andy who was already without a father and was on the brink of being motherless as well.

Under his vital influence, Ruth began to open her eyes to the merits of fighting for her life. It was to George Rogers that she confided her doubts about John Bickford, and she told him of her liking and trust for Victor Mishcon and Leon Simmons who had handled her divorce proceedings. It is possible that she was transferring blame for the Findlater fiasco in court to the hapless John Bickford since Melford Stevenson was out of her frame. Rogers and Mishcon, both of stalwart socialist persuasion, were already acquainted with each other, and George Rogers promised Ruth he would pass on her feelings to him.

Meanwhile Jacqueline Dyer and Granville in particular allowed no let-up in the pressure they placed on my mother to tell the truth. Nobody had swallowed the story of how she came by the gun, but it was the only explanation that she had offered. Behind the scenes, the activists on her behalf worked feverishly, and her suspicions or doubts about John Bickford were unfair and unfounded as he beavered away, even to the neglect of the rest of his practice, to penetrate the wooden cranium of the pompous arbiter of justice, Major Gwilym Lloyd-George, who was more concerned with homing to Wales for the Eisteddfod and taking tea and cucumber sandwiches with his sister than he was with the affairs of State.

There did appear on the horizon one glimmer of hope in the outcome of another case that had run parallel with Ruth's, but which, for one reason or another, had merited very few column inches. On Friday, 6 May 1955, 40-year-old Mrs Sarah Lloyd, the mother of a daughter aged 13, had been sentenced to death at Leeds Assizes for the murder of a neighbour. The neighbour was a widow, Edith Emsley, who was 86 years old. The two women had feuded in silence for two years over Mrs Emsley's allegations that Mrs Lloyd was responsible for an anonymous, venomous letter relating to her son. She also blamed Mrs Lloyd for a series of incidents in which bricks and marbles had been thrown through her window. On 7 February the two women had a flare-up with one another, and Mrs Lloyd battered Mrs Emsley with a garden spade. Before she died later that day, the old lady was able to tell police that prior to the spade attack, Mrs Lloyd had poured boiling carrots and onions over her.

Neighbours who were witnesses at her trial said that Mrs Lloyd stood chatting casually as the street inhabitants watched incredulously as Edith Emsley was carried into an ambulance. Cool as they come, that night Mrs Lloyd went out with her daughter to the cinema. The next day she was arrested. She awaited her fate in Manchester's Strangeways prison, where her execution had been scheduled for 7 July, just six days prior to that set for the hanging of Ruth Ellis. On 5 July, Mrs Lloyd was granted a reprieve by Major Lloyd-George.

The deadline for petitions to reach the Home Office was 8 July. Mrs Dyer and George Rogers soldiered on as did many others. London was in the grip of a scorching heat wave that sapped the energies of many people but not of those labouring on Ruth's behalf. One woman who had never even met my mother gave up her job to collect signatures on a petition. She was 29-year-old Frieda Platt who spent twelve hours each and every day at London main line stations encouraging travellers to append their names to the cause. She explained that four years previously she had been accused of the attempted murder of her own husband. She was convicted and bound over to keep the peace and then released. However, she had suffered a terrible ordeal while imprisoned on remand awaiting trial, and her heart went out to Ruth in her current predicament.

The more time Mrs Dyer spent with George Rogers, the more he began to see how badly Ruth's defence had been conducted. He learnt how Jacqueline could have offered evidence about Blakely's violent treatment of Ruth on numerous occasions. He discovered that Jacqueline had helped my mother pack each time she moved flats and that she had never seen a gun during any of those moves. She told him that Ruth had intimated, but later withdrawn the intimation, that Desmond Cussen had given her the revolver.

Ruth, meanwhile, buried her head deeper and deeper into her Bible. Gone was all the glamour of her court appearance. Her hair had yellowed and was tied in a pony-tail. She wore no make-up and was attired in the blue regulation-issue prison overalls. She attended the prison chapel for the Sunday service.

She entered with two wardresses before any other prisoners entered, and she was the last to leave. She sat in a pew at the front of the chapel, which was hung on three sides by thick green curtains, screening her from the other inmates. Only the padre could see her.

Time was running alarmingly short, as the tabloid head-lines were at pains to stress. On the morning of 11 July, the *Daily Mirror* ran the front-page headline: I'M CONTENT TO DIE SAYS RUTH ELLIS. By that evening, for the first time, she dramatically changed her mind after governor Dr Charity Taylor personally delivered the news that Lloyd-George had refused a reprieve. The headline of the same newspaper on Tuesday 12 July was: RUTH ELLIS'S DRAMATIC CALL FROM DEATH CELL.

She had told her brother Granville the truth for the first time. John Bickford was dropped from the case, and Victor Mishcon, the former Chairman of London County Council, was called in to head the desperate eleventh-hour efforts. How proud my mother would be today to see that same Victor Mishcon, now Lord Mishcon, representing Princess Diana's legal interests as a very different national press seeks to destroy the poor woman.

With the truth out, the hunt was on to find Desmond Cussen. Lawyers, my family members and the police cast what net they could, but wily old Desmond was not to be trawled. Ruth's reaction to the tidings brought by Charity Taylor had been hysterical; as though she had been anaesthetized since sentence was passed, she now lay on the bed in the condemned cell screaming: 'I don't want to die.' Victor Mishcon saw her on the evening of the 11th, and he and Leon Simmons saw her again first thing on the Tuesday morning, at which interview, I have reason to believe, she admitted that she had told lies to the police in order to honour the law of the Soho underworld, which decrees that one does not 'grass'.

With less than 24 hours to go, she set them a hopeless task. The police failed to locate Cussen and gave up the search. They informed the Home Office that there was no new material evidence, and Ruth's fate was sealed. The Home Secretary's official statement that he 'could see no sufficient grounds to recommend any interference with the due course of law' was not going to be amended.

On her last day she had a stream of visitors, with Jacqueline Dyer and a trio of friends from the Little Club and my grandparents and Granville calling twice for heart-rending farewells. Albert Pierrepoint and his assistant sneaked into the prison to begin their gruesome rituals, and the crowd of inevitable ghouls, voyeurs and protesters gathered outside the great oak gates of Holloway Prison. One visitor who did not get access to the inner sanctum of the condemned suite was Ruth's eldest brother, Julian, who arrived bearing flowers. She sent him a message of reassurance that she was all right and that he should not become involved. Later that night, thousands of people came together in Hyde Park to speak and hear the arguments against capital punishment.

No doubt Major Lloyd-George sat down to a nice dinner, and Sir Frank Newsam, the Permanent Under-Secretary to the Home Office, probably counted his winnings from his jolly day out at Ascot races. Desmond Cussen, wherever he was holed up, must have breathed his last sigh of relief that he could no longer be brought to justice for his crime. There was no food eaten in the Neilson house. Neither my grandparents nor any of my aunts and uncles had any stomach for it. There were tears of hopelessness for the frail little woman they all loved. Another who had no stomach for food that night was John Bickford, who had been on the receiving end of an astronomically unfair tirade of abuse from Ruth at the height of her hysteria. That she was going to die, she told him, was entirely his fault, and she put it in such a cruel and callous way that he later admitted it affected him for the remainder of his life.

Ruth herself, once she was becalmed, spent much of her final evening reading her Bible, unaware that the reptilian Albert Pierrepoint was staring at her through a secret peep-hole, sizing up her neck and getting ready to have a practice with a sandbag just as soon as she was taken out for exercise. He was all set to hang the last woman he or any other executioner would hang in Britain. I hope he had a good dinner, too.

CHAPTER NINETEEN

The Execution

On the morning of 13 July 1955, another article by William 'Cassandra' Connor appeared on the front page of the *Daily Mirror*. It began:

> It's a fine day for haymaking. A fine day for fishing. A fine day for lolling in the sunshine. And if you feel that way – and I mourn to say that millions of you do – it's a fine day for a hanging. . . .
>
> In this case I have been reviled as being a sucker for a pretty face. Well, I am a sucker for all human faces because I hope I am a sucker for all humanity, good or bad. But I prefer them not to be lolling because of a judicially broken neck.

By first light following a sticky, humid night, the small crowd outside the prison gates, which had kept an all-night vigil, had swelled to several hundred and continued to grow with each ticking minute. Police, both mounted and on foot, were called into action when hundreds of women tried to storm the prison gates. Some of those more depraved than others had taken their children along for the sport. Scuffles broke out frequently between abolitionists and those in favour of capital punishment. A couple of such scuffles involved one

Mrs Van Der Elst, known to her detractors as VD Elsie, who encouraged and incited abolitionists to cross the police lines.

Violet Van Der Elst had attracted a great amount of press publicity since she made her debut outside the gates of Pentonville Prison on 13 March 1935 on the occasion of the hanging of Charles Lake for the murder of a bookmaker. Though that case in itself was not sensational, VD Elsie used it to seduce an army of eccentrics who followed her for more than twenty years to take up their disruptive posts, kneeling in prayer together on the stroke of the hour of execution. She became a regular client of the magistrates' courts, where she faced minor charges of obstructing police, passers-by and prison officials. She always dressed in black and was at the ready with a provocative quote for any journalist in her vicinity.

Holloway woke at its usual hour of 6.30 a.m., but Ruth was left to sleep out her sedated sleep. The other inmates were confined to their cells for the reason that they all understood only too well. There was an eerie silence within those austere red-brick walls except for the clamour from outside the doors in Parkhurst Road. The incessant chant was 'Evans, Bentley, Ellis'.

Major Gwilym Lloyd-George, the 61-year-old Home Secretary, sat down to breakfast secure in the knowledge that his luxury residence in St James's Court, Buckingham Gate, was under heavy police guard. John Bickford, reeling from the shock of mother's tirade against him and from the failure of all his considerable efforts, went for a long walk across Blackheath Common in an attempt to divert his mind from the inevitability of the morning. He was unable to rid his head of the haunting tune of 'La Vie En Rose' and the haunted image of Ruth's powder compact, which played that tune when she opened it. Leon Simmons, in despair equal to John Bickford's, read Ruth's penultimate letter to him:

> I am now content and satisfied that my affairs will be dealt with satisfactorily. I also ask you to make known the true story regarding Mrs Findlater and her plan to break up David and I – she should feel content now her plan ended so tragically.

Would you please ask my mother to go to David's grave and put flowers, pink and white carnations. (Ask her to do it for me.)

My grandmother sobbed quietly and inconsolably. On her last visit she had bought Ruth some red roses from a Camden street seller. She was unaware that Ruth was not allowed to have the flowers in her cell. The final farewell meeting had lasted no more than ten minutes, just long enough for my mother to beseech Bertha to look after Andy for her. The meeting ended with Ruth collapsing, screaming, 'I don't want to die.' That vision and the echo of those words haunted my poor grandparents for the rest of their days.

Aunt Elizabeth cried silently, but Muriel was too numbed and stunned to shed tears. She paced round her house, moving from room to room and back again, repeating the words 'No, no, no,' unable to come to terms with the harsh reality of the morning.

Andy was staying with Mr and Mrs George Rogers at their large country home in Sudbury. He was blissfully unaware of the events about to unfold and was, as far as he was concerned, enjoying a good holiday while his mother was away at work. George and Mrs Rogers had their work cut out making sure that no newspapers came into the house and that Andy was kept well away from the wireless. It had been decided between them and the family that the truth should be broken to him as gently as possible after the passage of a little time.

Albert Pierrepoint, the man who in his autobiography said that from the age of 12 it had been his ambition to follow his father and uncle in the executioner's trade, sat down to breakfast in Holloway, content in his professional pride that all his preparations had been completed. He described his job as a craft, even an art, and basked in the fame that being public hangman number one brought him. He had calculated the drop for Ruth Ellis and measured his rope accordingly. That calculation was vital as had been proved by one of his predecessors, one James Berry, whose miscalculation resulted in the full decapitation of some poor chap at Norwich gaol. Pierrepoint had his own formula based on the weight, height and physical condition of the condemned person. He had had his rehearsal the previous day while my mother was at exercise. It was done then so that she would not hear the trapdoors in the adjacent cell spring open. He rehearsed with a sandbag of identical weight to her own body, and afterwards the sandbag was left hanging on the noose to stretch the rope to its maximum. He had checked his equipment, examined his rope and made certain that he had in place the wrist-strap, leg-shackles and white hood. In recent years, I learnt that a pub of which Pierrepoint was once the landlord was called 'Help the Poor Struggler'.

It is impossible to say the exact time at which Ruth Ellis was awakened on her last morning. The reports are in conflict by a considerable number of minutes. She dressed quietly in the bathroom and reluctantly put on the Home Office issue canvas knickers that had been compulsory for every woman about to be executed since Edith Thompson died on the gallows in 1923. As Mrs Thompson dropped into the pit her under garments became drenched in blood, and it was feared she had been unwittingly pregnant and had miscarried on the end of the rope. Ever after it was canvas knickers for the girls. She refused offers of breakfast but accepted a brandy. She knelt in prayer before the crucifix on the wall, and the prison chaplain served her with communion. All histrionics from the day before had departed, and she was outwardly calm and collected.

With only minutes remaining, the non-stop clamour outside the prison gates subsided, and a still silence overtook the massed assembly. A lone violinist played Bach's 'Be Thou With Me When I Die'.

At twenty seconds before 9.00 a.m., the execution party of Albert Pierrepoint and his assistant, Dr Charity Taylor, the medical officer, the Under Sheriff of the County and the Chief Prison Wardress entered the condemned cell. Pierrepoint strapped Ruth's wrists behind her back, the wardrobe was slid back, and she was escorted into the execution chamber and on to the drop. Her feet were positioned on a marked spot with one foot either side of the division in the trapdoors. The assistant manacled her feet as Pierrepoint placed the white hood over her head. He secured the hood with the noose, tightened the rope around her neck and bent to take up a position similar to a sprinter on the starting-line. He removed the cotter-pin from the mechanism, pulled the lever, the trap-doors opened with a bang, and my mother was dead.

The medical officer immediately descended the flight of stairs into the pit below and pronounced her dead. The body was then left to hang for one hour. Pierrepoint dismantled his gear, another job done and £15.00 better off, his fee for ending a human life. At 18 minutes past 9 a.m., a warder came out to post the notices of execution on the prison gates, causing the crowd to surge forward beyond police control and bringing all traffic to a halt. Mounted police moved in, and two orderly queues of I cannot imagine what sort of people filed past the notices that were mounted in black wooden frames. One frame contained the Sheriff's declaration that the execution had been carried out in his presence, and the second contained the certificate of death signed by the medical officer, Dr H. R. P. Williams.

After the hour of suspension by the broken neck had elapsed, Pierrepoint adjusted his rope so that the noose could be removed from the neck, and the body made ready for the pathologist, in this case Dr Keith Simpson, who pronounced that death had been instantaneous. The corpse was then placed in a black coffin made of deal to await burial within the prison precincts during the dinner hour, when all the other inmates would be otherwise occupied.

If anyone wonders why I have gone into such gory detail about how my own mother met her death it is because, even as I write, there is still a lobby, and a powerful and growing one, to bring back the disgusting practice of hanging. The last executions in this country took place on 13 August 1964, when Peter Anthony Allen and Gwynne Owen Evans were simultaneously hanged at Walton and Strangeways Prisons for murder committed during the course of a robbery. From that date until now, the barbaric ritual has been confined to the history books.

To Granville fell the onerous task of formally identifying the body. He had not been in the prison throughout the morning but had spent it in floods of tears in the offices of the *Daily Mirror* in Fleet Street, watching the ticker-tape machine in the forlorn hope of seeing a last minute reprieve come through. On the stroke of nine, the desolate man, only 32 years of age himself, trudged to Holloway for the formality that was his duty. All he had witnessed on the ticker-tape was confirmation that the judicial sentence had been carried out according to the law. By the time he arrived at the prison, Ruth had been laid out, made up with lipstick and face powder and candles, a crucifix placed beside her. All swelling and distortion around the area of her neck had been carefully concealed by a scarf. Granville later reported what little comfort he could to the rest of the family that she looked as though her death had been from natural causes and that she looked beautiful.

Having made his formal identification, Granville was then taken upstairs to the Governor's office, where the inquest was conducted. He was appalled and angered that the insensitive coroner, H. Milner-Helme, referred to Ruth throughout as the murderess, and in his anger, he lost control and shouted at him to try and think of something else to call her. He was taken from the room, given a glass of water and then went home alone. He, like all the family, Jacqueline Dyer, Leon Simmons, John Bickford, Maurie Conley and the family of David Blakely, would never forget that morning. Where were Carole and Ant Findlater? Where was Desmond Cussen? They never said, but I trust they squirmed and ruminated on the parts they had played.

The crowd was slow to disperse, and Pierrepoint needed a police escort to leave the prison. He was hounded, jostled and pursued by reporters all the way to Euston Station. He ignored all their questions, but later admitted that hanging my mother had had a profound effect on him. In his book he accepted that the evidence from other countries and his own experience had taught him that the death penalty was no deterrent to murder. Seven months after Ruth's death he resigned from the post.

CHAPTER TWENTY

Mirror Image

After husband Eric had left our family home, I was in great distress and could not decide what action to take for the best. We had many debts, the mortgage and the domestic bills were all in arrears, and I had four children to support. There was no sign of any maintenance.

Around Christmas was especially difficult, and I hated not being able to provide the normal seasonal joys that a parent loves to give to the children. I did not know where Eric was. We had no money. Then, out of the blue, I received a phone call from him telling me he was on holiday in Antigua.

My job working for Chanel was our only financial salvation, but that, too, caused me much distress because it forced me to leave the children, even if they were ill, in the care of au pairs or child-minders. I made new friends in the job but was unable to accept their invitations to join them socially after work because of rushing home to prepare meals, do the washing and ironing, and flop into bed exhausted. Men asked me out on dates, but I always declined. Unlike the other girls, I was fully encumbered and had no chance to let my hair down. Apart from anything else, I could not afford a social life on the small income I received from Chanel. The job was only part time, but it was as much as I could undertake without serious neglect of the home.

One Friday the girls at work refused to take no for an answer. It was the birthday of one of them, and, after much coaxing, I agreed to go out to the party in a bar in Manchester's St Ann's Square. I went home to feed the children, having organized a sitter for the evening, and returned to town. I was walking across the square towards Ronnie's bar when I saw him; I just thought to myself, Oh, my God, who the hell is he? I know it sounds like a Mills and Boon line, but it is true, that is precisely how it happened. To me, he looked just like Clark Gable whom I had idolized as a young girl.

In the wine bar my colleagues tried to engage me in chat, but I kept looking over their shoulders, and there he was again, staring at me. He was talking to a man with fair hair, but his eyes were fixed on me and mine on him. Eventually I took the bull by the horns and strolled over to them. As if I had known him for years, I said: 'Hello. It's nice to see you again; it's been ages. How are things?', as I looked into the most amazing set of honeycomb eyes I had ever seen.

He smiled in the roguish manner with which I was destined to become so familiar. The fair-haired man, Malcolm, made most of the conversation and was himself handsome, witty and interesting, but the powerful, mutual attraction between me and the one with the dark hair and moustache was undeniable. He told me his name was David Beard. Although I made no immediate connection between his initials and those of David Blakely, I came to call him DB. I found out much much later that Ruth often used to address Blakely as DB.

David Beard was a chartered surveyor, a founder partner in one of the north's leading commercial-estate agencies. He and I drifted off to another bar to chat alone together, and then he remembered that he had left something important in his office. The sexual chemistry between us was already bubbling, and when we reached his deserted office it was no more than a matter of seconds before our seduction was complete, and the fledgling relationship consummated on the floor of his board-room.

I was inescapably hooked, bowled over by this incredibly sexy man, and, as if I needed any extra persuasion to surrender myself fully, he drove me home in my favourite motor car, his XJS Jaguar. David Blakely had been a Jaguar lover too. The pattern was beginning to take shape. When Ruth met her DB, he was engaged to another girl; mine was already married with two children, though I was unaware of that fact at the time and did not dare ask for fear of learning something that I did not wish to hear.

A few weeks were to pass before we saw each other again, which was something of a relief once I knew the reality of his marital status. He and his family had gone to the South of France on a sailing holiday. In the meantime Malcolm, he of the fair hair, was phoning me to ask me out. He, too, was a married man, though such status seems these days to make little difference to either men or women.

I have never made a habit of seeing clairvoyants, but around this time I visited a psychic, whose revelations so surprised and disturbed me that I immediately consulted another. Both women told me the same thing: that I had recently met two men, one with dark hair, the other fair; that I should discount any ideas of happiness with the dark-haired man, and that the signs were more favourable towards him with the blond hair, whose marriage was foreseen to have but a short time left to run. I know it is silly to give great credence to such matters, but I was disturbed enough to want to get away and ponder my life. To this end I hired a car, and the children and I went to Cornwall, where we joined my recently found half-brother John, his wife Sue and our new extended family.

Quite what they made of us, I do not know, but I chatted ceaselessly and unburdened my anxieties about the fatal attraction that I felt for DB. They warned me in no uncertain terms not to get involved with any more 'bounders' and felt I had enough on my plate as a single parent with four children to care for. I should have listened more attentively. As soon as the Beards returned from France, David was on the phone, and, against my better judgement and regret to this day, I agreed to meet him. He bought me a huge bottle of Cartier perfume, the only scent I have ever used since, and I fell head over heels in hopeless, fatal love with him, seeing him as often as possible, arranging clandestine weekends away with him as I tried to block out thoughts of his other life.

He, also, was in a quandary. We took my children out often, and he was hurt, knowing he had left his own behind. The conflicts were intense but so was our passion, the latter to the extent that all sense and sensibility evaporated. We had embarked on a mirror-image adventure that so closely paralleled the story of Ruth and David Blakely and came so near to having the same tragic ending.

David Beard was leading a fraught existence, covering his tracks with difficulty. Eric had reappeared and sought a reconciliation for the sake of the children. I agreed to have one more shot at making the marriage work. Eric, however, was still unsure of me and accused me of continuing my association with David.

One of my distractions away from the pressures of *l'amour* was to sing in the local church choir, and one night choir practice went on longer than anticipated, and I failed to be home at the time I had said. Eric, fuelled by lager, suspected the worst and surrendered to it. Though I begged him otherwise, he left us again. What ensued was a sequence of vitriol of horrific proportions. Fights both physical and emotional between Eric and DB, with me the battered little prize who did not wish to be anyone's trophy. In tandem with the violence came police, bugging devices, private detectives, threats of malice, injunctions, all of which formed part of everyday life.

The battle for custody of the children then got under way. I was seeing David and more in love with him than ever, but he was still living with his wife. I was pregnant by him when he told me that he and his family were going on a reconciliation attempt to Morocco. I begged him not to leave me, but he was resolute. The night before they flew, I lost our baby, and, though David stayed with me as long as he felt he was able, he still flew off with his wife and children. I lay in hospital a completely broken woman. I had lost the baby of the man I loved, and all the signs were that I was about to lose my other children as well. I began to drink far too much to block out the horror.

DB came back from Morocco with presents for me, but told me that his wife had gone to bed early each night, and he had gone out to do his own thing. He assured me that his love for me had ensured his fidelity. Later, when he took me to Tenerife, I made sure he did not wander by hiding all his cash and credit cards in the bathroom cistern and clinging to him like a leech.

I was totally disconsolate and in need of a break, but I had no real money to pay for a jaunt and for someone to care for the children during my absence. My only disposable asset was my Cartier watch, which I had bought with the proceeds from the earlier *News of the World* features on my life as Ruth's daughter. I sold it, and the day after DB returned from Morocco I flew to Malaga by myself to spend a week on the Costa del Crime.

I was sauntering along the sea front in Marbella when a car drew to a halt beside me, and a middle-aged Englishman with a Cockney accent began to chat. I knew him only as Chas, and he introduced me to his North African girlfriend. I gleaned that he was a fugitive from British justice, and the two of them were running drugs from coast to coast across the Mediterranean. I do meet the choicest people. However, they were good fun, amusing and friendly and, in a nutshell, just what the doctor ordered.

One night, in Puerto Banus, the exclusive port where the rich and famous moor their gin palaces, I was out with them in Sinatra's bar, having drinks before dinner at Silks restaurant. Chas and the girl, well oiled with alcohol, engaged in the mother and father of a row, during which she threatened to ring the police and tell them where he hid his ill-gotten gains, and he promised revenge with the loss of her beauty. I stood up and walked discreetly away to the bar, where a good-looking man, who reminded me slightly of David Beard, started a conversation with me. He was well spoken, and among other things he told me he had a fine art collection. I know and care about art very much so I was able to converse on his level, about his Goyas, Toulouse-Lautrecs and Van Goghs. Despite his cultured English accent, I smiled inwardly and dismissed him as yet another bar-room bullshitter. A couple of times during his banter he pointed out to sea, but I paid little attention. I changed the subject and told him why I was in Spain and all about David, and then I excused myself and went back to my friends' table. He said: 'See you again some time,' and disappeared into the night.

When I sat down Chas said: 'You know who that was, don't you?' I shrugged no, and then he told me he was the son of Adnan Khashoggi, the billionaire arms dealer; his gesture out to sea had been towards the yacht *Nabilla*, named after Adnan's daughter. I failed to land the big fish. He had gone.

That night had a bizarre ending. Chas's girl had indeed tipped off the police, and as we headed back there were blue lights and police cars swarming round the area where Chas lived. He told me to go off alone, and I reluctantly walked away, looking like any other tourist. That was the last time I saw him, but I did receive a Christmas card from him. Not long after that I took a sharp intake of breath when I opened a newspaper and saw his picture. Charles Wilson, Great Train Robber, had been shot dead.

Back in England I told myself that DB was history after his Morocco trip, and I made the Royal Oak pub in Didsbury my second home. I freely confess that I was drinking far too much, but Eric was putting me under intense pressure as far as the children were concerned. The *Daily Express* got wind of our troubles, and once more I was the subject of headlines. This one read: KILLER'S GIRL IN DIVORCE TUG OF LOVE. Eric even gave them a quote saying: 'I don't want them growing up with their only claim to fame being Ruth Ellis's grandchildren. I'm not interested in the house. It's the children I want.'

David pestered me constantly to see him. After his wedding anniversary he had the effrontery to send me dozens of red roses. I drove round to his wife's house and left them on the front doorstep. I told David she deserved them for being married to such an idiot. It reminded me wryly of Ruth's drives out to Penn to the house of the 'married woman'. David met his match with me, and I will never allow myself to be humiliated by any man's ego. The words of my half-brother

Andy, when he told me I had inherited all Ruth's strengths, are true.

My spirit was strong, but my flesh was weak. Like a fool I agreed to meet David. He was bereft, telling me he would leave his wife that autumn. That was not what I particularly wanted, and I told him so. He gave me a present of diamond and ruby ear-rings.

I could drink with the best of them, and DB was never far behind. I nicknamed him 'Early Doors' because he was always there at opening time. He gave me a nickname, too, 'Jigsaw', because we lay together asleep and woke entwined each morning. I was seeing him on a regular basis, and he devoutly assured me that he and his wife had not had sex together for more than a year. A girlfriend of mine asked me casually if I had seen David's wife lately, and I said that I would not know her if I fell over her. When she told me where Mrs Beard could be found every Saturday, out of curiosity I went. I recognized the children from photographs, but when I saw their mother, I almost died. She must have been eight months pregnant if she were a day.

I fought Eric for the custody of our children, but we made an agreement prior to appearing in court on the advice of my barrister, whereby I would grant him custody and not pursue my case.

I was given a financial settlement by Eric, and I opted to blow some of it on a fortnight's trip to Paris for myself and DB. I was even more besotted with the man, I am ashamed to say, and we battled our way round the city, dinner at the Ritz, now having fun, now having an argument. One night, after far too much French 'loony juice', we had a tempestuous row, which resulted in David and I having the first of many fights. During the row an eminent French politician staying in the rooms below ours had complained, only to be treated to a volley of David's best Anglo-Saxon. David was asked politely to vacate the hotel the next morning, but they told me that I could stay; I was paying the bill, after all. But, vulnerable to the last, we left together, and for the rest of our sunny days in the city I looked Parisian chic in dark glasses day and night.

To begin with, before Eric turned awkward, I had visiting rights to the children, so I saw them at weekends, which was something to look forward to. I set up my home alone in a small place in Goose Green, Altrincham, and awaited the car that Eric had promised to provide for me as part of the settlement. My lawyer had omitted to specify any value, year or make of the car, and I was amused when a chocolate-brown Lada was delivered to my door. Word reached me that he was about to marry again. He did, but it was not very long before poor old Eric was going through his second acrimonious divorce.

At the time when Eric remarried, I was again pregnant by DB and about five months gone. The conception had taken place during a period of blissful happiness for David and me, when both our lives were in harmony. I was not trying to trap him with the baby, I just wanted a part of him and to give him the son that the tests I needed told me I was carrying. He began to take our relationship more seriously, and I had a gut feeling that he wanted to make some solid commitment and provide a home, if an unconventional one, for his 'alternative' family. The *Manchester Evening News* wrote a piece about me that ended by saying that I was pregnant, and David Beard and I had set up home together. This came as quite a shock to David's wife as he had forgotten to mention that aspect of his life.

Later on I came to know Liz Beard well, and when David drove me to my wits' end she would offer advice, warmly and sincerely, in the most unselfish way. We even looked after each other's children from time to time as we both danced to David's tune, both of us impotent since David held all the financial cards.

Our baby, Stephen, was born, named after David's brother who had died in childhood. Everything was wonderful, except that David made no move towards divorcing Liz, although he made it clear that the marriage was over in all but the piece of paper.

We had a battle over Stephen's christening, which I arranged. Phyllis and Peter Lawton and David's parents were all happy with their new grandchild, but David said he was against a christening because he felt guilt at having sired a child while still married to another woman. He claimed the ceremony would be a parody, but it duly went ahead with Malcolm, the fair-haired man of our first meeting, acting as godfather.

The fortune-tellers were ultimately proved right. Malcolm's marriage did not last long because, very tragically, his wife died of brain cancer; an event that not surprisingly traumatized Malcolm for some time.

I was cautious of any other relationship that DB had, even the one he enjoyed with Malcolm. Any suggestion that I join them was greeted with a lack of enthusiasm. I felt, rightly or wrongly, cut off from life, isolated and lonely.

DB still made no move towards a divorce, but Liz did it for him and started her own proceedings, something that threw David into shock. She and David had three children, and he complained about how restrictive maintenance was and that he could not afford to provide fully for both families. He reasoned that as Liz and her children had come along first, they must take priority, and we would have to make do. It beats me why anyone should have been expected to make do when David had his Jaguar, yacht and gold Rolex watch.

I was perplexed by his attitude, and as the property recession began to bite nationally, and I saw others in his field economizing, I could perceive no sign of David tightening his own belt. He was obviously successful and continued his lavish ways round town, never stinting on spending money on professional hospitality. I said little and withdrew for much of the time into my small world, which centred around Stephen. Making do, as David put it, only seemed to apply to our domestic set-up, and he was prepared to splash out on incredible holidays for us aboard the yacht and buy luxury convertible cars for my use.

I remained truly, madly, deeply in love with the man, and I proudly attended functions as the glamorous appendage on his arm. But I really wanted to be his wife. That was never to be.

Our times together, when not on holiday or out on parade, were torrid for most of the time with occasional ups to lighten the more frequent downs. During one such up, I again conceived. I hoped this new pregnancy would strengthen the bond between the whole extended family and hold us together. I clung to the belief that David and I would eventually marry, just as Ruth had tenaciously held on to the same belief in David Blakely.

Our second child, Chloe, was born on a Saturday. David was present and videoed the birth, and then he went off to a rugby match. David loves his children dearly, as do I, and he is a good father. However, the atmosphere between the two of us went into steep decline following Chloe's birth and was not helped when I stumbled upon David in a compromising position with another woman at Christmas. He tried to fob me off with the usual lame excuses of excess alcohol, Christmas spirit and office life, but I knew she was the new moon on the horizon, and the sun was setting on me.

I was doubly furious, both at his deceit and by the fact that he had despatched me that evening to go late-night shopping to buy all his presents for Liz and the children. I never trusted him again, and my life was once more in tatters. I know how my mother felt when she was tipped off about the woman in Penn and then watched Blakely leave her house first thing in the morning after he had spent the night there. It is a truly sickening feeling as all who have been duped in this way will understand. There was worse to come.

CHAPTER TWENTY-ONE

Like Mother, Like Daughter

Once I came to terms with David's affair, everything else slotted into place and made retrospective sense; the Sundays at the office and the fact that he often sounded out of breath if I rang him there. People were aware of the ups and downs and the intensity of our relationship, and it was the subject of much discussion and speculation in the Royal Oak pub.

We swung into our most violent episode one Saturday night. We had argued over what to do that night, DB wanting to go over to Malcolm's house, but I was tired out and simply wanted to go home. In the end he dumped me and the children at the house with no intimation as to what time, or even if, he would return. I sought solace, much of it liquid, with some friends, and when David eventually returned he had drunk sufficient to be spoiling for a fight, and I was highly inebriated myself. The inevitable squabble began and grew heated very quickly.

For some reason he began to put all the furniture outside in the garden. The children became terrified, and I put them in the nursery out of harm's way while I endeavoured to placate him. We both lost all semblance of control, and one of us could have been killed. My injuries were such that I had to go to hospital, and the police were called.

Our neighbours have since told me that they grew accustomed to hearing our fights, the children's screams and my sobbing for hours on end. The police were among our more regular visitors. The next outburst proved to be the last in that house. At the height of it he picked me up by the hair and tried to drag me out of the house. I managed to pick up a rolling pin from the kitchen table, and my only thought was that I wanted to kill him. If I could have got a swing in, I swear I would have battered my lover to death. Had my equivalent of a Desmond Cussen been on hand to furnish me with a revolver, I would have joyfully shot him.

The children were crying hysterically in the nursery, and I was equally distraught. We battled on until he managed to throw me outside. I fought to get back in but to no avail. My only coherent thoughts were to get my children out of the place as their cries of anguish tore through the air.

I smashed windows downstairs to try to reach Stephen and Chloe, but it seemed as if each time I attacked a window David was there to repel me. I was cut, bruised and battered, although in my uncontrolled panic I was not aware of the extent of my injuries. Crying and completely drained I somehow staggered to the Royal Oak, where the landlord, Arthur Gosling, dropped his jaw in horrified amazement. The staff and regulars had seen me in a state before but never as bad as the one they beheld that night. Someone bandaged my hand. I remember somebody else asking me where I wanted to go, and all I had about my person was £5.00. Then a saint whose name I do not know even now asked me where my parents lived. I told him Warrington, and he drove me to Phyllis and Peter's house where those ever reliable, wonderful people cleaned me up and put me into a warm bed.

I went to see a lawyer who depressed me by saying that I had no automatic right to the children just because I was their mother. Equally depressing was that David had bought the house in his company's name and rented it to himself. I had no claim on the property. As far as the children were concerned, the lawyer continued, the onus would be on me as an unmarried mother to show that I had a home to offer them and could care for them as well if not better than their father. I was on a hiding to nothing. It was no contest between me with £5.00 and a plastic bag containing bits and bobs and him, a wealthy businessman who could show any court that he had the means and desire to look after them. Once more I was robbed of my children.

Phyllis berated me as a fool, but, nonetheless, she gave me £100. I signed on the dole and rented a freezing cold room in a run-down house in Didsbury; I often stayed in bed to keep warm with a bottle for company. I reflected on DB's behaviour, and I tried in vain to contact him. He would not return my calls, and I did not set eyes on Stephen and Chloe until custody was agreed. It broke my heart, and I came perilously close to losing what little sanity I had left. I talked to the Samaritans all night long. Friends, especially those in the Royal Oak, propped me up, and I slowly pulled myself together and found work as a cleaner, with a view to setting up an agency. I moved eventually to David's place in Bowdon, near Altrincham.

Although we were under the same roof, he told me that he was planning to go to court for full and exclusive custody, and he offered to make me a financial settlement prior to a hearing. He briefed the same lawyer as Eric had used, one already well versed in blackening my name. David provided a deposit on a single modern bedsit for me in Withington, which was at least warm and had a telephone. We went shopping, and he bought me a bed settee, a collapsible wardrobe and about £600 worth of other goods. We took them back to the bedsitter. Believe it or not, just like my mother with her DB, there was still a strong sexual chemistry between us, and, fool that I am, I took him back into my bed and cooked for him and hoped that one day we could live and love together in peace and harmony. In spite of these regular close encounters of the sexual kind, I did not see the children once he had moved me out of his own house.

After he had installed me in Withington, I had to fend for myself. He would even drive me in his XJS to a house where I made a few pounds as a cleaner. For my fortieth birthday, 2 October 1991, we went to Amsterdam, where David and I did the tourist rounds of the red-light district, amazed yet fascinated by the endless supply of female flesh flaunting itself for sale in the windows. He offered to buy me a diamond ring, but we saw none that took my fancy other than an antique one that was too expensive.

That evening we dined in the most fabulous restaurant I have ever experienced, Maxim's included, and when the first course arrived at our table, a waiter lifted the silver dome that covered my plate and there beneath was a leather box containing the antique ring with which I had fallen in love earlier in the day. David placed it on the third finger of my left hand, and, though no words were exchanged, I presumed we were engaged. The pianist played something romantic, and the other diners clapped spontaneously. I was in seventh heaven, and I stayed there for at least eight hours. He wasted no time in the sobriety of the following morning in dispelling my illusions. He said he had given me the ring to make me feel better about not being married, and that it was a token of his intention. I did not believe him but vowed to keep the ring, come what may, in the hope that one day it would belong to Chloe.

Back in England, David and the children were living in a modern, rented house in the smarter part of Bowdon. For David this was ideal as the area is full of up-market wine bars and élite pubs, which attract the young, footloose and fancy free, and where he was able to practise his charms. David was to be found in the Griffin on certain days, a pub known to attract both those with high disposable incomes and those with highly curvaceous assets, and Thursday nights would see him in the Hale Wine Bar, where young spring lambs sweat it out alongside mutton dressed as lamb, and the pickings are easy. I, on the other hand, had to scrimp to exist, and on one unforgettable occasion had nothing in the house to eat other than bird food. I was on the floor, sometimes quite literally, and I fretted for my children so much that I drank too freely if and when I had any money in my pocket.

My life had to change, and one morning I gave myself a good talking to. I made certain resolutions, which included never to be poor again, never to feel sorry for myself again and never again to humiliate or subordinate myself for the sake of a man. I took a long, hard look in the mirror and saw the degradation that had been my mother's ruin. I summoned up all those strengths that Andy had reminded me I had inherited from her and went out with my head held high and a fierce determination to put an end to the wasteland that my life had become. In Didsbury I saw a window that proclaimed 'Health Studio'. That's it, I thought to myself, first things first; I will get myself fit.

In all innocence, I rang the bell and said I would like to use the gym and a sunbed. The woman who had opened the door looked at me as though I had just landed from outer space. I repeated my request, and she said she thought I had made a mistake but invited me in anyway.

Of course, they did not have a gymnasium, nor did they have any sunbeds. Instead they had a pleasant lounge, where a couple of girls sat in rather skimpy outfits, and several massage tables. The woman who had shown me in said I could have a job there if I wished, and slowly the penny began to drop. She left me with the other girls, and we started to chat. They explained what went on, and when they told me the sort of money they were earning, my eyes popped out on stalks. Four figures a week for a few hours seemed to be quite normal; the lure for someone fighting for existence on something like £40 per week was considerable. On the spur of the moment I decided; why ever not? And that was how it started. I was about to discover that sex is a highly saleable commodity.

Reporting for work on my first day at the health studio, I knew I could not go through with it. There were three of us, one middle-aged, plumpish woman, another very young and thin as a beanpole and myself. The first punter arrived; though well dressed and well spoken, he was physically unattractive. I sat there thinking, Please God, don't let him pick me. He went outside with the boss, and when she returned my worst fears had materialized; I was the chosen one. I went to her office and told her I just could not do it. 'Nonsense,' she retorted and immediately sent for a bottle of vodka. I swigged half the bottle in world record time. Thereafter it was easier, never pleasant, but the money was simply wonderful.

It was the turning-point for me, and I know Ruth was watching and approving my efforts to extricate myself from the trough into which I had sunk. Working the health studios, or high-class massage parlours as some call them, vacillated between the sinister, when the perverts called, and the highly amusing, when the fun-and-games gentlemen came to visit. Each and every one of them is a story in itself, and that is another book, but all those highly respectable professional men, lawyers, accountants, property tycoons and merchants can sleep easy in the knowledge that their names and their secrets are safe with me; their generous wads of money have been well used to re-establish myself to the point where I no longer have to undertake such work myself. I now manage three escort agencies and have a network of attractive people of both sexes available for global assignments.

Of the women who became my friends in these places, most had been abandoned by men, and all had children to provide for. They worked to try to put a home together, and I can say in all honesty that I have yet to encounter a bunch of more good-natured, down-to-earth girls and women. They do the job of psychiatric nurse and more, listening to problems, giving comfort and affection as well as the physical relief that might otherwise find release in a real schoolgirl or whatever fantasy decrees. It is, in truth, an awful job, physically and mentally draining. I am a great advocate of legalizing prostitution under stringent controls, and the government must be aware of missing out on so much potential revenue.

I look back on those days as golden ones in so many ways. I became a better, more considerate person, and I acquired a degree of humility that I had not previously found. I learnt to understand others better and to accept that women can be as cruel to men as men are to women. Setting aside the perverts, the majority of men who pay for sexual services are short on love and looking for the fun that has probably disappeared from the matrimonial bed. Working girls provide an outlet for many men who, though intelligent and successful and husbands of loyal wives, find the daily routine, both professional and domestic, slipping into a rut of tedium. Surely it is preferable that they pay a professional, without any emotional encumbrance, than become embroiled in a steamy romance with the secretary and all its incumbent hurt on all sides? The unfortunate side-effect of my work is that my attitude to men has changed, and I know I will find it difficult to give myself completely to a relationship with a man, at least in the immediate future.

Less than a year after our trip to Amsterdam, David Beard persuaded me to give back the antique ring he had bought me there, which he then sold to a dealer. I hated him at this point with more venom than anyone should rightly be able to muster and, if I had been in possession of the wherewithal, would have killed him without a second thought.

The woman to whom he had sold the ring said that if I could raise £850 I could buy it back. I can honestly say that every man whom I escorted professionally, or catered for in one of the 'health clubs' (the greatest euphemism in the English language), was a knife in David Beard's back as far as I was concerned. I died a thousand deaths in the execution of the oldest profession in the world, but I bought back the ring. I wear it on my right hand with pride, and it is bequeathed in my will to Chloe.

In spite of everything, DB remained staunchly possessive and jealous if I so much as talked to another man. I still found him sexually attractive, but there was no way I would contemplate going back to a life with him after I had crawled out of the gutter, worked the health clubs, graduated to executive escort and, finally, opened my own agency in Paris. One evening we were out together, and David thought I had been over familiar with one of the men in our company. In his anger he gave me a good hammering, and I ended up in hospital with a broken nose. It transpired that I had given as good as I got, and he, too, had his nose broken.

How David Blakely hurt Ruth Ellis. How David Beard has hurt me. But just like my mother before me, I cannot help but feel for him. How I have not killed him is beyond my understanding, but I am more than pleased that it did not come to that. I wish David Blakely had found the courage to face Ruth that Easter weekend, and then it would not have come to that for them either. As long as the human race inhabits this earth men and women will be consumed by jealousies, and there will always be crimes of passion. I hope all who read of my own and Ruth's experiences will think twice before they pull the trigger.

CHAPTER TWENTY-TWO

Post-mortem

Mention of the name Albert Pierrepoint makes me shudder, and photographs of him make my skin crawl. Facially he resembles Donald Pleasence in some of that great actor's most sinister roles. What motivates a human being to want to become an executioner is beyond my comprehension but once Pierrepoint resigned in February 1956 there was no shortage of volunteers to step into his shoes.

As far as Ruth Ellis is concerned, the pulling of the lever to plummet her to her death was the end of her life but the beginning of a role she has had to play that is far more important than anything she tackled in life. When cabinet papers were published thirty years after her hanging it was revealed precisely how troubled the government had been by the public revulsion that enveloped the event. Sidney Silverman was the prime mover against her execution, and it was his Death Penalty (Abolition) Bill 1956, a bill passed by the Commons but thrown out by the Lords, that first introduced the phrase 'diminished responsibility'. Sidney Silverman worked tirelessly for the cause in which he so fervently believed until the last two men were hanged in 1964, and parliament finally outlawed the death penalty once and hopefully for all.

Silverman had some strong advocates in support, not least of which was Quintin Hogg MP, now Lord Hailsham, who eloquently argued, prior to abolition, that the prerogative for granting a reprieve should not be solely in the hands of the Home Secretary. He said: 'I say that not only because I myself feel wholly inadequate to face that responsibility, as indeed I should, but because I think that in the past Home Secretaries have proved inadequate . . . I say that they demonstrably made mistakes . . . One has only to mention some of the cases such as Evans, Bentley and Ruth Ellis.'

The response to my mother's execution was immediate and global. Among the sickest that I have encountered happened while she was still hanging in the pit on the end of the rope. Just forty minutes after her instantaneous death, Louis Tussaud's, the waxworks located on Blackpool's notorious Golden Mile, announced that a wax effigy of her wearing a black evening dress would be on display in the Chamber of Horrors the next day.

The headlines in the British popular press on the morning of 14 July 1955 led, without exception, with Ruth Ellis. One columnist, whose blushes I will spare by not naming him, wrote: 'In the rush of life the particular case of Ruth Ellis will be forgotten.' How wrong could he be? In America there was unanimous agreement that she would not have been executed under the laws of any state within the United States. In Australia the *Melbourne Argus* carried a leading article that stated: 'Hanging shames Britain in the eyes of the civilised world.' Sweden's *Aftonbladet* said: 'The continuance of the death sentence in England is a burden for England's good name in the world.'

French journalists, as might be expected, were struck by the fact that a case that under English law left no grounds for appeal would, in French courts, have been punishable by a few years' imprisonment at most. This was vividly illustrated only two days later when a woman in Corsica, also charged with the premeditated murder of her lover, was convicted and sentenced to two years' imprisonment; the sentence was suspended, she was immediately released on probation. French juries always applied the widest of interpretations to attenuating circumstances, and emotional stress was taken into account without question. Jean Wetz, correspondent for *Le Monde*, wrote: 'As everyone knows, the Englishman is, or believes himself to be, a creature of sang-froid, and the legal system in force supports this fiction in overruling once and for all any emotional troubles or irresistible impulses. As seen by the upholders of tradition, the place accorded to so degrading a concept as the *crime passionnel* seems precisely to be the true measure of French decadence. But the doubts which begin to be felt will certainly be stimulated by yesterday's event.'

Another French journalist wrote: 'Passion in England, except for cricket and betting, is always regarded as a shameful disease.' The leader in the *Observer* on the Sunday following my mother's death included: 'Consider the task of explaining to the late Ruth Ellis's ten-year-old son what has happened. This boy, who is fatherless, has had something done to him that is so brutal it is difficult to imagine. We should realise that it is we who have done it.'

In a letter to the same newspaper, Hugh J. Klarf, the then Secretary for the Howard League for Penal Reform, wrote: 'It is difficult to see what has been achieved by the execution of Ruth Ellis. The case for abolition is based on the solid, factual evidence of the many countries where it has been abandoned that the murder rate has not been affected one way or another.'

And so the arguments raged and, forty years on, the name of Ruth Ellis is famously synonymous with judicial execution. She was the fifteenth and last woman to be hanged in England in the twentieth century. For those readers who would like to know who the other women were who suffered the same fate, they were as follows:

Louisa Josephine Masset, 9 January 1900 at Newgate Prison for the murder of her four-year-old son. Hangman: James Billington.

Ada Chard Williams, 9 March 1900 at Newgate Prison for drowning a child which she had adopted for a small sum of money. Hangman: James Billington.

Emily Swan, 29 December 1901 at Armley Gaol, Leeds, for the murder of her husband. Hangman: William Billington.

Annie Walters and **Amelia Sach,** 3 February 1903 at Holloway Prison for the joint murders of an unknown number of children of whom they had taken charge for a fee. Hangman: William Billington.

Edith Jessie Thompson, 9 January 1923 at Holloway Prison for the murder of her husband. Hangman: John Ellis.

Susan Newell, 10 October 1923 at Duke Street Prison, Glasgow, for the murder of a newspaper boy. Hangman: John Ellis.

Louie Calvert, 26 June 1926 at Strangeways Prison, Manchester, for the murder of her landlady. Hangman: Tom Pierrepoint.

Ethel Lille Major, 19 December 1934 at Hull Prison for the murder of her husband. Hangman: Tom Pierrepoint.

Dorothea Nancy Waddingham, 16 April 1936 at Winsom Green Prison, Birmingham, for the murder of a patient whom she was nursing. Hangmen: Tom and Albert Pierrepoint.

Charlotte Bryant, 15 July 1936 at Exeter Gaol for the murder of her husband. Hangmen: Tom and Albert Pierrepoint.

Margaret Allen, 12 January 1949 at Strangeways Prison for the murder of an elderly woman. Hangman: Albert Pierrepoint.

Louisa Merrifield, 18 September 1953 at Strangeways Prison for the murder of her employer. Hangman: Albert Pierrepoint.

Styllou Christofi, 13 December 1954 at Holloway Prison for the murder of her daughter-in-law. Hangman: Albert Pierrepoint.

That then is the roll of dishonour, with my mother bringing up the rear. Hopefully there will never be new names to add, and the chapter is closed once and for all. All the years that I have spent delving into my mother's background to try better to understand my own foreground has, I think, been time well spent. I am left admiring her guts and hating one or two people who helped shape here final destiny. I weep for those of my immediate family who could not come to terms with the execution and whose own lives were reduced to rubble by it.

What remains for me is to get on with my own life as positively as I can and put my shambolic years firmly behind me. I also have six children who come, first and foremost, above all else. While no mother can dictate a modus vivendi to her children, I am quite determined to afford mine every opportunity to learn from my mistakes. Already I am overwhelmed by their capacity to forgive my past indiscretions and neglect. They have all, without exception, benefited from the tenderest of loving care from their respective fathers. I do not deserve their unqualified love, but I am resolved to merit their devotion in the way that I live out my remaining years. It is, I hope, never too late.

Finally, it seems highly unlikely that the issue of capital punishment will disappear once and for all. I would like to remind all those clarion trumpeters who demand an eye for an eye that, whenever a person is sentenced to death, the family and unborn innocent heirs of that family are sentenced to live their entire lives in the valley of the shadow of death. I hope it never happens to you.

Index

NOTE: Ruth Ellis is abbreviated to RE, Georgina Ellis to GE and David Blakely to DB.